KNOWN
by
NATURE

KNOWN by NATURE

*Thomas Aquinas on
Natural Knowledge
of God*

ANNA BONTA MORELAND

A Herder & Herder Book
The Crossroad Publishing Company
New York

The Crossroad Publishing Company
www.crossroadpublishing.com.

© 2010 by Anna Bonta Moreland

All rights reserved. No part of this book may be reproduced, stored in a retrieval system, or transmitted, in any form or by any means, electronic, mechanical, photocopying, recording, or otherwise, without the written permission of The Crossroad Publishing Company.

In continuation of our 200-year tradition of independent publishing, The Crossroad Publishing Company proudly offers a variety of books with strong, original voices and diverse perspectives. The viewpoints expressed in our books are not necessarily those of The Crossroad Publishing Company, any of its imprints, or of its employees. No claims are made or responsibility assumed for any health or other benefit.

Printed in the United States of America.

The text of this book is set in 11/14 Sabon.

Cataloging-in-Publication Data is available from the Library of Congress

ISBN-13: 978-0-8245-2481-4

1   2   3   4   5   6   7   8   9   10   16   15   14   13   12   11   10

Juan Pablo Bonta
in memoriam

Begin by believing these things,
advance and persevere;
and though I know thou wilt not arrive,
I shall rejoice at thy advance.
For he who devoutly follows in pursuit of the infinite,
though he never come up with it,
will always advance by setting forth.
Yet pry not into that secret,
and meddle not in the mystery of the birth of the infinite,
nor presume to grasp that which is the summit of understanding:
but understand that there are things thou canst not fully grasp.*

Hilary, *De Trinitate* ii. 10, 11.
Cited by St. Thomas in
the *Summa Contra Gentiles* I, viii.

---

*Haec credendo incipe, procurre, persiste: etsi non perventurum sciam, gratulabor tamen profectorum. Qui enim pie infinita prosequitur, etsi non contingat aliquando, semper tamen proficiet, prodeundo. Sed ne te inferas in illud secretum, et arcano interminabilis nativitatis non te immergas, summam intelligentiae comprehendere praesumens: sed intellige incomprehensibilia esse [*Opera Omnia*. Editio altera Veneta..., t. 18: IV Libros de Veritate Catholicae Fidei Contra Gentiles etc. (Cudebat Simon Occhi, Venetiis, 1753)]. This translation, and all subsequent ones, are from *On the Truth of the Catholic Faith: Summa Contra Gentiles*, trans. Anton C. Pegis (New York: Hanover House, 1955), 76 [henceforth *SCG*].

Contents

Acknowledgments xi

Chapter One
Postliberal Interpretations of Aquinas 1

    The Problematic Situation / 1
    Central Problem / 4
    Method / 5
    Structure / 6
    1. George Lindbeck / 8
    2. Bruce Marshall / 21
    3. Eugene Rogers / 31

Chapter Two
An Initial Natural Knowledge of God:
The Remote Context (*ST* I, 12, 12) 38

    Introduction / 38
    Title of the Work / 38
    General Prologue / 39
    Prologue to Question One / 47
    Prologue to Question Two / 50
    Prologue to Question Three / 58

Chapter Three
Natural Knowledge of God Affirmed:
The Proximate Context (*ST* I, 12, 12) 66

    Introduction / 66
    Prologue to Question Twelve / 66

Chapter Four
The Development of Natural Knowledge: Parallel Texts 79

    Introduction / 79
    Scriptum super libros Sententiarum / 80
    Expositio Super Librum Boethii de Trinitate / 91
    Summa contra gentiles / 103
    Conclusion / 115

Chapter Five
The Mature Fruit of Natural Knowledge: Central Texts 116
    Introduction / 116
    Scriptum super libros Sententiarum Revised Text / 117
    ST I, 12, 12: Can We Know God by Natural Reason
            in This Life? / 124
    Article Twelve / 124
    Question Thirteen / 128
    In epistolam ad Romanos / 134

Epilogue
Thomas Reexamined: The Contemporary Conversation 143
    Sacra Doctrina / 144
    The Philosophers / 150
    Religio / 153

Notes 157

Select Bibliography 197

Index Bibliography 205

Acknowledgments

This book grew out of a doctoral dissertation at Boston College directed by Michael J. Buckley, S.J., to whom I owe more than I could possibly express in these acknowledgements. Those of us who were fortunate enough to study under him can only hope to emulate him as a teacher, an advisor, and a mentor. I am grateful to Thomas Hibbs and Louis Roy, O.P., for serving on my dissertation committee and for providing thoughtful and detailed comments to each chapter. I would also like to thank to David Burrell, C.S.C., for his work and for his encouragement of me during this project.

John Given patiently read over and improved my Latin translations of Thomas' work. Grant Kaplan read the manuscript for publication and offered valuable insights both with respect to content and style. Kevin Hughes read over a draft of the epilogue, and offered incisive reflections. My husband, Michael, read through a final draft of this manuscript. His support throughout the development of this study was invaluable. Finally, I am grateful to John Jones at Herder and Herder for inviting me to submit this manuscript, and for guiding it through the process of publication.

– One –

Postliberal Interpretations of Aquinas

The Problematic Situation

For two millennia the question whether God can be known through human reason has divided the Christian church. Against Alexandrians maintaining that knowledge of God is reached through faith alone, Clement of Alexandria countered that Christians and Greeks "know the same God, though not in the same way."[1] The Reformation renewed the repudiation of any natural knowledge of God and would claim that "[f]aith alone, and not reason, is able to think rightly about God."[2] At the end of the nineteenth century, the First Vatican Council's Constitution *Dei Filius* attacked rationalism on the one hand and fideism on the other.[3] While defending the sphere of faith, it insisted upon a positive evaluation of human reason's ability to come to the knowledge of God.[4]

Thomas Aquinas' influence upon this discussion has waxed and waned in Catholic theological circles since the thirteenth century. Leo XIII's encyclical *Aeterni Patris* in 1879 launched a renaissance in the study of Thomas Aquinas, one that might not have occurred were it not for Leo's influence.[5] For roughly a century this renaissance was intensely felt at Catholic universities. But it was still an insular achievement, as it scarcely touched the religion curriculums, for example, at Yale or Chicago. As a direct result, though, of both the work and effects of the Second Vatican Council, Protestant theologians became interested in Catholic theology in general and the thought of Thomas Aquinas in particular. Fresh readings of Thomas have begun to emerge on age-old theological questions. So now Protestant and Catholic theologians are reading Thomas together. A new portrait is taking shape of a medieval thinker for whom scriptural commentary, preaching, and Christ are central to his theology. This is an exciting development — both for ecumenical inquiry and for Thomistic studies.

This book seeks to engage one segment of this new conversation. It addresses those who have been coined "postliberal" theologians, notably George Lindbeck and two of his students, Bruce Marshall and Eugene Rogers. Their renewed attempt at a more accurate and sympathetic understanding of Thomas has resulted in a startling development: while maintaining a traditional Protestant reserve about natural reason, they have begun to claim Thomas as a party to this reserve. They disagree with standard Catholic interpretations, arguing that Thomas does not support anything that can be called a natural knowledge of God. These theologians argue that Thomas' understanding of the natural knowledge of God resembles — quite surprisingly — Karl Barth's position on this issue. This appropriation of Thomas has introduced a radically new situation for ecumenical inquiry.

The claim on the Thomistic heritage by Protestant theologians has been incremental. In the elaboration of his own theology, George Lindbeck, for example, has both reinterpreted and appropriated Aquinas. Lindbeck writes in the *Nature of Doctrine* that decades of ecumenical discussions led him to propose a new context within which to make sense of these discussions. He argues that religions are cultural and/or linguistic frameworks or mediums that shape one's life and thought.[6] According to this postliberal theology, religions shape and sometimes constitute the way one experiences religious truth.[7] Divergent religions, therefore, cannot be understood as offering different objectifications of the same basic experience.[8] Lindbeck enlists Thomas Aquinas at various stages in his argument, suggesting that Thomas' theology is "no longer incompatible" with the approach to religious knowledge outlined in the *Nature of Doctrine*.[9] Lindbeck affirms that Thomas was a "constant, even if background, presence"[10] while he composed the *Nature of Doctrine*. He even claims that his "cultural-linguistic" account of religious belief is "in part a clumsy rendition in modern philosophical and sociological idioms of what Aquinas often said more fully and more precisely long ago."[11] At the end of his book, Lindbeck also reveals that Karl Barth's theology was "at second hand" and a "chief source" for the cultural-linguistic proposal of his book.[12] Lindbeck has even characterized himself as a "Wittgensteinian Thomistic Lutheran."[13]

Some of Lindbeck's students have taken up his cues and have begun to reread Thomas in light of "postliberal" theology. For example, in an article entitled "Aquinas as Postliberal Theologian," Bruce Marshall explores the relationship between Lindbeck's project in the *Nature of Doctrine* and Thomas' understanding of truth and justification of Christian belief.[14] Marshall states that Thomas and Lindbeck share an understanding of the justification of ontological truth that would rule out any possibility of natural knowledge of God. In fact, for Thomas there is no "external standard of truth" or "independent vantage point" from which Christian claims can be assessed, even of the existence of God.[15] For the Christian belief system is comprehensive: "there is no practice or proposition which cannot be understood and evaluated in Christian terms."[16] In addition, Thomas distinguishes between *scientia* before and after faith to show that "in relation to God, *scientia* is only possible after faith."[17] Consequently, "only the believer means by 'God' what one must mean in order to refer to God at all."[18] Therefore, to seek *scientia* for Thomas is to do "intratextual theology" for Lindbeck, in which one " 'redescribes reality within the scriptural framework rather than translating Scripture into extratextual categories.' "[19] Marshall claims that if Lindbeck is a fideist or irrationalist, then so is Thomas Aquinas.[20]

Another student of Lindbeck, Eugene Rogers, has published a comparative work on Thomas Aquinas and Karl Barth that began as a dissertation under Lindbeck.[21] He argues for a convergence between Thomas and Barth on the natural knowledge of God. For his interpretation of Thomas, he relies on continental theologians Otto Hermann Pesch and Michel Corbin and on his own teacher Victor Preller.[22] Rogers seeks to "displace" the traditional interpretation of Thomas. Although he does not identify the representatives of this tradition, he claims that the tradition both reads Thomas as a Christian philosopher who allows for the natural knowledge of God and uses the *Summa theologiae* rather than Thomas' scriptural commentaries as evidence for this claim.[23] In contrast to this tradition, Rogers proposes a "genuinely 'evangelical' Thomas, in the German sense of the word, as one who in the *Summa* speaks always and everywhere as a theologian rather than a philosopher."[24] According to Rogers' reading, Thomas makes sacred doctrine "a matter of 'taking every understanding captive into obedience to Christ.' "[25] Thomas means for theology to regard "all things as belonging to the one world depicted within the Bible."[26] Sacred doctrine, then, is intratextual in the sense that it not only confines itself to the scriptural realm, but it absorbs the whole world into this realm.[27]

For evidence, Rogers draws upon Thomas' commentary on Romans 1:20, and analyzes Questions 1 and 2 of the *Prima pars* of the *Summa theologiae* in light of this scriptural commentary. He concludes his study by comparing his findings in Thomas' commentary with Barth's reading of Romans. This interpretation of Thomas "create[s] a convergence . . . between Karl Barth and Thomas Aquinas just where both modern Barthians and modern Thomists would have thought convergence least likely: on the natural knowledge of God."[28] George Lindbeck in an implicit way, Bruce Marshall in a more suggestive study, and Eugene Rogers in an extended analysis have argued for such convergence.

Central Problem

One may wonder, however, whether Lindbeck, Marshall, and Rogers read Thomas through lenses decidedly Barthian, and whether these lenses actually focus or distort the meaning of Thomas' work. In hopeful attempts to forge ecumenical agreements, are we forcing an actual or artificial convergence between Thomas and Barth on the question critically important to the whole of Christianity: is there a natural knowledge of God in Thomas' theology, and if so, what is its character?[29]

The importance of this question goes far beyond the Roman Catholic–Barthian dialogue, for it touches upon the fundamental problem about the significance of "nature" in the Christian's self-understanding. While this question immediately concerns itself with God, the root of the issue lies in the relationship of the human person to God and the nature of the human person. Does the human person have a natural capacity for God, implanted by God and addressed by everything that is? Is this capacity brought to completion utterly beyond itself by grace and revelation and yet remaining true to itself? Is that natural capacity fundamentally destroyed by the fall, or is it seriously debilitated? If it is fundamentally destroyed, then how does grace become effective in the human person?

These questions move beyond intra-Christian conversations into dialogue with other faiths and with contemporary secular culture. For if human reason can attain *some* knowledge of God, indeed if reason is naturally and irrevocably oriented to this knowledge, no matter how inchoate and elusive, communities of faith have a particular context within which to begin conversations with non-believers. If not, then the irreducibility of one religion to another that Lindbeck maintains will necessarily govern both ecumenical inquiry and inter-religious dialogue. In an age in which inter-religious concerns are so pressing, foundational questions about nature and grace take on a renewed significance in Christianity. How a Christian understands human nature radically alters the way in which she seeks conversation with a Jew, a Muslim, a Hindu, or an atheist.

What will emerge from this critique of a postliberal reading of Thomas on natural knowledge of God? The thirteenth century might provide a much-needed model for inter-religious dialogue. Indeed, it is the burden of this study to argue that Thomas Aquinas provides such a surprisingly contemporary model.

Method

The question about the Barthian interpretation of Thomas that forms the background of this book could be met by a hermeneutical argument about the unavoidability of contemporary lenses. The questions and presuppositions ("prejudices") that the interpreter brings to the subject always shape the interpretation of a text.[30] Hans-Georg Gadamer insists that the interpreter "is always performing an act of projecting."[31] Or, as Bultmann writes, every interpretation is guided by the interpreter's "preunderstanding."[32] The rise of hermeneutics has uncovered an enormous challenge to textual interpretation, and this, in turn, has led to the renewed insistence on the importance of the historical study of philosophical and theological texts. Gadamer himself insists that "the effect of a living tradition and the effect of historical study must constitute a unity, the analysis of which would reveal only a texture of reciprocal relationships."[33] Historical studies, therefore, are needed as a corrective to contemporary biases, just as contemporary questions can elicit incisive interpretations of historical texts. Consequently, the following study engages the contemporary proposals on Thomas' treatment of the natural knowledge of God through a historical and systematic study.

To guard against contemporary biases, the methodology for this study takes its paradigm from I. T. Eschmann's textual analysis in *The Ethics of Saint Thomas Aquinas*.[34] It is not the only method one could choose for this study, but it offers a way to carefully read a text, as it attends to both systematic and historical concerns. Eschmann's method proceeds in two major stages in the examination of a text. First, one must examine the presuppositions of the text and second, the text itself.[35] The presuppositions or "terms of comparison" include (1) the "coordinated texts," (2) the set of "parallel texts," and (3) other writing by thinkers who influenced Thomas on the subject.

These "terms of comparison" need a word of explanation. First, the set of "coordinated texts" comprises the context within which Thomas' treatment of a particular article occurs, a context often explicitly set down in the prologues in which the author states the intention of each section.[36] These passages are examined in order to illumine and contextualize the selected text within the larger framework of questions, under the conviction that the part attains its intelligibility in terms of the whole. Next, the study of "parallel texts," where Thomas treats the same subject in different sections of the *Summa* and in other works, clarifies semantic terms that in turn bring focus to his argument, and reveals any possible intellectual development on this subject. Finally, the positions of other writings known to Thomas and with which he is explicitly or implicitly in dialogue will be investigated in order to obtain some sense of the particular character and originality of Thomas' treatment. To understand fully the selected text, one must understand the thinkers with whom Thomas is in dialogue. After investigating these three terms of comparison, the argument in the focal text will be examined in detail. The selected text for this study is: *Summa theologiae,* Question 12, article 12 (whether we can know God in this life through *rationem naturalem*).

Structure

To situate its inquiry within the contemporary problematic situation, this study opens with an initial review of the contemporary state of the problem, outlining recent attempts to reinterpret Aquinas. It traces this interpretation from George Lindbeck's suggestions (1984) through Bruce Marshall's development (1992) and Eugene

Rogers' concrete proposal (1995), terminating in the articulation of the question.

Chapters 2 and 3 explore the "coordinate texts," focusing on how the issue that the article examines fits into the web of questions as a whole. The remote "coordinated texts" selected for analysis in chapter 2 include the prologue to: (a) the *Summa* as a whole, and (b) questions 1, 2, and 3 of the *Prima pars*. These prologues will offer a general framework within which the article central to this study will be examined. Chapter 3 then takes up the prologue and the first eleven articles in Question 12, providing the specific contextualizing environment of article 12.

The fourth chapter focuses upon the set of "parallel texts" in prior works of Thomas. This examination selects from the following works: the *Scriptum super sententiis*, which Thomas completed during his first period of teaching in Paris as a bachelor of the *Sentences*;[37] the commentary on Boethius' *De Trinitate*, written a few years later;[38] and the *Summa contra gentiles*, which he wrote upon returning to Italy.[39] This chapter allows any historical developments or shifts in emphases to rise to the surface and clarifies the terms and argument in the selected text.

Chapter 5 turns to the theological and scriptural foci of this study. The theological focus consists of the revision of the *Scriptum super libros sententiarum* and the *Summa theologiae*, both written while Thomas was setting up a *studium* in Rome.[40] The scriptural focus is comprised of the selection from *In epistolam ad Romanos* that examines Romans 1:20. This commentary most likely was completed during his last period of teaching in Naples.[41] Each objection in Question 12, article 12 will be examined with respect to the tradition it represents, the force of the objection, and the way it is incorporated into Thomas' response. Then, the argument in the *respondeo* will be analyzed in detail, taking into consideration Thomas' prior treatment of this subject. Finally, the position of the article within the structure of Question 12 and the surrounding questions in the *Prima pars* will be analyzed. An examination of the objections highlights other thinkers on this same subject with whom Thomas was in dialogue. As will be shown, Thomas' treatment of this issue consists in a set of answers to particular questions of his time. The medieval *quaestio* format of this article exemplifies what Alasdair MacIntyre calls "tradition-constituted inquiry,"[42] for the objections that open

Thomas' treatment of this article represent three significant voices of the tradition in which Thomas is firmly planted: Boethius, Aristotle, and Augustine.

The epilogue returns to the ecumenical discussion of the first chapter. My postliberal interlocutors — Lindbeck, Marshall, and Rogers — are taken up anew and reconsidered in light of this textual study, and their claims about the convergence between Thomas and Barth are reexamined. The contemporary implications of this reading will then be introduced, with particular emphasis upon its effects on inter-religious dialogue.

1. George Lindbeck

Throughout the past five decades, George Lindbeck has focused his theological work around ecumenical issues. These concerns have led him to address fundamental questions about religious knowledge and belief. His most celebrated contribution has been the "cultural-linguistic" proposal for ecumenical dialogue found in his constructive work *Nature of Doctrine* (1984). In order to understand the development of Lindbeck's thoughts on the natural knowledge of God in Thomas, it is necessary to cull his reflections on Thomas that thread throughout his entire corpus. Lindbeck's work can be divided into three moments: (1) his early articles in the sixties and seventies on Thomas, (2) his constructive proposal in *Nature of Doctrine,* and (3) further reflections on *Nature of Doctrine* from articles that have appeared since its publication.

Lindbeck in the 1960's and 1970's: Rethinking Aquinas in Light of Vatican II

Lindbeck's published articles from the 1960's reveal a profound optimism about the possibilities of an ecumenical dialogue between the Lutheran and Roman Catholic Churches. In his autobiographical sketch decades later Lindbeck observes that more than anything else, this dialogue "mostly with Roman Catholics" shaped the context of his thinking.[43] Being a Delegated Observer from the Lutheran World Federation during the first three sessions of the Second Vatican Council had a marked effect on his attitude toward the Roman Catholic Church.[44] As a result, he wrote a series of articles on Thomas Aquinas including: "The Evangelical Possibilities of Roman Catholic Theology" (1960), "The *A Priori* in St. Thomas' Theory of Knowledge" (1965), and "Discovering Thomas (1): The Classical Statement of Christian Theism" (1967).

Even before the opening of the Second Vatican Council, Lindbeck began to notice changes in Roman Catholic theology that would necessitate "a complete re-study of exactly where the difference lies" between Roman Catholic and Protestant understandings of such questions as the function of dogma, the doctrine of justification, the authority of Scripture, and the nature of faith and reason.[45] In "The Evangelical Possibilities of Roman Catholic Theology," for example, Lindbeck drew upon Yves Congar and Hans Küng to show that Roman Catholic theology had begun to change with respect to the development of dogma and the doctrine of justification.[46]

In this article Lindbeck reflects on the Catholic understanding of the nature of faith and reason. The rise of historical-criticism worked revolutionary changes in twentieth-century neo-Thomism. Among these effects lies an important change in the significance of "natural theology:"

> Even some Thomists now treat natural theology, not so much as a preamble and support of revealed truths, but rather the reverse. It is admitted that in modern society it is generally a waste of effort to try to bring men to a belief in the existence of God by philosophical argument. As a matter of fact, and perhaps even of necessity, it requires the operation of grace to overcome the social effects of sin in a man's mind so that he can gain a natural knowledge of God. In short, at least in most cases in our contemporary society, it is only when a man has supernatural faith that he will also be able to have natural knowledge of God. Further, the importance of the natural knowledge of God apart from supernatural faith is strictly limited. It gains its true significance only in believers who, by means of their purified reason, now rejoice to see the glory of God in the things which he has made. Thus philosophical work becomes an act of adoration and obedience, rather than of human self-assertion.[47]

Even before the Council, the reexaminations of their own theology by Catholic theologians encouraged Lindbeck's study of the relationship between Roman Catholic and Protestant theology. Among these reexaminations, one notices a particular effort to re-evaluate the Catholic understanding of the natural knowledge of God. Lindbeck suggests in this article that Roman Catholic theology had begun to move in a direction more congenial to Lutheran theology.

In order to understand this movement within Catholic theology, Lindbeck insists that one must look not simply at its conclusions. Rather, one must consider its epistemological foundations. Among a series of articles after Vatican II that deal explicitly with the theology of Thomas Aquinas, Lindbeck wrote an article on Thomas' theory of knowledge.[48] He argues that Thomas does not reject and "to a certain extent" supports the position that metaphysical knowledge is *a priori*.[49] *A priori* knowledge, here, is understood in a particular way. The Thomistic insight — inherited from Aristotle — that all knowledge was *a posteriori* "was directed against the objective *a priorism* of Augustinian Platonism and does not exclude a Kantian nonobjective variety."[50] In other words, Thomas insists that all human cognition happens through *conversio ad phantasma*. Kant echoes this insistence by affirming that concepts without percepts are blind. Neither Thomas nor Kant espouses the Platonic *a priorism* of innate ideas and direct apprehension of pure intelligibles.[51] Against this kind of *a priori* knowledge, Thomas and Kant affirm that all knowledge is *a posteriori* such that all knowledge is attained through the senses. But while Thomas rejects *a priori* knowledge of the Platonic variety, he does not exclude the kind of *a priori* knowledge that Kant would affirm centuries later. It is therefore legitimate to read many Kantian and post-Kantian views into Thomas, even if they might go against the "rhetorical grain" of the Thomistic texts.[52] If Thomas rejects *a priori* objects of knowledge, he continues to accept nonobjectifiable *a priori* knowledge. For example, Thomas' epistemology excludes knowledge of cognitive objects that are not known through the senses, but it does not exclude the possibility that the " 'form,' the intelligibility of objects of intellectual knowledge is contributed by the mind."[53] It also leaves open the possibility that the necessity and universality of certain concepts and judgments arise from the intellect rather than from sensible things. In fact, Thomas did not reject the Kantian view that "intelligibility is 'projected' into the sensible content of our knowledge rather than 'extracted' from it."[54]

While this article is primarily a defense of Maréchal and Rahner's interpretations of Thomas on the structure of human knowledge *in general* (against their contemporaries Etienne Gilson and Jacques Maritain), it concludes with an argument for *a priori* knowledge *of God*. For Thomas the "agent intellect can be best understood as an 'openness' to being which is the direct source of our knowledge of being."[55] To understand fully its import, this statement must be examined. First, whatever is potentially knowable becomes actually knowable through the agency of something already in act. This "something" is a "kind of openness to the full actuality of being."[56] In addition, the agent intellect is described as the "intelligibility of *ens* present *a priori* in the mind."[57] Second, the agent intellect is the human participation in the divine light, or intelligence. God's *intelligere* is primarily the knowledge that God has of Godself; we participate in God's *intelligere* in any act of human understanding. Therefore, in each act of understanding we implicitly know God as the horizon against which we complete an act of understanding. This means that the "*a priori* anticipation of the divine plenitude which is the agent intellect is a precondition for every act of knowledge."[58]

Thomas rejects here any understanding of *a priori* knowledge of God in the form of an innate idea or concept, but he accepts an *a priori* knowledge of God that can be neither objectified nor conceptualized:

> ...the natural desire for the beatific vision is said to presuppose some kind of knowledge of the beatifying object, God. It is true that St. Thomas explains that this is a confused knowledge which is incapable of serving as the basis for a demonstration of God, but it would seem that the sort of *a priori* knowledge of which we are speaking is quite sufficiently vague to satisfy that condition...I shall, therefore, simply record my belief that this doctrine of natural desire does lend credence to the theory that there is an *a priori* knowledge of being.[59]

In sum, a human being's conscious knowledge of being is a "reflection in experience of the light of the agent intellect" which is a "preconscious anticipation or openness to the fullness of being, to God."[60] For Thomas, then, the agent intellect points to a natural desire for God, and this natural desire is the ground of *a priori* knowledge. We see here in Lindbeck's early work on Thomas an admission of the authentic role that natural knowledge plays in Thomas' theology, even as it is anticipatory and inchoate.

In 1967 Lindbeck wrote a series of four articles commenting on the recently published Blackfriars edition of the *Summa theologiae*. Lindbeck's considerations of St. Thomas immediately ran counter to some of the assertions in the newly minted interpretive appendices found in the back of each volume of this edition. The first three articles comment upon the *Prima pars* of the *Summa:* God as One, God as Triune, and the origin of man. The final article takes up the question of hope found in the *Secunda secundae*.

In the first article, "Discovering Thomas (1): The Classical Statement of Christian Theism,"[61] Lindbeck discusses issues concerning the natural knowledge of God and its relationship to faith. After claiming Thomas as one of the "fathers of Protestant theology,"[62] he discusses how Thomas uses natural reason in the first 18 questions of the *Summa*. Thomas does not divide the single science of *sacra doctrina* into revealed and unrevealed parts.[63] In fact, there is nothing in Thomas that resembles what we think of today as autonomous natural theology or philosophical theology.[64] While Thomas employs arguments from natural reason in these questions, Lindbeck asserts that for Thomas "reason unaided by faith can know nothing."[65] Even in those areas where people can "know something of divine things apart from faith, philosophical reasoning has no autonomy, no independence."[66] *Sacra doctrina* uses philosophical reasoning to provide extraneous arguments from probability in order to, as St. Paul states, bring " 'into captivity every understanding into the service of Christ' (2 Cor. 10:5)."[67]

The *quinque viae* of Question 2, then, only interest Thomas as a commentary on Rom. 1:20, especially since Thomas devotes but a few pages to these arguments. They are certainly not proofs or demonstrations in any strict sense, since they function only as probable and extraneous arguments.[68] The arguments for the existence of God do not achieve anything of importance for salvation. Each argument ends with something that human beings call God, but there is no way to know whether these arguments all end with the same God.[69]

Lindbeck concludes that "there is perhaps no fundamental conflict between St. Thomas and the reformation tradition on the relation of faith and reason, of philosophy and theology."[70] According to this interpretation, Thomas uses Aristotle like Augustine uses Plato and Barth uses Kant:

> In all these cases theologians have employed the thought patterns of their times in order to help their contemporaries make sense of the faith even while recognizing that revelation vastly surpasses the insights of unaided reason, and must therefore, in part at least, be expressed in categories peculiar to it.[71]

On this basis Protestants should not immediately dismiss Aquinas as a philosopher rather than a theologian. They should, instead, read him anew with a critical eye and genuine seriousness.

This, of course, raises questions about the contemporary usefulness of the first 26 questions in the *Summa theologiae*. While it is true that Thomas was able to translate biblical language about God into the Aristotelian language pervasive in the thirteenth century, other idioms now dominate. In particular, contemporary systematic theology need not be as metaphysical as Thomas' theology.[72] Furthermore, seen through this new lens, Thomas' theology refutes one of the standard criticisms lodged against him, namely that beginning with the most abstract divine name, *Ipsum Esse*, is misleading because it suggests that one can know something significant about God based solely on reason. Thomas emphatically denies this claim. Textual evidence can be found in II-II, Q2, a2, *ad* 3 where he states that unbelievers " 'do not believe that God exists under the conditions which faith defines;' " therefore, " 'they do not really believe that there is a God.' "[73] Given this evidence, questions about autonomous natural theology or philosophical theology lose their importance.[74] Asking, then, whether Thomas' arguments "when judged at the bar of reason" are demonstrable is the wrong question entirely; one would be right to ask simply whether he has done justice to the faith.[75]

To conclude this review of Lindbeck's articles throughout the 1960's, one notices a serious effort to engage in ecumenical dialogue with the Roman Catholic Church. As part of this effort, Lindbeck reexamines the theologian who represents the classical expression of Roman Catholic theology, Thomas Aquinas. Within his reexamination one finds an initial attempt to reconcile Thomas' understanding of the relationship of faith to natural reason with the Reformation heritage. An examination of Lindbeck's theological development will reveal how he relies on Thomas for his own constructive proposal.

The Nature of Doctrine *and Thomas Aquinas*

Lindbeck is perhaps most known for the "cultural-linguistic" approach outlined in his 1984 work *Nature of Doctrine: Religion and Theology in a Postliberal Age*. When commenting on this work, he suggests that his "cultural-linguistic" account of religious belief is "in part a clumsy rendition in modern philosophical and sociological idioms of what Aquinas often said more fully and more precisely long ago."[76] To understand this claim one must first investigate Lindbeck's cultural-linguistic approach in detail.

Dissatisfaction with the ways religious dogmas or doctrines have been understood in contemporary ecumenical discussions drives the *Nature of Doctrine*. The problem is one of conceptualization. A new "postliberal" approach is needed to address the inadequacies of both modern and preliberal ways of thinking about religious dogmas. This postliberal approach conceives of religion as a cultural and/or linguistic framework or medium that shapes one's life and thought.[77] Contrary to the "propositionalist" approach, religion is not primarily a set of beliefs about the true and the good; contrary to the "experiential-expressivist" approach, religion is not fundamentally a set of symbols that express basic attitudes and feelings. Rather, a postliberal understanding of religion is:

> ...a communal phenomenon that shapes the subjectivities of individuals rather than being primarily a manifestation of those subjectivities. It comprises a vocabulary of discursive and nondiscursive symbols together with a distinctive logic or grammar in terms of which this vocabulary can be meaningfully deployed. Lastly, just as a language (or "language game" to use Wittgenstein's phrase) is correlated with a form of life, and just as a culture has both cognitive and behavioral dimensions, so it is also the case of a religious tradition. Its doctrines, cosmic stories or myths, and ethical directives are integrally related to the rituals it practices, the sentiments or experiences it evokes, the actions it recommends, and the institutional forms it develops.[78]

But what are the characteristics of this postliberal approach to religion?

First, this postliberal approach is distinguished from "experiential-expressivism" in that it inverts the inner and outer features of religion. Instead of deriving external features of a religion from inner experience, the inner experiences are derived from its external features:[79]

> A religion is above all an external word, a *verbum externum*, that molds and shapes the self and its world, rather than an expression or thematization of a preexisting self or of preconceptual experience. The *verbum internum* (traditionally equated by Christians with the action of the Holy Spirit) is also crucially important, but it would be understood in a theological use of the model as a capacity for hearing and accepting the true religion, the true external word, rather than (as experiential expressivism would have it) as a common experience diversely articulated in different religions.[80]

The focus here, then, is on the external rather than the internal word, so that the actual practices of a religion cannot be easily swept aside in the search for a common inner core experience.

Another characteristic of this postliberal understanding of religion is that the cognitive aspect of religion is important but not primary. In contrast to the "propositionalist" approach to religion, in this postliberal approach truth claims are important, but they are not the fundamental aspect of the religion: "[I]t is, nevertheless, the conceptual vocabulary and the syntax or inner logic which determines the kinds of truth claims that the religion can make."[81] Becoming religious, then, is more easily compared to learning a *language* than to learning a *set of propositions*. It is only when one achieves competency in the particular religious language that one is able to make coherent and true religious statements. As a result, religious statements divorced from the rituals and practices that ground them are meaningless. This move away from propositions and toward practices enables one to see that becoming religious does not primarily involve learning *about* the religion but rather learning *how* to become religious.[82]

A third characteristic of this approach is that the acquired skills or practices needed for becoming religious function as a kind of Kantian *a priori*.[83] While these skills certainly vary according to the religion in question, every religion includes a set of necessary skills and practices: "[T]he means of communication and expression are a precondition, a kind of quasi-transcendental (i.e., culturally formed) *a priori* for the possibility of experience."[84] A prelinguistic or unreflective experience, therefore, is impossible. In addition, changes or developments in religion are due to adaptations to new cultural-linguistic situations rather than responses to new private experiences. Finally, the "objectivities" of religion, or its language, doctrines, liturgies, etc., are primary; it is through these "objective" aspects of religion that religious experience arises at all.[85]

The most crucial consequence of this postliberal outlook for our purposes, however, concerns the "meaningfulness of the notion that there is an inner experience of God common to all human beings and all religions."[86] There is no room for such a core experience in this outlook because the interpretive frameworks, i.e., the cultural *a priori* of different religions simply give rise to different experiences. If experience is dependent upon language, and if religions do not share a common language, then there is no way that people of different religions have a generic core experience of God. The postliberal approach, in fact, argues that this claim is illusory. All religions do share, however, a formal cultural-linguistic aspect, rather than a material experiential core. Consequently, comparing religions is like comparing languages: what is common to all languages is the fact that they are spoken. But this universal formal feature tells us nothing significant about the languages themselves.[87]

This final characteristic of the postliberal approach to religion gives rise to further questions. If religions are cultural-linguistic frameworks or mediums that shape one's life and thought, rather than being different expressions of a universal capacity to experience God, then questions about religious truth claims immediately come to the fore. First, truth claims in a cultural-linguistic religion are based, at least in part, on "categorial adequacy."[88] In other words, when deciding whether or not a specific religious claim is true, one must first ask about the adequacy of the categories or the grammar of the specific claim. But since categories are specific to particular religions, there is no way to compare two different religions:

> The cultural-linguistic approach is open to the possibility that different religions and/or philosophies may have incommensurable notions of truth, or experience, and of categorial adequacy, and therefore also of what it would mean for something to be most important (i.e., "God"). Unlike other perspectives, this

approach proposes no common framework such as that supplied by the propositionalist's concept of truth or the expressivist's concept of experience within which to compare religions.[89]

Religious truth (or any truth for that matter), then, is utterly context-dependent. Until one has mastered the skills needed for the Christian faith, for example, one has no way of either affirming or denying the statement that "Jesus is Lord": "One must be, so to speak, inside the relevant context; and in the case of religion, this means that one must have some skill in *how* to use its language and practice its way of life before the propositional meaning of its affirmations becomes determinate enough to be rejected."[90]

Within this concept of religion, theological or doctrinal statements are, like grammatical statements, second-order activities. They affirm nothing true or false *about the world*. Rather, they are, like grammar, statements about statements. Theology and doctrine are, of course, propositional; but they are second-order propositions that "affirm nothing about extra-linguistic or extra-human reality."[91] Lindbeck asserts:

> [P]ropositional truth and falsity characterize ordinary religious language when it is used to mold lives through prayer, praise, preaching and exhortation. It is only on this level that human beings linguistically exhibit their truth or falsity, their correspondence or lack of correspondence to the ultimate mystery. Technical theological and official doctrine, in contrast, are second order discourse about the first-intentional uses of religious language. Here, in contrast to the common supposition, one rarely if ever succeeds in making affirmations with ontological import, but rather engages in explaining, defending, analyzing, and regulating the liturgical, kerygmatic, and ethical modes of speech and action within which such affirmations from time to time occur.[92]

Note here that for Lindbeck theology does not deal primarily with ontology or truth; it is strictly a second-order discourse. In addition, theological statements have an intratextual character. In other words, intratextual theology "redescribes reality within the scriptural framework rather than translating Scripture into extratextual categories."[93]

Finally, what has become the dictum of postliberal theology: "[I]t is the text, so to speak, which absorbs the world, rather than the world the text."[94] This does not mean, however, that theology simply repeats the words of Scripture and disregards non-theological knowledge. Quite the contrary, theology makes use of philosophical, historical, and other resources on an *ad hoc* basis. These other disciplines are always subsumed under the theological task. There is no outside standard from which to measure the truthfulness of theological statements. As a result, there are no independently formed standards of reasonableness in postliberal theology:

> Reason places constraints on religious as well as on scientific options even though these constraints are too flexible and informal to be spelled out in either foundational theology or a general theory of science. In short, intelligibility comes from skill, not theory, and credibility comes from good performance, not adherence to independently formulated criteria.[95]

In Thomas revelation dominates every aspect of theology, but it uses philosophy and other knowledge in defense of the faith.[96] Thomas even argues that reason in support of the faith is only meritorious after faith. Or, in Lindbeck's terms, "[T]he logic of coming to believe... like that of learning a language, has little room for argument, but once one has learned to speak the language of faith, argument becomes possible.[97]

The present study asks, however, whether the "cultural-linguistic" dismissal of the natural knowledge of God really coheres with what Thomas himself insists in his own treatment of this issue.

Lindbeck since the Publication of Nature of Doctrine

Since the publication of *Nature of Doctrine* in 1984, Lindbeck has continued to craft his cultural-linguistic proposal for understanding religion and religious doctrine. This development has served to further isolate individual religions from an external world that would supply evidence and argument. It has also served to answer questions arising from the *Nature of Doctrine*. In particular he has attempted to answer the following questions: (1) how does the postliberal approach affect scriptural interpretation? (2) what does intratextual theology mean? and (3) how does this approach engage in interreligious dialogue?

In an essay written for the 1988 Ratzinger Conference on Bible and Church, Lindbeck argues in favor of the "consensus and community-building potential of the 'classic' pattern of biblical interpretation."[98] In other words, he suggests that Scripture be read today "as a canonically and narrationally unified and internally glossed (that is, self-referential and self-interpreting) whole centered on Jesus Christ, and telling the story of the dealings of the Triune God with his people and his world in ways which are typologically ... applicable to the present."[99] The contemporary crisis in biblical interpretation arises from the gap between what historical-critical methods of interpretation tell us about the past, and how Scripture should be interpreted today. The contemporary theological scene, dominated by "translation theology," fails to encourage biblical literacy among the faithful with its insistence on translating the faith into current idioms.[100] Theologians today attempt to translate diverse historical reconstructions of Scripture into equally diverse contemporary parlance. In contrast, premodern theology escapes this problem:

> The only major source of theological diversity in premodern theology is the historical situation. The biblical message as classically interpreted is relatively stable: what chiefly changes are the philosophies and other culturally conditioned outlooks which are interpreted within the framework.[101]

Premodern theologians were able to put non-Christian philosophy to Christian use because they understood that "texts project worlds in which entire cultures can and have lived."[102] Thomas, for example, was able to put Aristotelianism to Christian use by absorbing the Aristotelian idiom into the biblical world. But what does it mean to live in a text?

> A habitable text need not have a primarily narrative structure..., but it must supply followable directions for coherent patterns of life in new situations. If it does this, it can be considered rational to dwell within it: no other foundations are necessary or, in the contemporary climate of opinion, possible.[103]

This proposal coheres with the contemporary post-Enlightenment situation that has caused both a loss of faith in autonomous reason, and a better understanding that we live in a socially, linguistically, and textually constructed world.[104] For Lindbeck, a return to classical biblical hermeneutics would imply a return to a more unified Christian community where Scripture grounds the community of faithful believers.

In another essay, "Toward a Postliberal Theology," Lindbeck further develops some of the conclusions of the *Nature of Doctrine* since its publication. He pushes the ramifications of his cultural-linguistic proposal further than he had done in his book by presenting a detailed analysis of intratextual theology. Specifically, he deals with the dogmatic problem of faithfulness by arguing that faithfulness in religion — at least in the three great monotheistic religions — primarily involves remaining faithful *to the text*. This discussion of faithfulness hinges on theology as intratextual. While Lindbeck had already established that intratextual theology "locates religious meaning within a religious system or text"[105] this article establishes what it means to be religiously faithful:

> [I]n the instance of religions more than any other type of semiotic system, description is not simply metaphorically but also literally intratextual. This is true in some degree of all the world's major faiths. They all have relatively fixed canons of writings that they treat as exemplary or normative instantiations of their semiotic codes. One test of faithfulness for all of them is the degree to which descriptions correspond to the semiotic universe paradigmatically encoded in holy writ.[106]

Different theologies could have an intratextual norm of faithfulness while at the same time maintain their material disagreements.[107] This intratextual norm of faithfulness is formal in that it deals with how we should live and understand our lives in light of the biblical narratives. The material conclusions to which we arrive could be different, but the formal concern to interpret our lives biblically holds the religious community together.

Finally, Lindbeck takes the cultural-linguistic alternative and moves from prolegomena to implementation in an article in *Modern Theology*.[108] Lindbeck asks how the postliberal approach engages interreligious dialogue. He contends that much attention has not been paid to religions as community-forming semiotic systems and to their uniqueness as "formally untranslatable and as materially consisting of the unsubstitutable memories and narratives which shape community identities."[109] Classical hermeneutics was able to maintain the primacy of Scripture for interpretation. While every reality could be translated into the "biblical universe of discourse" without losing its truthfulness, the same was not true in the other direction.[110] Nothing could be translated out of the biblical universe into an "independent communicative system" without damaging its truthfulness.[111] In particular, Thomas Aquinas maintained that "all entities and truths of whatever nature are *revelabilia,* that is, capable of entering into the sphere of revelation, of being seen in relation to God as known in and through the scriptural witness."[112] Lindbeck concludes that the untranslatability of religion should be understood in the following way:

> [T]he Bible as interpreted within the Christian mainstream purports to provide a totally comprehensive framework, a universal perspective, within which everything can be properly construed and outside of which nothing can be equally well understood. This double claim of comprehensiveness constitutes the general form of untranslatability.[113]

In scriptural hermeneutics the formal rules stay the same while the lexicon expands indefinitely. Lindbeck, then, brings a religion's untranslatability into focus, and calls his readers back to classical biblical hermeneutics — among whose practitioners Thomas is the fullest expression.

To understand Lindbeck's pivotal importance before, during, and after the publication of *Nature of Doctrine* one must recognize that he: (1) lays the initial framework for the establishment of a postliberal theology; (2) consistently uses Thomas as a theologian who coheres and sometimes expresses this new theology; and in particular (3) brings Thomas' understanding of the natural knowledge of God into compatibility, if not into full agreement, with this postliberal approach to theology.

2. Bruce Marshall

Bruce Marshall writes three important essays that culminate in a book, furthering this postliberal reading of Thomas begun by his mentor, George Lindbeck. In an essay entitled "Aquinas as Postliberal Theologian"[114] (1989), Marshall offers the first extended presentation of a postliberal Thomas, sparking considerable debate within circles of Thomist interpretation.[115] A second essay, "Absorbing the

World: Christianity and the Universe of Truth,"[116] (1990), further clarifies Lindbeck's proposal of theology as intratextual. A third essay, "Faith and Reason Reconsidered: Aquinas and Luther on Deciding What is True," takes the interpretive work begun in his 1989 essay and extends it into a comparison with Reformation theology. In his book, *Trinity and Truth,* Marshall engages in an extended study of the concept of truth and justification of such truth in Christianity.[117] After the publication of his book, Marshall continues to apply this constructive reading of Thomas to contemporary theological concerns.

In "Aquinas as Postliberal Theologian," Marshall explores the relationship between Lindbeck's and Thomas' understanding of truth and justification of Christian belief, arguing that Thomas and Lindbeck share the following fundamental claim:

> [U]tterances of Christian belief are ontologically true *only* if they cohere with specific linguistic and practical paradigms *internal* to the religion itself, and indeed that this coherence is an adequate justification of their ontological truth [italics mine].[118]

Lindbeck certainly agrees with Thomas that truth is a *correspondentia* or *adaequatio* of the mind to reality. When considering the *justification* or criterion for truth, Lindbeck's "criteria of linguistic and practical coherence" is similar to Thomas' position on the justification of religious truth.[119] In other words, while the referent for religious statements is objective reality, the criterion for these statements is intratextual. Therefore, there can be no philosophical or experiential basis for justification of religious knowledge.

How does Thomas consider the conditions under which one can assert a true proposition, or the "justification" for such a belief?[120] For Thomas, God is both the formal and material object of faith. God is the formal object of faith by being the "first truth." In other words, God is the measure and standard of all truth: for something to be true it has to be in accord with God's knowledge. Consequently, faith as such can involve no error or falsity since God is its formal object. In addition, since the *veritas prima* is *a Deo revelata,* the creeds, as a summary of Scripture, express the formal object of faith.[121] In order to establish the connection between God as *veritas prima* and the creeds, Thomas "argues that the formal object of faith must be linguistic in character."[122] He does this by applying the Aristotelian principle that "things known are in the knower in a way appropriate to the knower," or that humans know things by forming propositions about them.[123] Now, the formal object of faith, or the *prima veritas*, can be considered both from the point of view of the reality believed (God), and from the point of view of the believer. In this second way, the object of faith is " 'something composite (*complexum*), in the form of a proposition (*enuntiabilis*).' "[124] While the formal object of faith for Thomas is God, we can only apprehend God in faith through the language of Scripture and the creeds. Stated differently, the *prima veritas* is "linguistically embodied."[125]

For Thomas the material object of faith (God and anything created in its relation to God) is only reached through assent to propositions. Christians affirm only those propositions that are warranted by the formal object of faith. The propositions of God's self-communication are found in Scripture and summarized in the creeds. As a result:

> [C]oherence or agreement with the linguistic paradigms of the religion, especially key ones enunciated in the creeds, is for Christians a necessary condition for any sentence about God or creatures in relation to God being a true proposition.[126]

This is both a necessary and *sufficient* condition for Christian truth: any proposition that coheres with Scripture and the creeds must be true or correspond to reality. It is plausible, therefore, to interpret Thomas as holding that the "criterion of truth for Christian beliefs is their coherence with other beliefs, especially certain central ones."[127] Marshall pushes this interpretation further by claiming that this is "the *only* way Christian beliefs can be justified, since faith alone ... is the virtue by which the intellect is 'rightly ordered' to God — that is, which entails the *correspondentia* by which truth is defined."[128]

Consequently, unbelievers cannot utter true statements about God. Unbelievers do not believe that God exists "or hold any other beliefs about God which Christians hold" because 'they do not believe that God exists under those conditions which faith determines (*determinet*).' "[129] Pre-Christian philosophers held "beliefs about God" on the basis of demonstrative arguments.[130] They cannot believe that God exists without also believing in Scripture and the creeds. An unbeliever, then, can know nothing meaningful about God. For Marshall knowledge is subsumed under belief.

According to Marshall, not only do Lindbeck and Thomas agree on the linguistic coherence necessary for creedal ontological truth, but they also agree on the practices that are necessary for ontological truth. Since faith is an assent of the intellect moved by the will, the act of faith is rooted in *caritas,* or love. As a result, this intellectual assent is accompanied by a desire to act in ways appropriate to what is believed. Religious propositions, then, require both a linguistic context and a set of appropriate practices. These conditions are sufficient for an act of faith.

What should we make of Thomas' disjunction between *scientia* and *fides?* How is an act of faith an act of religious knowledge? Since for Thomas, *scientia* about God is only possible after faith, Marshall concludes:

> If faith is the necessary beginning of the process which ends in complete *scientia,* then there simply is no *scientia Dei,* no correspondence of the mind to God, outside of faith...only the believer means by "God" what one must mean in order to refer to God at all.... The Christian and the philosopher both say "God is one," but because they do so under different "conditions," they in fact hold different beliefs about God.[131]

Even a philosopher's formally valid argument cannot bring about any *adaequatio mentis ad rem* in relation to God, while the same demonstration can yield such knowledge when it happens in the context of faith. For Thomas *scientia* about God, then, occurs only within the context of faith. As a result, to seek *scientia* for Thomas is to do "intratextual theology" for Lindbeck, in which one " 'redescribes reality within the scriptural framework rather than translating Scripture into extratextual categories.' "[132]

Since for Thomas the Christian belief system is comprehensive, everything can be understood in Christian terms. As a result, there is no "external standard of truth" or "independent vantage point" from which Christian claims can be assessed, even of the existence of God.[133] In Thomas' context, Aristotelian philosophy was the "prime candidate" for external standards of truth. But Thomas did not appeal to these external standards. Instead, he evaluated Aristotle by understanding him in Christian terms, or to use Lindbeck's terms, by drawing him into the biblical world.[134]

In this article Marshall further weaves a thread begun by Lindbeck. He argues that Thomas can be understood in postliberal terms exactly where we would not expect him to: in his position on the natural knowledge of God. If statements about God are as context-dependent as Thomas maintains, then no unbeliever can utter anything true about God. Marshall maintains that Lindbeck successfully translates this Thomistic claim into contemporary postliberal terms.

Marshall writes a second important essay, "Absorbing the World: Christianity and the Universe of Truths" (1990), in which he further explains Lindbeck's metaphor that Scripture absorbs the world. Marshall maintains that the Christian community primarily tests and reforms its beliefs and practices by appealing to the "plain sense of Scripture."[135] Scripture has "justificatory primacy" such that the closer a statement stands to the central Christian beliefs, the more it must cohere with the plain sense of Scripture. In addition, this primacy means that the internal beliefs and practices of Christianity are the main criteria of truth.[136] Absorbing the world into the scriptural text means:

> ... the ongoing effort by the Christian community and individual members to construe novel, unfamiliar, or "alien" sentences in a way which *both* (a) constitutes the best available interpretation of those sentences and (b) allows them to be held true.[137]

This translation may involve changing the meaning of a discourse that is external to Christianity. Thus, Thomas' transformation and expansion of Aristotle creates a "superior Aristotelianism by his massive effort to interpret (or 'redescribe') Aristotle so that he can hold as much of Aristotle as possible true within a distinctively Christian and scriptural universe of discourse."[138] Christians attempt to engage in discourse by interpreting external data by their own internal criteria. In this case Scripture becomes " 'not simply a source of precepts and truths, but the interpretive framework for all reality.' "[139]

As a result, a religion is reasonable if it can offer an intelligible interpretation of the diverse situations that believers encounter. In Lindbeck's terms reasonableness is weighed according to a religion's "assimilative power." This power is accessible to people both within and outside the Christian community. One need not believe in Christianity in order to understand that its "assimilative power" is a criterion for truth, nor need one believe in order to apply the test. Non-Christians, for example, might be committed to the notion of assimilative power for their own philosophical reasons, or they might adhere to a religion that employs this notion internally. Rather, one need only become sufficiently acquainted with the religion's discourse and practice in order to make a judgment about its truth claims.[140]

Marshall then takes up the criticism of fideism that is often charged against this approach. First, this metaphor of Scripture absorbing the world does not replace the world with the text or escape from the world. Rather, it interprets the world through the text. Consequently, it encourages an open-ended engagement with whatever claims are made that are external to the Christian community.[141] We come to understand these external claims by a principle of charity that seeks to find truth in these claims.[142] But we judge these claims against the horizon of Scripture. Second, the appeal to external criteria that is often raised against this postliberal approach begs the question of what comprises adequate criteria. If we are to judge Christianity by external criteria, it cannot be criteria that are internal to any other web of beliefs. The question is whether there exist absolutely external criteria at all. Finally, criticisms have been raised that this postliberal approach prematurely rejects any truth claim that is too foreign to its web of beliefs, and does not recognize that beliefs are always placed in danger when entering into conversation with nonadherents to those beliefs. This criticism, however, offers a standard for rational conversation that is impossible to meet, for we cannot place all of our beliefs open to doubt at the same time.[143]

Marshall does allow, however, for the possibility that encounter with alien belief systems may cause Christians to either reject or revise some of their beliefs. Thomas' attempt to absorb aspects of Aristotle's physics, metaphysics, and cosmology into Genesis 1 is a case in point. But while external truth claims may change how Christians interpret the plain sense of Scripture, they do not benefit from justificatory primacy, since there is no external standard against which these claims can be assessed.

In this article Marshall further explains how Scripture can absorb the world without necessarily falling into fideism. The crucial issue here is the justificatory primacy that is ascribed to Scripture over everything else. Marshall's defense of this postliberal approach claims that it can ascribe this kind of primacy to Scripture while at the same time take external truth claims seriously. The assimilative power of Scripture that Marshall proposes here, while not enabling people to decide among alternative religions on the basis of reason alone, helps " 'provide warrants for taking reasonableness in religion seriously.' "[144]

Marshall published a third important article, "Faith and Reason Reconsidered: Aquinas and Luther on Deciding What Is True" (1999). In this article Marshall provocatively argues that Aquinas and Luther hold the same view of faith and reason: "the view that the most central Christian beliefs, those generated by communal interpretation of Scripture according to creedal rules, enjoy unrestricted epistemic primacy."[145] These central beliefs are, of course, held by faith rather than by reason.[146] Both Thomas and Luther answer the question that governs this article, "How should we decide what sentences and beliefs are true?"

For Thomas, a person learning about the chief matter of Christian faith, the salvation brought about by the cross of Christ, employs reason in a particular way. This person, by " 'presupposing the foundations of the true faith, if he finds anything true in the teachings of the philosophers, takes it into the obedience of faith.' "[147] Marshall interprets Thomas here to be affirming that:

> ...we ought to decide whether other beliefs are true by seeing whether their contents agree with those interpreted sentences which together identify and describe "the salvation accomplished by the cross of Christ."[148]

The content of faith that is expressed through the creeds of the Christian community is to be treated as an indivisible whole. Faith "clings to the incarnate and triune God who manifests himself to us as first truth by way of the scripturally normed discourse of the Christian community."[149]

When dealing with the concrete example of the pre-Christian philosophers, Thomas admits that they knew certain things about God available to human reason while not knowing about the Trinity and the incarnation. However, " 'Even if [the Gentiles] err in the smallest way regarding the knowledge of God, they are said to be completely ignorant of him.[150] Believing that God exists and that God is one, then, are only true when one also believes that God is Triune and Incarnate.[151] Marshall concludes that the pre-Christian philosopher and the Christian believer mean two *contradictory* things when they say that God exists.

While Thomas thinks that creatures could have known God, God has withdrawn this knowledge after the fall of sin.[152] As a result, a believer who reaches knowledge about God primarily relies on God's self-testimony rather than on her own intelligence. If a conflict arises between the articles of faith and one's own reasoning, epistemic primacy belongs to the former. Even statements that appear to be self-evident principles (*principia per se nota*) need to be tested for consistency against the articles of faith.[153] Wisdom for Thomas, therefore, is the "practice of interpreting and assessing everything else in light specifically of Scripture's identification and description of the human being Jesus Christ, and above all of the salvation accomplished by his cross."[154] The Son teaches us, and the Holy Spirit enables us to be taught.

This interpretation of Thomas leads Marshall to conclude that Thomas' and Luther's position with respect to deciding what is true was the same: they were both scripturalist and creedalist in their epistemologies. In fact, "[L]ogically, if not rhetorically and stylistically, Luther did just what Aquinas would have done if Aquinas had been living and writing in Luther's very different situation."[155]

While his 2000 book *Trinity and Truth* is not put forth as an interpretation of Thomas, Marshall himself notes that "Aquinas is the deepest influence on the book,"[156] stating, in fact, that he has "learned to think about truth and justification of belief in a trinitarian way by reading Thomas Aquinas,"[157] especially by reading Thomas' commentary on the Gospel of John. This reading of Thomas suggests that "on the questions at issue here, as on most others, [Thomas] presents a far different and more compelling figure than is often supposed nowadays by his admirers and detractors alike."[158] A brief sketch of the argument of the book should reveal Marshall's most fully detailed approach to issues in epistemic truth and justification, and where he disagrees with Thomas on such issues.[159]

Marshall employs tools from the contemporary analytic tradition, particularly from Donald Davidson and Alfred Tarski, in order to argue that Christian doctrine, especially the doctrine on the Trinity, should serve as the primary criteria of truth.[160] He criticizes five epistemological assumptions characteristic of modern theology:

interiority, foundationalism, epistemic dependence, pragmatism, and correspondence. Against these, he presents a "coherentist" view of justification.[161] On such a view the biblical narratives are primary: "[t]he narratives which identify Jesus are epistemic trump; if it comes to conflict between these narratives and any other sentences proposed for belief, the narratives win."[162] The church's central beliefs based on these narratives have "unrestricted epistemic primacy" that "can be stated only negatively: no sentences which are *in*consistent with those beliefs can be true..., but consistency with the church's central beliefs does not normally guarantee, all by itself, that other beliefs are true."[163] Justifying Christian beliefs on the whole could be based on the belief system's "assimilative powers." If Christianity shows the ongoing capacity to assimilate alien beliefs into its web of beliefs, it is "holding its beliefs in an epistemically responsible way."[164] While rejecting a correspondence theory of truth, correspondence comes into play, not between ideas or sentences and reality, but through a correspondence between Jesus and the Father, and between creatures and God. While Christ is the "truth-bearer," creatures can become conformed to Christ by grace, and therefore themselves become bearers of the truth.

After putting forth an extended argument on the justification of Christian truth, Marshall takes up Thomas explicitly in order to disagree with him regarding what truth actually is. Marshall contends that Thomas, like many of his contemporaries, holds two different accounts of truth without explicitly distinguishing them. Thomas sees truth as a correspondence of the mind to reality. But sometimes forms bring this about "when they come to exist in the intellect by passing through different media which link the intellect to the world."[165] At other times, though, sentences bring this about — in those articles, for example, that decide whether particular sentences are true under certain interpretations. Today, however, since everyone agrees that sentences exist, and knows how to use them, the notion of truth bearers "of the more dubious and obscure sort" as exemplified in "non-linguistic mental entities"[166] should be abandoned. Marshall concludes by arguing:

> According to our theologically disciplined notion of truth, beliefs justified according to these standards will generally be true just in case the triune God — and especially, in his distinctive way,

the risen Christ — undertakes his truth-bestowing act (1) with regard to belief in the narratives which identify him, (2) with regard to no belief inconsistent with these narratives, and (3) with regard to beliefs which there is otherwise good reason to hold. Truth will be *accessible* to belief if we can *count* on the triune God to do just this — if, when it comes to our own beliefs, his truth-bestowing act is not for the most part inaccessible to us.[167]

Both in his articles and in his book, Marshall furthers the postliberal approach first enunciated by Lindbeck by both clarifying what this approach entails, and by more concretely presenting Thomas Aquinas' theology as an intellectual precursor to postliberal theology.

After the publication of his book, Marshall has continued to apply this provocative reading of Thomas to pressing contemporary problems in theology, most notably to theological interpretations of Israel.[168] The essay most central to our purposes, however, develops his reading of Thomas' understanding of theology: "*Quod Scit Una Uetula*: Aquinas on the Nature of Theology."[169]

In this essay, Marshall compares the knowledge held by an old lady — a *uetula* — by faith to the knowledge gained through the science of theology. Here Marshall furthers his observation that Christians are the only ones who are able to maintain that God exists. Marshall reexamines his analysis of the passage in the *Secuda secundae* about unbelievers (*infideles*) not able *really* to believe that God exists, since they do not assent to the "scriptural and creedal faith of the Christian community."[170] Marshall adds, "When it comes to God, the web of belief is so tightly woven that for any one statement to be true, it has to be believed with many other statements, above all the articles of Christian faith."[171]

This provocative reading concludes: "[T]he bold coherentism for which Aquinas argues here effectively rules out natural theology (unless, of course, it is practiced by Christians)."[172] Marshall then characterizes the Thomists who would object to this claim — naming Gilson as their representative — as those who think Thomas put belief in God's existence and nature "on a firm rational foundation, whence it could ... serve as a basis for the acceptance of revealed truths about God beyond reason's grasp."[173] Against this school of Thomism, Marshall defends Thomas. He chooses Scripture — especially

Rom. 1:19-21 — as his main tool for such defense. The attributes about God *could have been* rationally demonstrated, had human beings not sinned. But now with their minds lost and their hearts darkened, they can only see clearly through a restorative light — the *lumen fidei*.[174]

Marshall admits that this "bold coherentism" faces significant challenges, for if the unbeliever and the believer mean two different things when they state that God exists, then the unbeliever is ignorant about God. She could not disbelieve Christian claims about God, since she would simply be holding different beliefs. On this account, then, she does not even succeed in being an *infidelis*.[175] Marshall admits these challenges, but maintains that this bold coherentism is Thomas' position, at least in his later writings.

Marshall furthers Lindbeck's initial suggestions about Thomas' epistemology in significant ways. His most marked contribution has been to argue for a bold coherentist view of truth in Thomas. We will see if such a coherentist account holds up to our own analysis of Thomas' texts in chapters 2 through 5.

3. Eugene Rogers

Eugene Rogers has presented the most extended analysis of this postliberal reading of Thomas in his recent work, *Thomas Aquinas and Karl Barth: Sacred Doctrine and the Natural Knowledge of God*. Rogers seeks to "displace" the traditional interpretation of Thomas by proposing "a genuinely 'evangelical' Thomas" who "speaks always and everywhere as a theologian rather than a philosopher."[176] He analyzes Questions 1 and 2 of the *Prima pars* of the *Summa theologiae* in light of Thomas' commentary on Romans 1:20. The study concludes by comparing Thomas' commentary to Barth's reading of Romans. This interpretation of Thomas creates a curious convergence between Karl Barth and Thomas Aquinas on the natural knowledge of God.[177]

Rogers' main argument relies upon a hypothesis (1) established about *sacra doctrina* in Question 1 of the *Summa theologiae*, and (2) tested through an interpretation of Thomas' commentary on Romans. Thomas understands *sacra doctrina* as an Aristotelian *scientia*:

A science is the more Aristotelian, the more it proceeds from first principles. Unitary first principles take propositional and real forms. For sacred doctrine, those first principles are respectively scripture and Christ.[178]

Sacra doctrina takes its first principles from divine revelation, which, in turn, is not simply identified with Scripture, but with Jesus Christ.[179] Just as an Aristotelian science offers demonstrations by means of its first principles, *sacra doctrina* "finds its 'most fitting' demonstrations in Christ incarnate."[180] *Scientia*, therefore, is a tool that relates theology and Jesus Christ.[181]

How does this understanding of *scientia* emerge in Thomas' writings? First, a science is Aristotelian when it proceeds from first principles.[182] While these principles are expressed through syllogistic reasoning, they do not simply exist on paper or in propositions. Rather, they "pervade everything that is."[183] Thomas understood first principles to exist both in the mind and in the world. First principles are "unitary beginnings (*archai*) that make both things and ideas work. They identify a single necessity, of which we are accustomed to distinguish two aspects":[184] in real things and in propositions. Consequently, *scientia* proceeds from first principles in these two aspects. In addition, these first principles "inhere in actually existing things as their forms, and thingly forms begin in actually existing things as their first principles."[185] Since the principles of things can exist in the world before they exist in *scientia*, intelligibility can exist in itself before actually existing in us. Therefore, Aristotelian science can exist in the thing to be studied as well as in the mind studying it.[186] The *existence* of first principles is what makes a science Aristotelian, not the fact that the conclusions are drawn from its first principles.[187] The logic that connects the first principles with the conclusions adds nothing new to the first principles. The scientific character of *sacra doctrina* "proceeds from first principles not on account of the (discursive) *linkages* they boast with a higher science, but on account of the (principial) *light they shed*, even if it lies beyond us."[188] These first principles can be understood as "revelations" such that *sacra doctrina* proceeds from formal "revelations" or from the "self-manifestations of real forms, real first principles."[189]

Second, in his discussion of *sacra doctrina*, Thomas transforms the Aristotelian concept of *scientia* from a discipline whose teleology is without intention, to one whose teleology is centered on Christ.[190] Aristotle speaks of the divine without a will: "the whole point of form is to explicate teleology without intention, as of the unmoved mover to explicate causation without extension. Both *telos* and prime mover attract, that is, without willing."[191] This transformation turns what was originally an Aristotelian science into a radically *un*-Aristotelian science: "So Christology has assumed teleology, rendering Aristotle's account a deficient, reified case of itself."[192] The difference between Aristotle and Thomas lies in this: "For Aristotle human beings were made by impersonal form for the world; for Thomas human creatures were made for God by God, a person capable of direct address in words like 'Father.'"[193] In Thomas the structural first principles both of the world and of one's own understanding lie beyond themselves, for they are found in the mind of God. In this life, sacred doctrine is a borrowed science whose first principles are taken from authority. As a result:

> Sacred doctrine is a science with believers only. That situation constitutes a contradiction in terms to Aristotle. Yet in this life we are united to the subject of sacred doctrine only in the habit of faith, not in that of *scientia* (I.12.13 *ad* 1)... the answer to the question, whether those things that are of faith can be known (*scita*), is "no" (II-II.1.5).... Among the perfections of *scientia*, sacred doctrine lacks the one Thomas calls *plena possessio* by human beings (I-II.68.2c). That is, although the *discipline* of sacred doctrine is a science (I.1.2), the *habit* (II-II.1.5) is not. Thomas presents us with a paradox. In sacred doctrine we have a science without scientists.[194]

The science of *sacra doctrina* is not a human inquiry that leads to knowledge of God. Rather, it is a science that is established by the "*subject's* inquiry after *us*."[195] While we have a natural desire to know God, we receive a provisional answer in this life by a "*praecognitum finis*" and in the next, by the "*scientia Dei et beatorum*."[196] Since we do not have the ability to know God on our own, "the effective structure of the soul that results from revelation is the infused habit of *formed faith*."[197] This faith is formed into propositions by the discipline of sacred doctrine whose first principles are revealed and then *believed*. In fact, the "intelligible structure of reality to which the science's intelligibility corresponds remains altogether unknown to us in this life even as faith unites us to it (I.12.13 *ad* 1) by a self-revelation of God—climaxing in the Word become flesh—to which we now enjoy only textual access."[198]

A problem arises, however, in that if *sacra doctrina* is to be an Aristotelian science, it must be unified. But in *sacra doctrina* "[t]he end of inquiry, the habits of the soul, the axioms of deduction, the forms of things in the world and our access to them have all come radically apart."[199] *Sacra doctrina* is considered unified, however, because it borrows its first principles from a perfect science, the knowledge that God has of Godself, and that the blessed have of God. For Rogers *sacra doctrina*:

> ...to proceed from first principles must therefore mean to proceed from borrowed, that is, *revealed* first principles — no longer in the straightforward sense in which all science proceeds from the revelations of existing things, but now in the radically theological sense in which a revelation sheds a light that goes beyond the created tendency to associate being with the deliverances of our natural conceptual scheme and requires an intentionality empowered by God's elevating agency.[200]

Since God is the first principle of all things, and all things can be considered as they relate to God, *sacra doctrina* treats all things in this way. In other words, it views all things not as *revelata,* but as *revelabilia. Revelata* are things that have been revealed, while *revelabilia* are things that contain a natural form of revealability regardless of whether or not they are written about in Scripture.[201] All things that exist can be considered as *revelabilia.*

Article 10 of Question 1 lays out the first principles of *sacra doctrina,* namely, Scripture and Christ. The four senses of scriptural interpretation all center around Christ, for the fundamental teaching of the Christian faith is the salvation brought about by the cross of Christ.[202] As shown above, *sacra doctrina* treats its objects as *revelabilia;* Christ is the exemplar, the demonstration, and the central *revelabilium.* For, only through Christ do human beings reach *scientia beatorum.*[203] In addition, through knowing Christ "we get a foretaste (the *praecognitum finis* of I.1.1) of what friendship with God is like."[204] Finally, while *sacra doctrina* in a sense provides a "science without scientists," Christ, "as God, *is* such a scientist, does possess the beatific vision, does enjoy the fruits of the demonstration his humanity provides, even in the strictest sense: and he does so *for us*."[205] Thus, Christ is the *demonstratio,* the *via,* leading Christians to *scientia Dei.*

Thomas primarily tries to establish the logic internal to revelation rather than to establish a theological methodology in Question 1.[206] That question has a circular structure in which article 1 asks something foreknown about the end that is found in article 10, and article 10 lays out the scriptural authority upon which article 1 depends.[207] In addition, while *sacra doctrina* began as an instantiation of Aristotelian science, it became the norm against which Aristotelian science is an imperfect realization.

Rogers then asks whether Thomas abandons his scriptural and Christological principles when he moves from Question 1 to Question 2. He analyzes Thomas' interpretation of Romans 1:20, "the invisible things of God are known from the things God has made," since Thomas cites this passage as a warrant for the problematic enterprise that will be instantiated in his *quinque viae.*

This analysis concludes that Thomas' discussion of the natural knowledge of God should be understood as "objectively trinitarian" and as "issuing effectively in justice, piety, and gratitude."[208] This natural knowledge

> ... represents nature as completed and perfected by *grace*. Under conditions of sin, the completion and perfection of nature by grace involve the redemption that comes to the *faithful*.[209]

As a result, natural knowledge of God is always "*cognitio naturalis gratia evangelica Christi,*"[210] or natural knowledge by the evangelical grace of Christ. Natural knowledge can be both detained and redeemed, depending on the disposition of the will. In the first case, natural knowledge is not neutral. It is, rather, "feckless," ineffective, and culpable:[211]

> It exists only in order to show what is being denied. It does not show what people possess, but what they lack. Their cognition amounts, in Preller's words, to "a felt ignorance" and it is in that sense alone a cognition rather than a failure of cognition.[212]

This detained natural knowledge *would have* been effective had it not been destroyed by human sin. It is understood correctly as knowledge in what it is meant to have attained; but it has never actually been carried out. Redeemed natural knowledge of God, however, leads to charity, fruitfulness, and joy. Natural knowledge of God depends upon the will, which was created to "lean upon grace."[213] This natural knowledge of God, which functions only in the presence of grace, leads human beings to do the good. In addition, faith, not *scientia*, makes this natural knowledge effective.[214] In the Romans commentary, then, Thomas ascribes natural knowledge of God to the Gentiles only to point out the knowledge that they *would have had* if their wills had turned toward God. He refers to this as "knowledge" only out of "courtesy"; it actually turns out not to be knowledge *at all*, but sounds rather more like ignorance.[215] Rogers concludes:

> So in the concrete situation of human beings the natural cognition of God is explicitly and logically dependent upon the revealed cognition of God — that is upon the revealed cognitions of God properly and effectively so called or the *revelabilia* as God's form in the world, engaged in informing human beings toward their end of friendship with God.... Thomas uses the term *theologia naturalis* only in that negative sense. Thomas never uses the phrase "natural theology" to describe what he is up to in the Romans commentary or the *Summa*. He thinks of both as biblical, dogmatic theology.... After Deism, however, one thought that the whole point of natural theology was to be *the same thing* when believers and non-believers practiced it... one of Thomas' genres had been lost, and Barth rightly rejected it in theology as a category mistake. But Thomas did not make that mistake. Thomas made a distinction.[216]

Thomas' *quinque viae*, then, are written not in order to lead human beings up to God by their own ability. Rather, "it renders God world-enveloping"[217] by viewing the demonstrations as *"revelabilia, in which, through God-bestowed faith, they are joined with the first truth they cannot otherwise reach."*[218] Thomas co-opts Aristotelian language into the Christian language game in order to trace the relationship between the created order and its Creator.[219] In this way, Thomas makes the Lindbeckian move of absorbing the world into the scriptural text, and even of making the whole world intratextual.[220]

Rogers concludes that the way Thomas uses Scripture is not fideist because he deals with cosmology. In other words, there is a legitimate place in Thomas for the theology that pertains to metaphysics.

In addition, his use of cosmology is not foundationalist since he interprets the *quinque viae* through the text of Scripture. He does not try to prove the existence of God in a nineteenth-century foundationalist way. Instead, he is thoroughly Christological in his scriptural and cosmological observations.[221]

Rogers adds a few remarks at the conclusion of his work about the discussion that underlies this question about the natural knowledge of God: the nature-grace debate. He claims that for Thomas there are two lights (one of the intellect, and the other of faith) that come from the grace of God. There are, then, two kinds of grace. The first light is that by which the Gentiles have any knowledge of God:

> That a human being can have *cognitio* of some truth without grace, which Thomas affirms at I-II.109.1, does not deny that the cognition in question is defective, and does not affirm that the cognition in question has anything to do with our elevation — except as it gets taken up into the nature that is shot through with *grace*.[222]

While Thomas distinguishes these two types of grace for the sake of analysis, the first kind cannot achieve anything on its own. It simply works proleptically until God's plan takes place in us; "it is not a human power so much as a divine mercy."[223]

To conclude, Rogers provides a detailed interpretation of Thomas on the natural knowledge of God that brings the work begun by Lindbeck and Marshall to its logical fruition. The natural knowledge of God found in this reading of Thomas is true only within the context of Christian revelation. As a result, those untouched by Christian revelation cannot come to any true, effective knowledge of God. If this interpretation of Thomas is correct, contemporary assumptions about the differences between Protestant and Catholic understandings of the natural knowledge of God need to be substantially reevaluated. In fact, on this account Thomas emerges as a medieval precursor to Luther, Barth, and postliberal theology. The reading of Thomas outlined above — from Lindbeck's initial seeds to Marshall's elaborations to Rogers' full proposal — provides the contemporary problematic of this book. If it is in fact a plausible reading of Thomas, then age-old divisions between Protestant and Catholic theology might be healed.

– Two –

An Initial Natural Knowledge of God: The Remote Context
(ST I, 12, 12)

Introduction

Having outlined the postliberal reading of Thomas on natural knowledge of God — namely, that there is no such knowledge in Thomas' theology — we now turn to Thomas' texts themselves to see how they measure up to this interpretation. As mentioned in the last chapter, we will apply a historic-systematic method of analysis, one that takes the meaning of the text as a central concern, while attending to historical data that informs variances in the text. The first step in this method involves an examination of the remote coordinate texts.

The remote coordinate texts that bear importantly on the analysis of Question 12 consist of (a) the prologue to the *Summa* as a whole, and (b) the introduction to questions 1, 2, and 3 of the *Prima pars*. These prologues disclose the framework within which Question 12, article 12 must be examined, shedding light on how the article fits into the web of questions as a whole. This examination of the prologues offers the structural context for article 12.

Title of the Work

Before an analysis of the prologue, one might say a word about the title given to the work itself. In fact, it does not seem that Thomas himself gave the work its title. Nevertheless, this work soon acquired *Summa theologiae* as its most ancient and widely attested title.[1] The title reveals at least how his contemporaries and the immediate subsequent generations received it.

As a result of the rise of the medieval universities, the context within which theologians worked changed. Their teaching and disputations distanced themselves from more immediate pastoral, spiritual, and confessional concerns, and moved toward greater systematization and conceptualization. Alexander of Hales was the first Master of Theology at the University of Paris to lecture on the *Sentences* of Peter Lombard, a practice that quickly became commonplace at the university.[2] Originally, a *summa* meant a "brief, synthetic and complete collection of 'sentences' in which one aimed at presenting the truths of Christian doctrine (or any body of doctrine)."[3] It replaced the older *sententiae* and *florilegia,* and came to be the dominant form of twelfth-century theology.[4] The first *summas* were distinguished from the previously dominant *libri sententiarum* in that they were no longer simple compilations of the writings of the Fathers and other ancient writers. Rather, they put forth organized presentations of materials, while still remaining close to the texts that they coordinated. In commenting on his résumé of Christian history, for example, Honorius of Autun remarks that he named this work *summa totius* because the events ocurring throughout Scripture were presented in a summarized fashion.[5] The *summa,* then, became the principal work of the twelfth century, moving beyond the older *sententiae* and *florilegia.*[6] Chenu finds three characteristic purposes of a thirteenth century *summa:* (1) to expound, in a concise and abridged manner, the whole of a given scientific field (original meaning); (2) to organize, beyond any piecemeal analysis, the objects of this field of knowledge in a synthetic way; (3) to realize this aim so that the product would be adapted for the teaching of students.[7] What characterized a thirteenth-century *summa,* then, was an effort at pedagogical, comprehensive and systematic treatment of a given subject matter in a concise manner. Thomas offered his *Summa theologiae* as a contribution to this textual tradition.

General Prologue

An examination of this general prologue to the *Summa* should note (1) the capacity in which Thomas puts forth this work, (2) the audience that he intends to instruct, (3) the purpose he sets out to fulfill, and (4) the method employed to reach that purpose.

When turning to the prologue, the first question that arises involves the capacity in which the author sets forth this work. The prologue explicitly states that Thomas writes as a *Catholicae veritatis doctor,* a teacher of Catholic truth. In other words, he sets forth this work as a theologian writing from within an ecclesial tradition:

> Aquinas was by vocation, training, and self-understanding an ordained teacher of an inherited theology. He would have been scandalized to hear himself described as an innovator in fundamental matters and more scandalized still to hear himself — or any Christian — called a "philosopher," since this term often had a pejorative sense for thirteenth-century Latin authors.[8]

Thomas wrote as a theologian who was in charge of teaching both young Dominicans and students at the University of Paris. Pedagogical concerns, then, were at the forefront of his purpose in writing the *Summa*.

The question of author logically engages that of audience: what was the audience that Thomas sought to teach? The prologue emphasizes that the intended audience was comprised of *incipientes* or *novitii*. But who exactly were these medieval beginners, these new students of the Christian religion? Leonard Boyle's important study of the setting of the *Summa theologiae* offers an in-depth look at these thirteenth-century beginners. Boyle argues against the traditional interpretation, namely, that the *Summa theologiae* was intended for students at the University of Paris. Since the prologue is not clear about who these beginners were, Boyle looks to the *Summa theologiae*'s historical context to clarify the composition of Thomas' audience. He proposes that the students mentioned in the prologue to the *Summa* had not received the educational opportunities of someone like Thomas or Albert, and were, as a result, "young, run-of-the-mill Dominicans."[9] Thomas began writing the *Summa theologiae* between 1265 and 1268 at Santa Sabina where he was in charge of setting up a *studium personale*. This *studium personale* was "no more than an attempt by the Roman Province to allow select students to prepare themselves under a single master, Thomas, for the priesthood and the Dominican apostolate."[10] The courses offered at this *studium* had the same pastoral motivations as the courses Thomas had been teaching at Orvieto (1261–1265) before moving to Santa Sabina.[11] The training that the *fratres communes* received during that time was comprised mainly of practical theology, with moral issues being at the center of such teaching.[12] Teaching the *fratres communes* at Orvieto led Thomas to choose to contribute to the already existing manualist tradition in his order.[13] In these earlier years he became aware of the weak formation that these Dominican preachers were receiving. Their formation lacked coherence as a whole, solid grounding in the Scriptures, and serious dogmatic training.[14]

In September of 1265 the annual Chapter of the Roman Province to which Thomas belonged instructed him to set up a *studium* in Rome for students from various houses of the province.[15] This project offered Thomas the opportunity to develop a curriculum of his own, one that did not necessarily follow the Dominican educational procedures of his time. During this period Thomas lectured on God, Creation, and Trinity (the topics of the first book of Lombard's *Sentences*), rather than on the customary topics taken up by the practical theology of his time. The fact that Thomas begins his *Summa theologiae* with doctrinal rather than "practical" matters (such as those heard within the confessional) suggests that he was trying to place the practical theology of earlier Dominican manuals in their wider theological context:

> Christian morality, once for all, was shown to be something more than a question of straight ethical teaching or of vices and virtues in isolation. Inasmuch as man was an intelligent being who was master of himself and possessed of freedom and choice, he was in the image of God. To study human action is therefore to study the image of God and to operate on a theological plane. To study human action on a theological plane is to study it in relation to its beginning and end, God, and the bridge between, Christ and his sacraments.[16]

Boyle concludes that the *incipientes* referred to in the prologue were Dominicans studying at the *studium personale* at Santa Sabina, not the select few who were sent to Paris for university education.

The *Summa theologiae*, however, does not immediately strike the contemporary reader as pedagogy for *beginners*. Chenu admits this incongruity, and suggests that "[t]here is perhaps in this intent some of that illusion which is common to professors as regards the capacities of their students — even university students."[17] Another reading of this incongruity, however, has appeared in a provocative study that is not satisfied with Chenu's suggestion and takes particular issue with Boyle's interpretation of the *incipientes* mentioned in the *Summa*.

John Jenkins, C.S.C., argues that these students were no "run-of-the-mill Dominicans" for four main reasons. First, the *Summa*'s structure and content are sophisticated and demanding, addressing the most controversial issues of Thomas' time. A comparison of discussions in the *Summa* to earlier parallel discussions will indicate that the *Summa* treats questions in a more advanced manner than do Thomas' previous works. Next, the *Summa* was written as second-level pedagogy; it was designed so that the student would learn to move from the fundamental causes to the conclusions about the subject matter. In this second stage, the student begins to acquire intellectual habits that enable him to consider effects through their causes.[18] This is contrasted to first-level pedagogy where the student becomes familiar with the fundamental concepts in the discipline. In the first stage, the instructor teaches the student by using *quia* demonstrations: moving from what is most apparent to her (effects) to what is least apparent (cause). Third, the *Summa* seems to have been written to serve similar purposes as Peter Lombard's *Sentences*. Jenkins argues that, most likely, students of the *Summa* were at the same level as students of Lombard's work, the latter being engaged in a final and comprehensive course in theology.[19] Fourth, if Thomas meant his *Summa* for his Dominican *fratres communes,* he could have told the priories and provincial *studia* to use his work. Thomas profoundly influenced the educational policy of his province, so much so that the 1265 provincial chapter put him in charge of both establishing and running the *studium* at Santa Sabina.[20] From 1272 to 1274, he lived in his province where he could easily have disseminated the first and second parts of the *Summa* and asked that they be used in the province's schools.[21] There is no evidence, however, that the *Summa* was generally used in the province during this time or shortly thereafter. Jenkins maintains:

> There would have been reason to continue to teach the *Sentences* to those students destined for university study, for this was still the standard university text. However, for the *fratres communes* in the priories who were not destined for the universities, there would have been no reason not to substitute the *Summa* as the standard theological text — if, in fact, it was intended for this group.[22]

Jenkins compiles all his evidence, both circumstantial external clues and internal design of the text, to argue that the *Summa theologiae* was written for university students who had had extensive philosophical and classical training, particularly in Aristotle.[23]

While no definitive identification of these *incipientes* to the *Summa* may be possible, the historical and textual evidence seems to point in both directions. It is possible that when composing this work Thomas primarily had his students at Santa Sabina in mind, but he also assumed that it would benefit a more experienced university audience. He also could have hoped that the lucidity of the organization of the material would guide the *incipientes* at Santa Sabina through the complex questions that comprise the *Summa*. It is clear, however, that this *Summa* broke with the reigning textbooks of the day, as Thomas "devotes special attention to the philosophical, metaphysical, psychological, and ethical foundations of speculative theology, and this in a measure not equaled by any previous theological *Summa*."[24] In addition, the effective history of the audience to the *Summa theologiae* points in both directions. In the years that followed, the *Summa* circulated mostly through abridged and vulgarized versions throughout Dominican houses of study. In addition, Lombard's *Sentences* remained the standard text at the University of Paris for a long time, its place never challenged by the Dominicans, while the moral work in the *Secunda secundae* was widely diffused.[25]

Regardless of whether the primary audience in this work was the Dominican at Santa Sabina or the university student in Paris, it is evident that Thomas was deeply concerned with pedagogy. Thomas notes that the instructional use made of the theological books of his day introduced useless questions, articles, and arguments that led to frustration and boredom in new students of theology. The medieval *lectiones* did not allow for a treatment according to the order native to the subject matter (*ordinem disciplinae,* or the method of learning), but according to the organization of the text upon which one was commenting, or as the occasion demanded. Thomas has in mind here two kinds of works.

On the one hand, the twelfth-century textbooks were not written according to the logic of the discipline. Some, such as the books of *Sentences,* explored issues that arose from the *lectio* or the explanation of the major and normative texts from Sacred Scripture and the Fathers; others arose from disputed questions such as *quaestiones disputatae* and *quaestiones quodlibetales*.[26] Some have argued that books like Peter Lombard's *Sentences,* Alexander of Hales' *Summa universae theologiae* or Raymond of Peñafort's *Summa de casibus* lacked a coherent organizational pattern.[27] For example, Grabmann was of the opinion that:

> The *Commentaries on the Sentences* and the *Summae* composed before the *Summa Theologica* of St. Thomas, frequently present a homogeneous and very monotonous aspect. The same questions are but too regularly discussed and solved by means of the same authorities and reasons [sic]. The objections and difficulties are in large measure borrowed and handed down from one author to another. Not rarely entire articles or at least important fragments thereof are taken over verbatim.[28]

The teacher who commented either on Scripture or Lombard's *Sentences* was restricted to commenting on the content and arrangement of the text.

On the other hand, the medieval disputed questions and quodlibetal works were written according to the *occasio disputandi*.[29] On these occasions the speaker was similarly limited to the theme of the disputation:

> The disputation frequently also gave rise to a great many sterile questions which merely helped to confuse those who heard them and prevented them from forming any total picture of the faith which had passed down to them and which it was the purpose of teaching to provide.[30]

In this prologue Thomas has in mind the weaknesses of the medieval *lectio* and *quaestio* format, a format, of course, in which many of his other works are presented.[31] While these works do not fit the pedagogical needs of beginning students for an ordered progress in learning theology (the intended audience in *this* work), they can, of course, be of great theological value in themselves.

The third question the prologue must treat is that of purpose. The prologue explicitly states the purpose of the *Summa theologiae:* to teach beginners those things that pertain to *Christian religion* and *sacred doctrine* as clearly and briefly as the matter allows. In stating this purpose, the prologue refers to a passage from 1 Corinthians, chapter 3: *Being little ones in Christ, I gave you milk, not solid food.*

In this passage Paul refers to the burgeoning Christian community at Corinth. He had given them the fundamental Christian message of the cross and resurrection of Christ, but they still needed guidance in their relationships, both within and outside the community. Food is a metaphor for this guidance, but Paul doubts they have the stomachs for it.[32] In his *Super epistolas S. Pauli lectura,* when treating this passage, Thomas comments that Paul must accommodate his message because of his audience's "impotence" and "weakness."[33] Thomas had drawn on this same passage a few years earlier[34] in his *Commentary on the Gospel of St. John* when discussing Jesus' proclamation to the disciples that "I have food to eat of which you do not know" (John 4:32). He draws on Origen's insight that just as the same amount of bodily food is not appropriate for everyone, spiritual food should be distributed according to each person's capacity:

> Solid food is for the perfect; thus Origen says that the man who understands the loftier doctrine, and who has charge of others in spiritual matters, can teach this doctrine to those who are weaker and have less understanding. Accordingly, the Apostle says in 1 Corinthians (3:2): "Being little ones in Christ, I gave you milk, not solid food."[35]

This reference to 1 Corinthians suggests, then, that the manner in which the subject is taught should be suited to its audience, in this case, to *incipientes.*

With respect to the subject of the *Summa,* the prologue explicitly states that Thomas will treat *christianam religionem* and *sacra doctrina.* First, what does the prologue mean by "Christian religion"? In the *Secunda secundae* Thomas discusses religion within his treatment of the virtue of justice. Generally speaking, religion implies a habitual relationship between the believer and God:

> For it is He to Whom we ought to be bound as to our unfailing principle; to Whom also our choice should be resolutely directed as to our last end, and Whom we lose when we neglect Him by sin, and should recover by believing Him and confessing our faith.[36]

But how does this relationship take shape in religion? Like piety and gratitude, religion is a moral virtue considered under justice. First, the virtue of justice is the perpetual and constant will to render to each one his right.[37] Since the purpose of religion is to render to God what is His due, it falls under the virtue of justice. But religion in some sense falls short of justice because the human person is never fully able to render to God what is owed to God.[38] As a result, religion is understood only as a "potential part" of justice, not justice itself. Second, a virtue is an operative habit that makes both the act and the person performing the act good.[39] To render anyone her due is evidently an aspect of the good: through giving someone what properly belongs to her one becomes more properly ordered to her.[40] Finally, religion is a moral virtue — as opposed to, for example, a theological or intellectual virtue. It resembles intellectual virtues in that it is an acquired, not an infused, virtue, but it differs from intellectual virtues in that its acts arise from the will, not simply from reason. Religion is not a theological virtue because it deals with the acts that are directed toward the worship of God but not directly to God himself. Acts of religion are choices that are made of what is appropriate for the worship of God. Thus, religion does not reach out to God as faith reaches out to God when we believe. In other words, God is not the object of religion as God is the object of faith. Rather, God is the end of religion, as God is the purpose of religion. Therefore, when we worship through communal adoration or private prayer, we do so *as a result of* religion as a virtue.

In the *Summa contra gentiles* Thomas places religion beyond the reach of reason. Religion is necessary because it allows the human person to reach beyond the goods of this life:

> Wherefore since man is directed by divine providence to a higher good than human frailty can attain in the present life, ... it was necessary for his mind to be bidden to something higher than those things to which our reason can reach in the present life, so that he might learn to aspire, and by his endeavours to tend to something surpassing the whole state of the present life.[41]

Just like the philosophers urged people away from sensible pleasures and toward virtues, Christian religion urges people away from temporal matters, and promises spiritual and eternal goods.[42]

That the *Summa theologiae* teaches beginners those things that pertain to *Christian* religion means, then, that it teaches things related to what we today would call "Christian piety." The ecclesiological question of what pertains to *Christian* religion as opposed to other religions is, of course, not a medieval question.

Thomas also sets out to teach those things that pertain to *sacra doctrina*. Thus, the general prologue to the *Summa* inevitably leads into the prologue to Question One, which treats the nature of sacred doctrine. It is to this prologue that we must now turn.

Prologue to Question One

A whole tradition of interpretation has developed around the meaning of *sacra doctrina* in Question One of the *Summa*.[43] Interpretative difficulties arise from the fact that Thomas links *sacra doctrina* not only to faith, but also to theology and Sacred Scripture. Much ink has been spilled over just how *sacra doctrina* relates to the life of faith, the study of theology, and appeals to Scripture.[44]

Without attempting to address all of the many issues surrounding the meaning of *sacra doctrina*, it is necessary to investigate the actual character of *sacra doctrina*. Question One establishes the methodology for the entire *Summa theologiae*. With respect to the structure of the articles, James Weisheipl reads the ten articles as a whole, allowing Article One to set the terms of interpretation. Following the medieval format of inquiry, Question One includes: an investigation of the *an sit* of the subject (a1); its nature, or *quid sit* (a2–7); and its method, or *quale est* (a8–10).[45] Thus, the First Article discusses the necessity of *sacra doctrina*. There are two ways of knowing the *an sit* of any given subject: either by direct perception, or by demonstration of its necessity through cause or effect. This article demonstrates the hypothetical necessity of *sacra doctrina* through final cause:

> That is, from man's supernatural end one can demonstrate the existence of revelation, that is a *propter quid* demonstration by way of final causality. Granting that man has a supernatural end, it follows that the way to that end must be revealed, which revelation must be accepted by man through faith. Both the cause (ultimate end) and the conclusion (existence of revelation) are truths of faith, but there is a necessary connection between them. This argumentation alone shows that *sacra doctrina* is a *scientia*.[46]

Since the human person is directed to God as to an end that surpasses human reason, the human person must be instructed and thus come to know that end so that she can strive for it. Therefore, it is necessary for human salvation that certain truths that exceed the grasp of reason be divinely revealed, for salvation depends upon knowledge of the end. This teaching of such truths by God is *sacra doctrina*. The reasoning in this question is tied to the structure of the entire work — God as the source and final end of human life. A discussion of the nature of *sacra doctrina* follows. The discussion in this First Question moves from the most general to the most specific precision. By the end of article seven, the reader has learned that *sacra doctrina* is a single science (a2–3) that is both theoretical and practical (a4) and it excels [*digniorem*] all other sciences (a5). It is also a wisdom (a6) about God as God reveals Himself (a7).[47] Since this is the nature of *sacra doctrina*, it must be argumentative (a8), metaphorical, poetic (a9), and pluralistic (a10).[48] Sacred doctrine, then, is divine teaching — God teaches fundamentally through revelation. Thus, Van Ackeren points out that *sacra doctrina* is the active teaching process of God to God's listeners. The Church and theologians study this teaching in order to understand and preserve its meaning and to transmit it to each generation of Christians.[49] Weisheipl argues that this first question on *sacra doctrina* is not simply an introduction to the *Summa* itself, but rather to the "subject matter possessed by every Christian and studied by every theologian."[50] It presents the wider methodological context within which the specific method of the *Summa*, found in the prologue to Q2, sits.[51]

Sacred doctrine is the divine teaching that forms the basis of the theology in the *Summa theologiae*, and it is itself based on *scientia Dei et beatorum*.[52] Sacred doctrine is an invitation to participate in the knowledge that God and the blessed have of both God and the world. In Question 12 on knowledge of God, Thomas states that those people who are marked by charity will know God more perfectly than others in the beatific vision.[53] Who is marked by charity? They are the blessed, the saints. The kind of knowledge gained in *sacra doctrina*, then, is linked to the kind of love (*caritas*) exhibited in the lives of the saints. In being called to sanctity, Christians are called to know God more fully.

In addition, since God is the *subject* of *sacra doctrina*, God is the one who is met in reflection, not an object to be conceptualized.[54]

When Thomas concludes in Q1, a5 that *sacra doctrina* is principally speculative, he means that it is principally contemplative, for "the two words are practically synonymous in Thomas."[55] Sacred doctrine, then, is:

> ... not to be identified with scholastic theology, which is an artifact, but with the glimmer of light given to all who believe in him. In other words, sacred doctrine is that wisdom about God by which we lead our life to eternal glory. This is the wisdom of Sacred Scripture; it is the wisdom of the saints. There is no higher wisdom in this life.[56]

But while *sacra doctrina* provides the specifically Christian foundation for the *Summa,* does Thomas engage in *sacra doctrina* or in theology in this work?

Sacra doctrina provides the divine teacher and the teaching; the study of theology in the *Summa* arises out of that teaching. In other words, *Sacra doctrina* is God's revealing of Godself. The theology employed in the *Summa* is an attempt to understand that teaching. It begins from Sacred Scripture — the text that has documented such revelation. It expounds upon Scripture by using some passages to illuminate others and by drawing from other disciplines. It ensures that what God has revealed has not only been heard by the faithful, but that it has been understood.

Theology in this case is different in kind from *theologia quae pars philosphiae ponitur,*[57] or what was later called natural or philosophical theology. The theology that belongs to *sacra doctrina* in the *Summa* presupposes Christian revelation. As a result, it draws liberally from Scripture by incorporating scriptural passages as premises, appeals to authority, or examples. But it also incorporates insights from philosophy, from the sciences, etc., in order to illuminate and reflect upon the scriptural message. Sources other than Scripture, however, are used alone as extraneous and probable.[58] *Sacra doctrina* does not take its principles from these other disciplines, as its principles are fully provided by revelation. Rather, it uses these other disciplines for the greater clarification of its teaching. These disciplines, then, have a subsidiary and ancillary role. They are, in fact, brought into *sacra doctrina* not because of a defect or insufficiency within itself, but because human beings are more easily led to the things above reason through human disciplines.[59] These disciplines act as handmaidens or preliminary guides set forth to draw people into the study of *sacra doctrina*.[60] There is, then, an organic relationship between all knowledge and *sacra doctrina*.[61] The *Summa* is a grand attempt at doing theology that reflects upon *sacra doctrina*, an attempt that expounds the truths of *Christianam religionem*.

In Question One, then, *sacra doctrina* is the act of God revealing Godself. Scripture embodies this revelation. The theologian interprets and asks questions posed by Scripture, but not fully answered by Scripture alone. As a result, she uses other knowledge to interpret Scripture.[62] Scripture itself invites the reader to pose further questions.[63] It is this task that Thomas takes up in the *Summa theologiae*, namely, by doing the theology that arises out of and pertains to *sacra doctrina*.

Prologue to Question Two

The prologue to Question Two lays out the *ordo disciplinae*, or method of learning, of the work: we will deal first with God; second, with the rational creature's movement toward God; and third, with Christ, who, insofar as He is a man, is our way of going to God. This order is chosen because sacred doctrine teaches not only knowledge of God in Godself, but also God as the beginning and last end of every creature. The specific *ordo disciplinae* that Thomas chooses to adopt begins and finds its center of gravity with God: "all things are treated under the aspect of God[,] either because they are God Himself or because they refer to God as their beginning and end."[64] Since God is the subject of sacred doctrine, God forms the organizing principle of the text. Everything else is discussed as it relates to this principle. Thomas will treat other subjects but always in light of their connection to the origin and end, God.[65]

Most contemporary commentators agree with Chenu that the *Summa* is based upon a neo-Platonic scheme of exitus-reditus from God to creatures, although they disagree on the specifics of how the scheme develops in the work itself. According to Chenu's reading, the *Prima pars* treats the emanation of creatures from their principle, God. The *Secunda pars* treats their return toward their ultimate end, God, while the *Tertia pars* is not directly integrated into this scheme, as it provides the specific means willed by God to assure the creatures' return. Chenu readily admits that his interpretation converts the *Tertia pars* into an appendage.[66] This scheme suggests that the material on Christ in the *Tertia pars* is not integral to the pattern of the *Summa*. Most contemporary interpretations of the structure of the *Summa* adopt Chenu's exitus-reditus pattern, while adding slight modifications. M.-V. Leroy, for example, argues in favor of keeping the *exitus-reditus* scheme, but applies it only to the "economic" part of the *Summa*, beginning with Q44 of the *Prima pars*. The *exitus* (Ia, Q44–119) is followed by the *reditus* (*Secunda* and *Tertia pars*) which culminates in the human person's communion with God through the mediation of Christ. Torrell finds Leroy's interpretation the most convincing, and adds, " '[b]efore being Neoplatonist [this scheme] is quite simply Christian.' "[67]

Consequently, the examination of each question in the *Summa* must be undertaken against this general background of exitus-reditus of creatures to and from God. The main structure, then, is theocentric. The theocentric principle of this work incorporates such disciplines as metaphysics, geometry, and Scripture by both respecting their autonomy as disciplines and subsuming them into this larger theological endeavor: God as the principle and end of human life.

The next more specific division that this prologue introduces involves that which pertains to (1) *essentiam divinam*,[68] (2) *distinctionem personarum*,[69] and (3) *processum creaturarum ab ipso*.[70] Thomas has been repeatedly criticized for dividing his treatment of God into God's essence on the one hand and the Trinity on the other, leaving the impression that one can speak of the nature of God without speaking of the Trinity.[71] Among the most distinguished critics stands Karl Rahner. Concerning the *De Deo Uno* and *De Deo Trino*, Rahner maintains that "it is not as easy to distinguish these two treatises as was thought after St. Thomas and under the influence of his example."[72] Rahner argues that in speaking of the one God, one speaks of the unity of the three divine persons that is properly mediated through the Trinity. One does not speak, as it is often assumed, of God's essence and the "unmediated unicity of the divine nature."[73] Nicholas Lash makes the more guarded claim that "whatever Aquinas' reasons for preceding his discussion of questions concerning God's trinity by grammatical [sic] observations on what does and does not count as 'godness,' and by general remarks on God's 'operations', his would be an imprudent order of topics for a theologian to adopt today."[74]

While an extended analysis of this discussion is not within the bounds of this work, suffice it to say that criticisms of Thomas' treatment of the divine essence on the one hand and the distinction of Persons on the other arise from a subsequent accenting of the former over the latter, an accent that does not necessarily occur within the *Prima pars* itself. In fact, as will become clearer through this investigation, Thomas distinguishes in the *Prima pars* in order to hold together, not to create division. Furthermore, the structure of the whole *Summa* lends itself to an interpretation that the *Tertia pars*, which treats the subject of Christ, is the pinnacle and summit of the work.[75]

Taking up the *consideratio* of the divine essence, Thomas first establishes the *an sit*, namely whether God exists (Q2), then the *quomodo sit* or *non sit*, or the manner of his existence (Q3–13),[76] and finally the *operatio*, or the operations of God (Q14–26).[77] Q2 of the *Summa* establishes the *an sit* of the subject-matter of the entire work, God. Much ink has been spilled over the role Q2 plays in the overall scheme of the *Summa*, and whether Thomas was really trying to demonstrate the existence of God.[78] In the three articles that comprise Q2, Thomas negotiates between the two extremes of the self-evidence of the knowledge of God (a1) and agnosticism (a2). He settles on knowledge of the existence of God found in a general and confused way in nature,[79] and followed by rational deliberation. He employs *quia* demonstrations, or arguments that move from effect to cause.

The issue of whether the fact that God is, is self-evident (*per se notum*) was disputed not only in the Christian and philosophical tradition that Thomas inherited, but also in his own time. While Thomas only selects Damascene, Aristotle, and Anselm in the "objections" of article one, even such thinkers of his own time as Richard Fishacre and Alexander of Hales maintained that one could not truly think that God does not exist.[80] John Wippel, however, has shown that the more likely target in this first article is Thomas' contemporary, St. Bonaventure.[81]

Thomas resolves this issue by stating that something can be self-evident in two ways: either it is self-evident in itself and not to us, or it is self-evident in itself and to us. For a proposition to be self-evident means that the predicate is included in the intelligibility (*ratio*) of the subject. In the statement "man is an animal," for example, animal is contained in the intelligibility of a man. For this statement to be self-evident not only in itself but to us, everyone would have to know the meaning of the terms "man" and "animal." There are some things, however, that are self-evident only to a few — that incorporeal substances are not in space — because only the learned know the meaning of "incorporeal substances." With respect to the issue at hand, in the statement "God exists" the predicate is the same as the subject; in God *esse* and *essentia* are identical.[82] Thomas has already maintained in Q1, a7, *ad* 1 that human beings do not know the essence of God in this life. Therefore, the proposition "God exists" is not self-evident to us, but needs to be demonstrated by things that are more known to us, such as the effects of God. The existence of God, therefore, is self-evident in itself but not to us.

The three objectors in this article present arguments from the perspectives of experience, language, and reality. Objector one, recalling Damascene, argues that human beings are innately aware of the existence of God. Objector two, echoing Anselm, insists that once humans understand the meaning of the word "God" (as "that than which nothing greater can be conceived"), it follows that God exists; existence in thought and reality is greater than in thought alone. If God is "that than which nothing greater can be conceived," God has to be greater than a God who would only exist in the mind. The third objector argues from the nature of truth. Even denying that truth exists admits truth — were there no such thing as truth, then it would be true that there is no truth. Scripture reveals that God is truth itself. Therefore, the existence of God is self-evident.

The first objection is most central to the purposes of this examination. The reply to this objection distinguishes between knowledge of God that is implanted in us by nature and absolute knowledge that God exists. While human beings have a general, inchoate awareness that God exists [*in aliquo communi sub quadam confusion*], they lack absolute knowledge of God's existence [*simpliciter cognoscere Deum esse*]. This argument is framed in terms of the human person's ultimate end, happiness [*beatitudo*]. God is the ultimate happiness for the human person. The human person naturally desires this happiness, and what is naturally desired must be naturally known. Therefore, the human person must know God in at least a general way. This is like knowing that someone is approaching, but not to know that it is Peter who is approaching, even though it actually *is* Peter who is approaching.[83]

The reply to the second Anselmian objection argues that even if everyone understands that "God" means that than which nothing greater can be thought, it does not follow that they understand that "God" exists actually, but rather only that "God" exists mentally. One cannot therefore argue that God actually exists unless it is admitted that there *actually* exists something than which nothing greater can be conceived. This, most obviously, is not admitted by everyone.[84]

The reply to the third objector is brief: while it is self-evident that truth in general exists, it is not self-evident that there exists a First Truth, which will be the task of the *quinque viae* to demonstrate. Article 1, then, rules out one of the extreme positions of Thomas' day, namely, that the proposition that God is, is self-evident to us. It also introduces the subject of this study, namely, natural knowledge of God.

Thomas turns to the other extreme in article two where he considers whether the existence of God can be demonstrated at all. Here, his objectors emphasize the radical transcendence of God, positing what would later be called agnosticism or fideism with respect to what creatures can know of God through human reason. Thomas counters first by appealing to Scripture, in this case Romans 1:20: "The invisible things of Him are clearly seen, being understood by the things that are made." The second response turns to the nature of rational demonstration. Something can be demonstrated in two ways: either through its cause [*demonstratio propter quid*] or through its effect [*demonstratio quia*].[85] If the effects are more evident to us than the cause, as is the case in the existence of God, one can argue from the effects back to the existence of the cause. Since every effect depends upon its cause, if the effect exists, the cause must also exist. Arguments for the existence of God, then, can only be *quia* demonstrations.

But what, exactly, is the difference between two such demonstrations? In Thomas' *Commentary on the Posterior Analytics of Aristotle* (1271–1272), he distinguishes between scientific demonstrations that are *quia* and *propter quid*:

> A demonstration is a syllogism causing scientific knowledge and ... it proceeds from the first and immediate causes of a thing.

We should understand these words as applying to the why-demonstration. But knowing the fact that something is so differs from knowing why it is so. Therefore, since a demonstration is a syllogism which causes scientific knowledge, a demonstration which causes knowledge of the fact that something is so [*quia*] must differ from a demonstration which causes knowledge of the reason why it is so [*propter quid*].[86]

A *quia* demonstration begins with effects, while the *propter quid* demonstration begins with immediate causes or immediate principles (such as the essence). When the effect is more evident to us than the cause, we attain knowledge through *quia* demonstrations, rather than *propter quid* demonstrations. Thomas delineates Aristotle's example of *quia* demonstrations. We know through effects that planets are near because they do not twinkle. Non-twinkling is not the cause why the planets are near, but the planets do not twinkle because they are near. Stars twinkle because the distance clouds our image of them. Therefore, this syllogism is a *quia* demonstration: "Whatever does not twinkle is near; but the planets do not twinkle: therefore they are near."[87] When turning to knowledge that God is in this article, Thomas establishes that we gain *quia* knowledge that God is, not *propter quid* knowledge, for we do not know the essence of God. We can only come to know that God is through knowledge of God's effects.

The three objections in this article arise from the nature of faith, the method of demonstration, and the incommensurability between the cause (God) and the effects of God (creaturely things). Objector one argues that God exists is an article of faith and cannot be demonstrated. But *even* if it were not an article of faith, adds objector two, it cannot be demonstrated because the middle term of demonstration, the essence of God, is missing. Objector three concludes that we cannot demonstrate that God exists specifically because the effects of God are incommensurate to their cause.

To the first objector who claims that the existence of God is an article of faith, and articles of faith cannot be demonstrated, Thomas replies:

> That God is and other like truths about God, which can be known by natural reason [*per rationem naturalem*], are not

articles of faith, but are preambles to the articles; for faith presupposes natural knowledge, even as grace presupposes nature, and perfection supposes something that can be perfected.[88]

This should not prevent someone who does not grasp the proofs for the existence of God from taking the existence of God as a matter of faith. For something may be known as a matter of faith by one person and a matter of knowledge by another. In this reply, Thomas rejects what would later be called fideism, in which faith is asserted independently of historical certainty and theological analysis.[89] Fideists believe that the human intellect is incapable of attaining knowledge of divine matters and consequently they emphasize the act of faith,[90] reacting against anything that appears to diminish the supernatural and gratuitous nature of faith.[91] Faith here needs no justification from reason but is rather "the judge of reason and its pretensions."[92]

To the second objector who argues that the essence of God is the middle term of a demonstration, and since we cannot know the essence of God, we cannot demonstrate that God exists, Thomas replies: when a demonstration moves from knowledge of effect to cause, the effect takes the place of the definition of the cause in order to prove that the cause exists. In proving the existence of God, we take a nominal definition of God in the place of a quidditative definition. Since the question "What is it?" follows the question "Is it?" we can name God from God's effects, and thus prove the existence of God from the existence of God's effects. In this reply, then, Thomas rejects this version of what would later be called agnosticism.

Finally, to the third objector who emphasizes the disproportion between the infinite cause, God, and the finite effects of God, and argues that a cause cannot be demonstrated by an effect not proportioned to it, Thomas replies: from effects that are not proportionate to their cause no perfect knowledge of the cause can be reached. That a cause exists, however, may be ascertained through knowledge of any effect.[93] This second variation of agnosticism is thus rejected in this reply.

In sum, the first two articles of Q2 delineate the two poles within which Thomas will construct his third alternative. One group of objectors claim that the existence of God needs no demonstration; it is given. The other group, that God's existence allows for no demonstration; it is unknowable. In more contemporary terms the two poles taken to their extreme are expressions of agnosticism and fideism. Thomas strikes out on an intermediate juncture, one that allows knowledge of the existence of the incomprehensible God.

Article three gathers arguments for the existence of God already circulating at the time in order to construct a third alternative to those offered in the first two articles. This article lays out Thomas' famous "five ways" of demonstrating that God exists.

The five ways are encompassed by two very real objections to the existence of God. The first presents the problem of evil and the second suggests that human reason and nature suffice as explanatory principles for the world. The existence of evil in the world is often presented as contradictory to the teleological argument and as evidence against the existence of God. While admitting the existence of evil, the reply places limits on it: evil does not ultimately triumph over goodness. Given the reality of God as the origin and order of everything that exists, God allows evil to exist only in order to produce a greater good out of it.[94] Thomas cites Augustine's *Enchiridion* on this matter: "Since God is supremely good, he would not permit any evil at all in his works, unless he were sufficiently almighty and good to bring good even from evil."[95] That evil exists does not entail that God does not exist.

The second objector claims that natural causes suffice to explain the origin of things, making any discussion of God superfluous. The reply counters, however, that natural causes and human will alone cannot explain what exists in the physical world. As will be shown in the five ways, the becoming and being of things must be traced to their First Cause.[96]

The preceding article argued that when something is not known in itself but produces effects that are known, the cause may be inferred from the existence of its effects. This method of demonstration is preserved in the five ways. Each way demonstrates that God exists by showing that things are effects of a hidden cause, which we call God.[97] Each of the five ways takes as its point of departure something composite that is given to us in the world of sensible things.[98] The composition is of the very character of an effect. Thus motion, causation, corruptibility, perfection, and natural orientation can lead one to the existence of their cause, God. The five ways taken together establish an unmoved mover, a first efficient cause, an absolutely necessary being, an absolute maximum, and the source of the orientation of natural things within the universe. All these we call God.

Whether these *viae* form five variations of one argument, whether each stands on its own, and whether each argues to the existence of a Christian God — are all much controverted questions.[99] But what is important to note here for our purposes is Thomas' attempt to take effects evident to our senses that are composed and argue to the existence of their simple cause. Thomas establishes metaphysically the *an sit* of his subject-matter, God, by these *quia* demonstrations. The five *viae* are not presented here as articles of faith to be believed. Rather, they are offered as cogent arguments for the existence of the subject-matter of the entire work, and are offered as an alternative to what are now called agnosticism and fideism. Thomas was not "masquerading...as a pagan philosopher"[100] in these five ways. Instead, he sets forth these arguments in the context of Christian faith and theology. It does not follow, however, that they depend upon this context for their cogency. Thomas thinks he has demonstrated that God exists, but as will be seen, these five arguments depend upon Q3, a4 to achieve their metaphysical force, and on Q12, a12 to gain their theological significance.

Prologue to Question Three

While Q2 has traditionally provoked reams of interpretive work, Q3 has not received the same attention. Many have maintained with Alvin Plantinga that it is a "mysterious doctrine" that is "exceedingly hard to grasp or construe."[101] However, it has come under new appreciation, especially since it highlights Thomas' apophaticism.[102] David Burrell is chief among the contemporary theologians responsible for the resurgence in interest in Q3. He maintains that while Q3 was traditionally understood to introduce a doctrine of God, it is really a treatise on what God is *not*:

> If this be a "doctrine of God," it is a dreadfully austere one....
> We could expect a doctrine of God to state what God is like, yet Aquinas is clear enough in warning us not to expect that of him. Nevertheless, commentators and critics alike have assumed that he is offering us just that — a doctrine of God — in questions 3 through 11.[103]

Thomas had already asserted in Q1, a7 that no one can know the essence of God, or what God is, citing Damascene to this effect.[104] But the body of Q3 reveals what it means to know God through knowledge of what God is not. Whether or not this Question presents a "doctrine" of God remains to be seen.

Before examining the structure of the articles, however, we must examine the introductory statements of the prologue. Thomas opens the prologue to Q3 by claiming:

> When the existence of a thing has been ascertained there remains the further question of the manner of its existence, in order that we may know its essence. Now, because we cannot know what God is, but rather what He is not, we have no means for considering how God is, but rather how He is not.[105]

What does Thomas mean by *quid sit* and *quomodo sit?* Q2 established the *an sit* of the subject matter, God. But after ascertaining the existence of something, the question "what is it?" [*quid sit*] follows. Thomas will place restrictions upon this *quid sit* knowledge, but in reflecting back upon Q3–11, he states rather matter-of-factly in the prologue to Q12 that "hitherto we have considered God as He is in Himself." So however strong the restriction upon knowledge of God's essence, Q3–11 still appear to give rise to knowledge about God in Godself.

When Thomas states that we cannot know the *quid sit* of God, he does not mean that we cannot gain *any knowledge whatsoever* of who or what God is. Rather, *quid sit* here is taken very strictly as comprehensive, essential and defining knowledge of God. The *De veritate* attests to this strict sense of *quid sit* by claiming that our intellect knows what something is when it defines it:

> The intellect is said to know what a thing is when it defines that thing, that is, *when it conceives some form of the thing which corresponds to it in all respects*. From our previous discussion, it is clear that whatever our intellect conceives of God falls short of being a representation of Him. Consequently, the quiddity of God Himself remains forever hidden from us. This is the highest knowledge we can have of God during our present life, that He transcends everything that we can know of Him....[106]

Thomist epistemology dictates that no thing can be known without an appropriate *phantasmata* or form. Following Aristotle, Thomas insists that all knowledge begins through the senses. A later question in the *Prima pars* insists that "our intellect understands material things by abstracting from the phantasms; and through material things thus considered we acquire some knowledge of immaterial things."[107] Our knowledge of immaterial things, however, is mostly by *per viam remotionis* and by their relation to material things.[108] We can never attain quiddative knowledge, or essential knowledge of immaterial substances, for our knowledge is attained through material things. Since God is an immaterial substance, we cannot know the essence of God. We do not know, therefore, *quid sit Deo*.[109]

Thomas' claim that we cannot consider God as God is, but rather as how God is not does not eliminate entirely any knowledge of God, as Moses Maimonides argued. Earlier in his career, Thomas had criticized Maimonides' radical way of restricting our knowledge of God. For Maimonides the absolute distinction between God and human beings means that there can be no analogical predication of God.[110] Relation for Maimonides is always found between two things falling under the same species, whereas there is no relation between two things if they merely fall under the same genus.[111] The strongest argument against knowledge of God here arises from the fact that there is no composition in God, but there is composition in human beings. If a relation subsisted between human beings and God, it would necessarily follow that the accident of relation be attached to God.[112] Therefore, we can only determine what God is not:

> It is not possible, except through negation, to achieve even that [limited] apprehension of God which is in our power to achieve,...on the other hand, negation does not give knowledge in any respect of the true reality of the thing with regard to which the particular matter in question has been negated...God cannot be apprehended by the human intellect, and none but He himself can apprehend what He is, and our knowledge [of Him] consists in our knowledge that we are unable truly to apprehend Him.[113]

As a result, all predication of God is necessarily equivocal since the meaning of the qualitative attributes ascribed to God and the meaning of those same attributes known to us have "nothing in common in any respect or in any mode, these attributes have in common only the name and nothing else."[114] Maimonides concludes:

> Glory then to Him who is such that when the intellects contemplate His essence, their apprehension turns into incapacity; and when they contemplate the proceeding of His actions from His will, their knowledge turns into ignorance; and when the tongues aspire to magnify Him by means of attributive qualifications, all eloquence turns into weariness and incapacity![115]

For Maimonides, then, there is *nothing* that a human being can justly claim about God other than that God is.

In *De Potentia* Q7, a5 (1265–1268) Thomas counters "Rabbi Moses" by stating that the idea of negation is always based on an affirmation since every negative proposition is proved by an affirmative.[116] In fact, when considering whether terms like "good," "wise" and "just" signify the divine essence, Thomas states, "Unless the human mind knew something positively about God, it would be unable to deny anything about him."[117] Note that this claim is very different from an agnostic repudiation of all knowledge of God. If Maimonides were correct that God is said to be "wise," not because wisdom is actually in God, but rather that in bringing about his effects, God acts like a wise man, then, Thomas argues, there would be no difference in saying "God is wise" or "God is angry" or "God is a fire." For He acts like an angry man when called angry and like fire when called fire. But the saints and prophets affirm certain things of God (that He is living and wise) while denying others (that he is a body or subject to the passions). In Maimonides' view, however, anything may be affirmed or denied of God with equal reason. Further, for Maimonides claims about God depend upon the existence of God's effects. But before creatures existed, God was wise. Were Maimonides correct in insisting that human claims about God only mean to exclude something from God rather than assert anything real in Him, then these claims would not make any sense. For, as Thomas asks ironically, "[M]ight we say that God is a lion because he has not the mode of being a bird[?]"[118] Positive statements about God, that He is wise or just or good, then, have some epistemological value for Thomas in a way that for Maimonides they are empty. It remains to be seen how this value takes shape.

In his commentary on Boethius' *De Trinitate*, Thomas continues to carve a legitimate place for positive statements about God:

> We cannot know *that* a thing is without knowing in some way *what* it is, either perfectly or at least confusedly... For our knowledge of definitions, like that of demonstrations, must begin with some previous knowledge. Similarly, therefore, we cannot know *that* God and other immaterial substances exist unless we know somehow, in some confused way, *what* they are.[119]

Even with respect to immaterial substances, we cannot know them through genus and accidents. Rather, we know them also by negations. We add negations one to another in order to understand immaterial substances in a confused way because each negation limits and determines the previous ones.[120] This process leaves our knowledge less confused than what it was when it was naturally implanted in us by nature.[121] Finally, in treating the transcendentals in the *De veritate*, Thomas maintains with Aristotle that we only come to know non-being through being: "[B]eing is, in some way, predicated of non-being insofar as non-being is apprehended by the intellect. For, as the philosopher says, the negation or the privation of being may, in a sense, be called being."[122]

Contrary to Maimonides, by claiming that we do not know *quid sit* or *quomodo sit* of God, Thomas does not remain simply agnostic about God. This means, rather, that human beings can never gain essential or comprehensive knowledge of God. Human beings begin with a vague and confused awareness or consciousness of God. Some advance in knowledge through learning, others through connatural knowledge. But none come to know fully who God is in Godself. Human beings can eliminate imperfection, change, finitude and composition in God, but they cannot fully conceive what it means for God to be perfect, unchangeable, infinite, and simple. While Thomas joins Maimonides in his concern over the religious temptation of idolatry, he also warns against another temptation — one that "empties God of all content and thereby threatens the *availability* of God."[123]

In addition, if Thomas were pursuing purely apophatic theology, the next sentence in the prologue would prove a curious one: *Ergo considerandum est (1) quomodo non sit, (2) quomodo a nobis cognoscatur (3) quomodo nominetur*. If humans cannot say anything meaningful about God, why would Thomas discuss how God is known [*cognoscatur*] and how God is named [*nominetur*] after establishing that God is *not* known and therefore *cannot* be named in Q3–11, for surely humans cannot name what they do not know?

After the introduction to the prologue establishes what Thomas means by knowledge *quid non sit* and *quomodo non sit,* it presents the structure of the articles. Since each of the five ways in the previous question has moved from composed effects to their cause, it is essential to show that the cause, God, is not composed.[124] This is the task of Question 3. The articles remove intrinsic composition, logical composition, and extrinsic composition in God. Articles 1–4 remove all composition intrinsic to God. They establish that God: is not a body, is not composed of matter and form, does not have a nature different from Himself, and His nature is not different from His existence. Article 5 argues that God is not logically composed, for God cannot be conceived in the categories of genus and difference. Articles 6–8 conclude that God is not extrinsically composed or composed with something else. For God does not have accidents added to His substance. Rather, He is altogether simple, and He does not enter into composition with other things.

Even in his attempt to eliminate imperfections from God in Q3–11, Thomas recognizes yet another methodological difficulty. Speaking of God's simplicity is particularly challenging because human words are always derived from composite things, since human knowledge is by nature composite:

> We can speak of simple things only as though they were like the composite things from which we derive our knowledge. Therefore, in speaking of God, we use concrete nouns to signify His substance, because with us only those things subsist that are composite, and we use abstract nouns to signify His simplicity.[125]

Consequently, humans inevitably obscure the simplicity of God by speaking in composite ways, in subjects and verbs. To say that God is simple, then, is to make the negative statement that God is not composite. There arises a dialectical tension in such predication where the negative claims about God move in tension with each other. The first three articles of Q3 eliminate the categories of bodily composition, matter/form and essence/nature in God.

In the fourth article Thomas reveals his unique insight that God's essence is not different from God's existence. In other words, God is not composed in the metaphysical compositions characteristic of all effects: He is not being-by-participation, but rather God *is*. After stripping all composition in God in articles 1–3, article 4 unveils God as the divine *esse*. Three facts lead to this conclusion. First, in something whose existence differs from its essence, its existence could be caused by its own constituent principles or by something else. But its existence must be caused by something else: for a thing that is caused, nothing in it can suffice to be the cause of its own existence. As has already been proven,[126] God's existence cannot be caused by something else. Thus, it is impossible that God's existence should differ from God's essence. Second, existence actuates form or nature. Goodness and humanity, for example, are in act because they exist. Existence is distinct from essence as actuality is distinct from potentiality. Since there is no potentiality in God, essence does not differ from existence in God. Third, just as that which has fire but is not itself fire is on fire by participation, so that which has existence but is not existence is a being by participation. It is established that God is God's own essence. If God were not God's own essence then God would not be essential being but rather participated being. This would entail that God is not the first being, which is contrary to what has been proven. The response to the second objection clarifies how we know that God exists. *To be* contains two meanings. It may mean the act of essence, or it may mean the composition of a proposition effected by the mind in joining a predicate to a subject. While in the first sense we cannot understand God's existence or God's essence, in the second sense we can: "[w]e know that this proposition which we form about God when we say *God is,* is true; and this we know from His effects."[127] A4, then, is articulated out of a metaphysics of *esse,* where being signifies the highest perfection of all, since it is understood as the actuality of all acts.[128]

The next two articles of Q3 continue to eliminate composition from God by demonstrating that God is not composed of genus/difference (a5) or subject/accident (a6). A7 combines the evidence from the previous articles in this question with the data established in Q2 to summarize the arguments for the simplicity of God. Once the arguments for the simplicity of God have been drawn together, a8 then asks whether this simple God enters into the composition of other things. It establishes that God rules all things as their efficient and exemplar cause without commingling with them. Despite the radical difference between God who is simple and creatures who are composite, there exists a proper and ordered relationship between them.

Looking back to the initial questions of the *Summa,* Q1 introduced the subject-matter, God. Q2 established the existence of the subject-matter as the First Cause of everything that exists. Q3 explores the utter simplicity of this first cause. In order to purify further what the simplicity of *God* means, Q4–11 must highlight the differences between human and divine simplicities. Thus, they distinguish God in His simplicity from any imperfection, evil, change, finitude, and composition. These are all inevitable aspects of the human condition. With respect to method, Q4–11 continue the *viae remotionis* established in Q3, since human claims about God can only take shape as: God is *not* imperfect, evil, or finite, God does *not* change, and God is *not* composite. While the motion is one of negation here, the negation of the negation produces positive knowledge — for God is perfect, good, infinite, and complete. While humans cannot know the full ramifications of what perfection, goodness, or infinity mean in God, they can be confident that these things are in fact true of God. The claim "God is perfect" is but a pale shadow of what perfection really means in God; but if it is in fact a shadow, then it reflects something true about God. Q3–11 represent a systematic attempt to reject all idolatrous tendencies to place God into a class with creatures. These questions highlight the radical transcendence of God. By Q11, we know that God is simple, perfect, good, immutable, eternal, and one. Q12 and 13 represent a pause and reflection on the methodology of the previous questions. Specifically, they ask how we come to know the characteristics of God established in Q3–11, and how we name that which we know.

Already in this cursory introduction to the remote coordinate texts of Q12, a12, we find strong passages in Thomas that recognize an initial, confused natural knowledge of God. The question of natural knowledge of God already touches upon: (1) the meaning of *sacra doctrina,* (2) the way to interpret the *quinquae viae,* and (3) the extent to which the apophaticism in Thomas is marked. These passages offer initial suggestions that Thomas carves a legitimate place for natural knowledge of God in the *Summa.* We will have to trace these suggestions further in order to ask how they cohere with the contemporary postliberal reading outlined in chapter 1 of this study.

– Three –

Natural Knowledge of God Affirmed: The Proximate Context
(*ST* I, 12, 12)

Introduction

After the introduction of methodology (Q1), and the exploration of the subject itself, God (Q2–11), Q12 now examines the epistemology underlying that metaphysical investigation. This question constitutes a movement from ontological to epistemological inquiry. By reflecting upon the first level investigation that took place in Q2–11, it outlines the epistemological tools employed in such an investigation. It takes up the general problematic of this study, namely, how human beings attain knowledge of God. Once knowledge of God has been established, the issue arises of how to speak about this God whom we know — a move, then, from epistemological to linguistic concerns. Thus, a reflection upon the names of God in Q13 caps the first set of questions in the *Prima pars* as theology progresses from ontological to epistemological to linguistic inquiry.

Since Question 12 provides a retrospective analysis, it is examined separately from the previous questions. Articles 1–11 of this question lead to the central issue of this study, namely, whether God can be known through human reason. These articles, then, tightly provide the contextualizing environment of Question 12, article 12. Specifically, they examine the final goal toward which all knowledge of God tends — even that which is given by natural reason — namely, knowledge of God in the beatific vision.

Prologue to Question Twelve

The prologue casually opens, "As hitherto we have considered God as He is in Himself..." The prologue to Q2 has already made clear that sacred doctrine teaches knowledge of God in Godself. However, the prologue to Q3 radically limits this assertion, for the human person cannot know what God is, but only what God is not. She cannot know so much how God is, but rather how God is not. The prologue to Q12 now claims that Q3–11 have just considered God in Godself. *How can knowledge of 'what God is not' be knowledge of 'God in Godself'?* Specifically, how does the method employed in Q3–11 of *per modum remotionis* lead one to knowledge of God in Godself? It could be simply ironic that Thomas' claims to ignorance about God in Godself do not "reduce...him to silence,"[1] but this irony leads to a real difficulty within the text.

Some theologians have solved this difficulty by maintaining that in Q3–11 Thomas is doing grammar, not metaphysics. Theology as grammar serves a corrective function to the narrative of Christian life without providing direct knowledge of any given subject.[2] Thomas does not compile a list of God's attributes, as if one can know that God has *this* or *that* characteristic. Rather, Thomas clarifies his speech about God by clearing away conceptual idols. While grammatical theology cannot present a direct account of God, it can point to inappropriate articulations and attributions.[3] Therefore, it performs an *entirely* negative task. Thomas remains always an agnostic about who God is.[4] In the words of David Burrell, "Aquinas displays his religious discipline most clearly by the ease with which he is able to endure so unknown a God."[5] Nicholas Lash adds:

> If Burrell is justified in thus interpreting Aquinas' insistence that he is concerned, by reflecting "grammatically" on the limits of language, to elucidate what cannot be said of God, then the gulf between Aquinas and Kant is perhaps not so wide, at this point, as has usually been supposed. But if "we cannot pretend to offer a description of a transcendent object without betraying its transcendence," does it follow that there is nothing which we can truly say of God? It would seem so, for even the discussion, in Question 13, of those predicates which *are* acceptably used of God remains under the rubric of God's "simpleness," his "non-compositeness," according to which "all statements formed of subject and object — that is to say, all discourse — will falsify the reality which God is."[6]

This grammatical interpretation, however, leaves questions unanswered. Placing such an emphasis on Thomas' agnosticism neglects the importance of the five ways on the one hand, and Thomas' statement in the prologue to Q12 on the other, namely, that he has just finished talking about what God is in Godself.[7] While Thomas is concerned with God's transcendence in Q3–11, these questions need to be interpreted without neglecting the surrounding context, specifically, Aquinas' claim to be speaking about the divine essence [*considerabimus ea quae ad essentiam divinam pertinent*].[8] It is not enough to maintain as some do that each of the five ways does not necessarily point to the same god. It is not enough when analyzing the possibility of talking about God to state with David Burrell:

> The fact of God's existence may be side-stepped. We are not concerned whether statements about God be true or false; only with the possibility of their being meaningful. That it is at least in some sense "ordinary" to speak of a "principle of all things" is enough for us.[9]

In addition, highlighting Q3–11 without properly attending to the surrounding questions runs into particular difficulties. As Brian Davies states, "... if our talk of God is simply read as an account of what God is not, then there seems no particular reason for preferring one way of speaking of him to any other[.]"[10]

If religious believers can make only negative claims about God, then it is impossible to bring some order, some cohesive structure, to their language about God. In fact, as previously established, Thomas has argued specifically against this agnosticism, such as was argued by Moses Maimonides. Thomas does in fact formulate a cohesive structure for our language about God. He does so, and even explicitly, in the following question (Q13) on the divine names. The *via remotionis* of Q3–11, then, while placing important restrictions on any knowledge of God, must cohere with statements found in the contextualizing surrounding questions. The solution proposed by grammatical theologians fails to account for this important context. The problem still remains: how has the method employed in Q3–11 of *per modum remotionis* led one to claim a knowledge of God in Godself?

This first appears as a riddle in the text. Consider the following alternative solution. Q1 introduces the subject matter of the entire work, namely, God and everything that relates to God. Q2 establishes the existence of the subject-matter by employing philosophical tools in order to confirm and indicate the witness given by the world to the teachings of Sacred Scripture that God is.[11] It demonstrates the existence of God by exploring the implications of God's effects in the world. God is established here as first mover, efficient cause, necessary cause, cause of the graded perfection of things, and the intelligence that gives their orientation to all natural things. Thomas sets forth these five demonstrations in the context of his attention to *sacra doctrina,* but he employs philosophical reasoning in order to demonstrate a truth of this *doctrina,* namely that God is, insisting that there are certain truths a person can know by unaided or natural reason.[12] These demonstrations are not particular to St. Thomas,[13] and he spends less time on them here than in other works.[14] But in this work, where he engages in theology proper, they are simply meant to demonstrate the existence of his subject matter, which he has accepted from *sacra doctrina.* He thus uses philosophical tools in Q2 to lead one [*manuductio*] to infer the existence of God. Questions 3–11 take the reply to the first objection in Q2, a1 as already established.[15] They are guided by a vague sense of what God is, but can only proclaim that God is not *this* or *that*. Each of these ways leads to the insight of Q3, a4, to the One whose *esse* is His essence. These questions have disclosed that the God of the Five Ways is utterly simple, one, eternal, perfect, good and immutable.

Q12 then analyzes what has taken place in Q2–11, dealing with the epistemological issues that arose in the previous ontological questions. While those questions considered the subject-matter, God, the present one treats the various ways that creatures know and think about this God.

Question 12 follows the movement of the vague, inchoate and imperfect awareness of God of Q2, a1, to the fulfillment of this knowledge found in the beatific vision. This Question delineates the moments in one's journey to knowledge of God: through nature, grace, and the beatific vision. But instead of following the progression of the imperfect knowledge as made possible for human nature to the perfect knowledge of God, that is, how the beatified see God, this Question takes the opposite course. The first ten articles examine the perfection of human knowledge of God found in the beatific vision. Only then is knowledge of God in this life addressed.[16] Why this order of treatment? First, knowledge of any nature is obtained best in its state of completion.[17] Also, the structure of the articles protects against overconfidence in our human capabilities. There is an appropriate disjuncture between article 10 and article 11, emphasizing that what is given as sheer gift can never be earned through human resources. As will be seen, however, this does not mean that our human nature is either obliterated or feckless.

The first cluster of articles (1–10) provides the key to unlocking Thomas' position on natural knowledge of God, since it reveals how the desires that humans are given by nature are fulfilled in the beatific vision. These articles are thus concerned with *videre Deum* — as opposed to the *demonstrare Deum* of Q2. The first step establishes that the blessed can in fact see the essence of God (a1), while the second examines how this takes place (a2–10). Specifically, this second step examines the factors necessary for any such vision by establishing the reach and limitation of the created intellect and the consequent strengthening of that intellect by divine grace.

A1 establishes that the created intellect can see the essence of God by introducing the kind of knowledge that will occupy the first eleven articles of this question: *videre essentiam Dei*. To understand how "God exists in our thoughts," it is not enough to review the kind of inferential knowledge obtained in the last Ten Questions of the divine existence without any definitional understanding of the divine essence. Classically, Christian faith knows itself promised and called to much more than this: [w]e shall see Him just as He is.[18] To assert the opposite of this, i.e., that "the created intellect will never obtain the vision of God is either to say that it will never attain happiness or that its happiness consists in something other than in God, which is contrary to faith."[19]

Two facts are operative in this kind of knowledge: [1] that mediated immediacy that characterizes vision (this is to "attain God," but not to "comprehend God" or to infer God),[20] and [2] that God is "seen" in that vision, which is to know God "in Himself" as opposed to "in and through His effects."

The opposite of this assertion, namely, that the created intellect could never see God, also offends reason. Every person naturally desires to know the cause of any effect she encounters. Wonder [*admiratio*] about the world is born out of this inescapably human desire. But if the human intellect could not recognize the first cause of things, this perfectly natural desire would remain intrinsically frustrated and empty. That such a desire, intrinsic to being human, is totally incapable of being fulfilled runs contrary to human reason. The blessed, therefore, must become able to see the essence of God. The following nine articles pursue how this possibility is actualized in the beatific vision.

This *visio essentiae Dei* is liable to four objections that together reflect the concerns of agnosticism. They derive respectively from the understanding of (1) comprehension, (2) infinity, (3) existence, and (4) proportion. Each reply clarifies the language at issue, with the first introducing a crucial distinction in Thomas. To "comprehend" God [*comprehendere Deum*] is impossible. But the possibility of understanding something of God — a possibility that will be seized upon in later articles with the introduction of *attingere Deum* — remains open.

To reply to the other objections demands the kind of analogical reasoning that will be outlined in Q13. One begins with the language of ordinary discourse and then purifies the terms, thus enabling these to reveal something true about God. Once the terms "infinite" (*ad* 2), "existence" (*ad* 3), and "proportion" (*ad* 4) are stripped from their purely human connotations, they are able to be applied appropriately to God in an "eminent" manner. The term "infinite" does not refer to matter that is not made perfect by form, for this "infinite" matter is unknowable in itself. Here, the term "infinite" when attributed to God means perfect form not contracted by matter. Since being is the most formal of all things, and God is not a being received in anything, but is, rather, His own subsistent being, God is both infinite and perfect. Thus, when referring to God, the "infinite" is limited neither by matter nor by form.[21] The "infinite" in God, then, is supremely known. In addition, when one says that God does not exist, it is not as if a human person were to lack existence. Instead, since God is God's own existence, He is in some way above all existence, exceeding, then, every kind of knowledge. While this eliminates the possibility of comprehending God, it does not rule out understanding something of God. "Proportion" is the final term to be clarified. When applied to the relationship of creatures to God, "proportion" should not be understood to mean a certain relation [*habitude*][22] of one quantity to another (as twice, thrice, etc.). Rather, since creatures are related to God as effect to cause and as potency to act, the created intellect can be proportioned to know God.[23] This last purification of the term "proportion" touches upon what is most profoundly at issue in this question. The fact that human beings are proportioned to God as effect to cause creates the condition for the possibility of knowledge of God.

The assertion that the created intellect — to attain its own happiness and to realize the promise of God — must be able to see [*videre*] the essence of God inevitably raises the question: how is such a vision possible for a created mind that moves toward this goal within the previous parameters? If it is actual, as the first article demonstrated, how is it possible? Here in article 2 one must distinguish two factors that are always and necessarily present in any sensible or intellectual vision: (1) the visual or cognoscitive power itself [*virtus visiva*] and (2) the "information" of this power by the object that is to be seen.[24]

There is no vision unless the thing seen is in a certain way in the one seeing. In corporeal things the thing seen cannot be by its essence in the one seeing, but only by its likeness [*similitudinem*].[25] For instance, a stone is known by its similitude or form actualizing the vision of the stone in the eye. But when the source of the visual power and the thing seen are one and the same thing, the one seeing possesses from the one same thing both the visual power and the form whereby it sees. This is the case when God is both the author of his power of vision and the object of his vision.

Similitudo, however, ranges through two divergent references in the analysis of this question: it can indicate the created form that informs the intellectual power so that it sees this rather than that; or it can denote the visual or cognoscitive power itself, which like any created reality is a participated similitude of its divine cause. But human beings cannot see the essence of God by means of this first kind of similitude — as they know corporeal things through their representation in the intellect. No created or finite form can so modify the human intellect that it would see the infinite God instead of some created or finite object. This is impossible for three reasons. First, things of a higher order cannot be known through a likeness to things of a lower order, as, for instance, the similitude of a body cannot lead one to know the essence of an incorporeal thing. Second, while God's essence is God's existence, nothing in creation resembles this. The difference between God and creation is so radical here that nothing that is created can represent God. Third, the divine essence is simply beyond delimitation [*incircumscriptum*], containing every perfection to a transcendent degree. Human expressions of these perfections are only determinately this rather than that. It is impossible, then, for any created similitude to represent the essence of God.

Only God can formally enable the finite cognoscitive powers to see God. The human intellect is not capable of having this vision all on its own; it must be strengthened for such a vision. For human beings to come to the vision of God, then, two factors are required: [1] the gracing or strengthening of the human intellect so that it can see God, a strengthening by what has been classically called the "*lumen gloriae*"; and [2] the information of the intellect by the divine essence itself, which is above all human or created forms of God so that what one sees is God. The visual powers are a created similitude of the *intellectus primus*, a likeness that is the participation in the divine glory (*ad* 1); the second is the divine essence itself, united to the human intellect, informing the human intellect, and reducing it to act.

Once the conditions required for any created intellect to see the essence of God have been established, it is necessary to understand how the human being meets these conditions. How can the human intellect be disposed or modified so that it can receive the form that is God Himself?[26]

It is necessary to examine more closely the first of the two factors required for any vision, namely the visual or cognoscitive power (a3–6). The structure of this examination must follow a typically Thomistic pattern of *viae negativae* and *viae affirmativae*.

The *via negativa* is necessarily the first step in this pattern, for it is imperative to strip away any misleading connotations associated with this power. It is necessary to empty the "visual" (a3) and "cognoscitive" (a4) aspects of this power from any corporeal implications. Then, one is able to move to the broader argument that no finite faculty of itself, whether human or angelic, is capable of fulfilling the task of this power.

The elimination of ocular vision is obvious. But it is necessary to go further to recognize the profound limitations of all natural faculties because "whatever is received is received according to the mode of the receiver."[27] If the mode of anything's being exceeds the mode of the knower, then the knowledge of that being is above the capacity of the knower. The knower, then, must be changed in order to be able to receive such knowledge.

The human person possesses two cognitive powers: the senses and the intellect. Sense perception is an act of a corporeal organ that naturally knows things existing in individual matter. Intellectual knowledge, however, is not an act of a corporeal organ. As a result, the intellect can know natures that exist only in individual matter, but it is able to abstract from this matter and understand these natures as universal. The angelic intellect supersedes the human intellect in knowing natures not existing in matter. But to know self-subsistent being is beyond any created intellect, either human or angelic, for no creature is his own existence, but rather has existence by participation. The created intellect, therefore, cannot see the essence of God, "unless God by His grace unites Himself to the created intellect as an object made intelligible to it."[28] In addition, the light of glory strengthening the human intellect disposes it to be able to receive God as form. As the form of the stone unites itself to the intellect in order to actualize the vision of the stone, so does God unite Himself to the intellect, becoming in some way its form for vision, in order that God be seen by the intellect.

Having established the incapacity of the senses and the limitations of all natural faculties for the beatific vision, it is necessary to explore how God can raise the created intellect above its nature by becoming its form.

Everything that is raised up above its nature must be prepared by some disposition above its nature. For example, the grace of faith must prepare someone to believe. If a created intellect is to see the essence of God, the essence of God itself must become the intelligible form of the intellect.[29] In order that this be possible, it is necessary that some supernatural disposition raise the intellect beyond its natural powers. This illumination of the intellect is classically called the *lumen gloriae* (*ad* 3). It enables the intellect to understand in the same way that a habit makes a power more able to act (*ad* 1). By this light the blessed are made "deiform" for they can see God as God is.

Of those who are made deiform one can see the essence of God more perfectly than another as one intellect shares more in this *lumen gloriae*. One will have a greater power or faculty to see God than another, but this power is not attained naturally. Participation in the light of glory, in its turn, is determined by the strength of charity in a person, for she who has more charity participates more fully in the light of glory: "where there is the greater charity, there is the more desire; and desire in a certain degree makes the one desiring apt and prepared to receive the object desired."[30] Therefore, she who possesses more charity will see God more perfectly, and thus will be more beatified. The intellectual knowledge that the blessed have of God has now been placed in the context of love [*caritas*].

No human intellect, of course, can reach [*pertingere*] to the perfect knowledge of the divine intellect, to know God as God is is intrinsically knowable. What is comprehended is perfectly known, i.e., is known insofar as it can be known. For example, anything capable of scientific demonstration, if held as probable proof, is not comprehended. She who holds this demonstration on the authority of others, for example, does not reach [*pertingere*] that perfect mode of knowledge of which it is intrinsically capable.[31] To comprehend, in the strict sense of this term, is to know in a whole and complete way.

Though God, whose being is infinite, is infinitely knowable, no created intellect can know God infinitely. The intellect, rather, knows the divine essence more or less perfectly in proportion as it receives a greater or lesser light of glory. Since this created light is not infinite, it does not enable the human intellect to know God to an infinite degree, or to comprehend God. While no created intellect can know God to an infinite degree, "for the mind to attain [*attingere*] to God in some degree is great beatitude."[32] This crucial distinction between *comprehendere* and *attingere* is foundational to grasp Thomas' overall argument for natural knowledge of God.

Comprehendere, however, can be understood in two ways: the first, being more strict and proper, and the second, more general and loose. According to the first, the thing comprehended is "included" in the one comprehending. In this sense, a human intellect can never comprehend God because it cannot contain God infinitely. In its second meaning, "comprehension" is taken as opposed to "nonattainment." In this looser sense of "comprehension," the person in some way attains [*attingere*] God, and is therefore said to comprehend God. The blessed, then, "see [God], and in seeing Him, possess Him as present, having the power to see Him always; and possessing Him, they enjoy Him as the ultimate fulfillment of desire."[33] One must insist, however, that the Christian tradition uses the stricter understanding of "comprehension," and so calls God "incomprehensible." This is not because nothing is seen of God, but because God is not seen as perfectly as God is capable of being seen.[34]

While the *lumen gloriae* explains the strengthening of intellect enabling it to see God, it does not indicate how one sees God and not simply a created similitude of God. This problem draws attention to the second factor in any cognoscitive or visual act — the presence of the informing form. If one cannot comprehend God because God is infinite (a7), three consequences follow: [1] what one sees is not everything that is in God (a8), [2] the form by which one sees God is not by a created similitude (a9), [3] therefore, one sees God all at once (a10).

In the beatific vision all things are seen in God as an effect is seen in its cause. The more perfectly a cause is seen, of course, the more the effects are seen in this cause. An intellect can know all the effects of a cause and the reasons for those effects in the cause itself, if it comprehends the cause completely. But no created intellect can fully comprehend God. No created intellect, then, in seeing God can know all that God does or can do, for this would mean that the intellect could comprehend the power of God. But any intellect can know more of what God does or can do the more perfectly it sees God.

To see God, this created intellect must be united to the divine essence itself, rather than to any created similitude. Each thing is known insofar as its similitude is in the one who knows. A mirror and what is in it are seen through a similitude. All things are seen in God as in an intelligible mirror. If God Himself is not seen by any similitude but by His own essence, neither are the things seen in God seen by any similitudes or ideas.[35]

For as things that are like to one and the same thing are like to each other, the cognitive faculty can be assimilated to any knowable object in two ways. In one way it is assimilated by the object itself, when it is directly informed by a similitude. In this case, the object is known in itself. For instance, in seeing Peter approaching, the similitude of Peter becomes the form in one's eye. In this case one sees Peter himself. In another way, the intellect is informed by a similitude that is not derived from the object itself, but from some image of the object, i.e., from some likeness. In this second case, the knowledge is not said to be of the thing itself, but of the thing in its likeness. For instance, one sees Peter's photo, and one recalls Peter because of how the photo resembles him. Hence to know things thus by their own likeness in the intellect, is to know them in themselves or in their own natures. To know them by their similitudes pre-existing in God, is to see them in God. The blessed, therefore, see things in God Himself — not by any other similitudes — only by the divine essence present to the intellect as God Himself is seen.

The final consequence of God's informing the intellect, rather than the intellect's seeing God by virtue of a created similitude, is that everything is seen in a single view. If the things seen in God were seen by their own similitude, they would be seen successively, as the parts of a whole are understood successively, each by its own idea. But since they are seen by the one essence of God, they are seen simultaneously, as diverse parts are understood under the one idea of the whole. For example, in the concept of a man we understand "animal" and "rational" at the same time, just as in the concept of a house, we understand "wall" and "roof" simultaneously.

The possibility of the fulfillment of the human desire to see God in the beatific vision, therefore, can be established in a2–10 by examining the cognoscitive power that is necessary for such vision. Now it is necessary to turn from the vision found in the beatific vision to the knowledge of God found in this life. A11 establishes what is needed for human vision of God's essence, ruling out the possibility of such vision in this life.

As has already been established (a4), the mode of knowledge follows the mode of the nature of the knower. In this life, of course, the human soul resides in a material body. Therefore, it knows only "what has a form in matter, or what can be known by such a form."[36] And these it knows through created similitudes. But it already has been established (a2, a9) that the vision of God's essence cannot be known by means of any created similitude. It is therefore impossible for the human intellect in this life to see the essence of God. It is, however, possible for the intellect to receive abstract intelligible things through "dreams and alienations of the bodily senses," such things as "divine revelations and foresight of future events."[37] Such experiences as prophecy (*ad* 1) and rapture (*ad* 2), where God raises the minds of some living in the flesh beyond the use of sense, even up to the vision of God's own essence,[38] are exceptions that will be treated more fully later in the *Summa*.[39] Since we are concerned with knowledge of God through natural reason, however, these kinds of encounters are beyond the scope of this study.

This brings us to the end of the analysis of *videre Deum* that has constituted the first 11 articles of Q12. It has shown the goal toward which all human knowledge of God tends, a steady vision of God in which God strengthens the created intellect by the *lumen gloriae*. The divine essence so modifies the created intellect here, that it becomes the intellect's informing form, enabling it to attain the vision of God offered by Christian hope.

If the beatific vision is what awaits the blessed after death, what kind of knowledge, then, is possible *in this life?* The final three articles naturally address this question, first by ruling out the sort of knowledge *per essentiam* enjoyed in the beatific vision, and then by establishing what can be known of God both through natural reason and through grace. These last two articles will be taken up separately, however, in chapter 5, as they represent Thomas' most mature articulation of the issue of natural knowledge of God in his theological works.

One material and one formal observation can be made after considering the remote coordinate texts. First, the data gathered in a1–11 of Q12 already suggest that Thomas' distinction between *attingere* and *comprehendere Deum* will play a pivotal role in his understanding of natural knowledge of God. Second, the very structure of the Question reveals that when talking about knowledge of God, the *gravitas* of the discussion concerns the beatific vision. Upon an initial reading, the last three articles appear disjoined from the first ten. This disjuncture signals the move from the beatific vision to knowledge of God in this life — whether by nature or by grace. Thomas might turn out to be even more of a pessimist than our postliberal friends regarding knowledge of God in this life. For the limitations that constrain natural knowledge of God find their counterpart in the knowledge received in faith. But we will reflect upon this pattern in the upcoming chapters.

– Four –

The Development of Natural Knowledge: Parallel Texts

Introduction

The exploration of how God exists in human knowing focused initially upon the summit of this knowledge, its highest instantiation and realization, i.e., the beatific vision, so that one can understand this knowing in its completion. But that does not satisfy the issues that underlie this exploration. It does not account epistemologically for the prior progress in the knowledge about God that the initial Questions of the *Summa* advanced. To begin this inquiry one must move to the opposite end of the spectrum. Instead of beginning from the world of the blessed, the question must be located in this world. Instead of talking about grace and glory, one must talk about natural reason. Instead of vision, the cognitive activity is human knowledge. And out of these three considerations comes the problem set by the next article: "Whether in this life we can know God through natural knowledge?" This inquiry will reveal that the grace that is bestowed upon the human person in the beatific vision is not some foreign imposition upon her. Rather, it brings her to completion, enabling her finally to become fully what she was created to be.

This is not the first time that Thomas attended to this problem, and considering these prior treatments reveals the development of the question until it appears in the *Summa theologiae*. Aspects of Thomas' mature position were anticipated in these early works. A consideration of these works will (1) pick out the seeds that were firmly planted from early on in his career, and (2) observe the shifts in emphases and concern that occur in his more mature works. In these texts Thomas consistently seeks to carve out a third way — one that does not succumb to the despair of agnosticism and the pretensions of fideism.[1] His careful use of language leads to an important distinction in his early works between *attingere Deum* and *comprehendere Deum*, a distinction that will prove crucial in his later writings. Thomas also transitions from talking about the general role of a virtuous life in natural knowledge of God to his later recognition of the specific role of charity in such knowledge. Finally, the distinctions between the knowledge found in nature, faith and the beatific vision sharpen throughout his work. The initial divergence between the reading that emerges in chapters 2 and 3 of this study and the postliberal reading of Thomas will, in turn, receive greater clarity here.

The texts chosen for examination include selections from his *Scriptum super libros Sententiarum*,[2] a commentary that he completed during his first period of teaching in Paris as a bachelor of the *Sentences*. Next, it will analyze selections from the commentary on Boethius' *De trinitate* that Thomas wrote a few years later,[3] and from the *Summa contra gentiles* that he wrote upon his return to Italy.[4] It ends with an examination of Thomas' revised commentary on the *Scriptum super libros Sententiarum* that he completed as regent master at *Santa Sabina*.[5]

An analysis of the *Summa theologiae*, the revision of the *Scriptum super libros sententiarum* and the *In epistolam ad Romanos* will be postponed until chapter 5. The mature nature of each and their central importance for addressing the contemporary conversation of this issue demand a separate treatment. It is the task of this chapter to allow historical developments or shifts in emphases to rise to the surface, which will then assist in clarifying the terms and argument in the *Summa theologiae*, the revision of the *Scriptum super libros Sententiarum* and *In epistolam ad Romanos*.

Scriptum super libros Sententiarum

Thomas wrote his commentary upon Peter Lombard's *Sententiae* during his first period of teaching in Paris (1252–1256),[6] when he was approximately 27 years old. This comprised the second stage of his journey to becoming a master in theology, following his time as a bachelor of Scripture in Cologne.[7] The commentary on the *Sentences* was the chief task of a scholar wishing to become a master of theology.[8] After completing this commentary, Thomas would enter the final step of this process in assisting his master in disputes.[9]

Two selections in this commentary contain Thomas' early examinations of natural knowledge of God; one is found in Book I and the other in Book III. Lombard's *Sententiae* are divided according to the Augustinian distinction between *res* and *signa*. There are three kinds of *res*: things intended for enjoyment (the divine persons), things intended for use (the material universe and creatures), and things intended for both (the human soul and angels). The Christian sacraments comprise the *signa*. The three kinds of *res* form the basis for the division of the *Sententiae* into the first three books, with the *signa* comprising the fourth book: [I] God and the Trinity, [II] Creation and original sin, [III] Incarnation and redemption, [IV] Sacraments and eschatology.[10]

The first set of articles under consideration, which treat natural knowledge of God, is found in Book I about God and the Trinity. *Distinctio* 3, where our articles fall, treats the unity of the essence and the Trinity of persons "through reasons and similitudes."[11] Since this cluster of questions discusses knowledge of God through the vestiges of creatures, a set of issues need to be addressed about knowledge of God through human reason.

Four articles deal with human knowledge from natural reason, namely: [1] whether God can be known by a created intellect, [2] whether the knowledge that God is is self-evident, [3] whether the knowledge of God can be reached by means of creatures and [4] if by natural knowledge the philosophers could have knowledge of the Trinity by means of creatures. These four constitute the focus of the present study. Two observations should be made about the structure of these articles. While they are remarkably Abelardian in pattern, they grow in content from the potentiality to the full implications of knowledge. These articles *de facto* follow a *sic et non* pattern somewhat like that of Abelard. The argument first establishes the possibility of knowledge of God by the human person. Next, it rules out the surest kind of knowledge, or self-evident knowledge that God is. While this knowledge is denied, some other kind of knowledge through creatures is then affirmed. The question ends by setting limits on such knowledge. Within this *sic et non* pattern there is a movement from a modest question to radical implications of the answer. The potentiality or mere possibility of any knowledge of God is first posed. Once this is established, the next two articles ask about the method of such knowledge. While ruling out knowledge of God *per se* or self-evident knowledge, they establish that God can in fact be known *per creaturas*. Finally, the full range of this knowledge *per creaturas* is examined by asking the most radical question of natural knowledge: could the pagan philosophers come to some knowledge of the Trinity *per creaturas*? An examination of the articles themselves will fully reveal how natural reason enjoys a legitimate and proper place in Thomas' early understanding of how the human person comes to know God.

The first move in the argument of this cluster of articles establishes the *an sit:* God can in fact be known by the created intellect. One must pay close attention to the verb chosen to describe the act of knowing here. When discussing knowledge in the beatific vision, Thomas will use the verb *videre;* the verb *cognoscere* will usually be reserved for knowledge of God in this life. Here, however, *cognoscere* is taken in its widest sense, suggesting the possibility of any such knowledge at all and prescinding from the problem of whether it occurs in the present life or in the beatific vision. The article focuses upon the capabilities of the human intellect, either moved by evidence available to natural reason, or elevated by grace, or found in the beatific vision. In addition, the question at issue here is not whether God in God's essence can be immediately seen. Instead, a much more modest question is being posed: can we *in some way* know God?[12] Already in this early work the distinction between *attingere* or *pertingere Deum* and *comprehendere Deum* is established. Appropriate knowledge of God is always framed in terms of *attingere*. Comprehending God or knowing God perfectly [*perfecte cognoscatur*] is ruled out from the beginning of the argument.[13] This will become a refrain in Thomas' work on natural knowledge of God.

The *sed contra* sets up the problem. Knowledge of God is both what we are called to in the Christian life, and what is attested to by "the philosopher" Aristotle. Both *sacra doctrina* and philosophical evidence reveal that the end of human life is the contemplation of God. God does not encourage in vain: the prophet Jeremiah proclaims, "But let anyone who wants to boast, boast of this: of understanding and knowing me" (Jeremiah 9:24). A critical problem, however, inevitably arises: the human person is oriented toward knowledge of a subject — God — that far exceeds the capabilities of her intellect. How can the vector of her life point further than her abilities reach when Scripture itself exclaims that the human person was not created in vain?[14]

The resolution of this problem depends upon the distinction between sensible and intelligible objects of knowledge.[15] The intelligible differs from the sensible in a crucial respect: that which exceeds the sensible destroys sense, whereas that which exceeds the intelligible strengthens the intellect. Since the human intellect can know what is knowable, and God in Godself is the highest intelligible, the human intellect can know God. The intellect, however, needs to be strengthened in order to enable it to know God. How this is to take place is set aside for later discussion.

The rest of the argument is worked out in dialogue with the objectors,[16] who examine the act of human knowing, showing how the object-to-be-known, God, far exceeds the reaches of the human intellect. Meditating upon the reality of God on the one hand and the capacity of the human intellect on the other leads to the nexus of the problem. The five objections taken together argue that the inescapable limitations of any created intellect — but here especially the human — mean that knowledge of God is impossible. These stem from two sources, either the nature of God or the nature of human knowing, which emerge in the objections in alternating moments.

Three characteristics of the act of human knowing weigh against the thesis of the article: that any created intellect knows only existing things [*arg.* 1], that it knows by the information of the species [*arg.* 3], and that it knows only through phantasms [*arg.* 5]. At first glance these characteristics rule out human knowledge of God. But closer analysis reveals possibilities within the act of human knowing. First, since God does not exist as a created thing exists, to say that God is above all existence is only true in a specific sense. While God does not exist as another being in the universe, the nature of being [*entitatis*] exists in Him "*eminenter.*" Since, then, God is not without being [*entitatis*], and being is knowable, God can be known by means of those creatures that are comprehended by the created intellect. Second, all human knowledge occurs through the assimilation of some species by the knower; but no species can be abstracted from God, for God is most simple. Knowledge of God, however, happens not through the abstraction of some species, but rather by the "impression" of God Himself upon the intellect.[17] While phantasms are a necessary component of any act of human knowledge, Scripture attests to the fact that no phantasm can be formed about God. The Book of Isaiah [40:18] exclaims, "What image can you give of him?" Knowledge through phantasm, however, is the kind of knowledge that is connatural to us in this life, where God is understood through phantasms, not of Himself, but of the effects by which we reach Him.[18] This does not rule out a higher way to come to knowledge of God, namely, through the influence of divine light for which a phantasm is not necessary. Exactly how God impresses Himself upon the intellect through this divine light is a question not yet taken up here.

When considering the nature of God, two characteristics weigh against the thesis that Thomas advances: the fact that God is beyond all intelligible things [arg. 2] and that God is infinite [arg. 4]. These characteristics properly understood, however, leave open the possibility that the created intellect can in fact know God. First, God is more distant from anything intelligible, according to the property of God's nature [secundum naturae proprietatem], than are intelligibles from sensibles. According to the way of knowing [in ratione cognoscibilis], however, God can be known by the human intellect, for everything that is separated from matter has a *ratio* such that it is understood as an intelligible. Second, infinity can be understood in two ways: as privation or as negation. Infinity by privation is imperfect, whereas infinity by negation simply has no finite mode, and therefore extends itself to everything and is most perfect. The created intellect does not have the power to comprehend this kind of infinity, but it can just attain [attingi] it.[19] Consequently, the intellect cannot perfectly see God. This is the crucial insight of the article, an insight upon which Thomas' later work will depend.

By wrestling with the objectors, Thomas establishes the epistemological foundation for the intellect's capacity to know God. God does not exist as a creature exists, but the unique beingness [entitas] of God, if you will, establishes the knowability of God, a knowability that will become a resounding theme throughout Thomas' work. This God is affirmed as the *maximum intelligibilis quantum in se est*.[20] But God is also immaterial and infinite. So while the created intellect can in fact know God, that same intellect always betrays human limitedness in this act of knowledge, and never perfectly understands that which it seeks. While the human limitations are real — we will see how they remain even in the beatific vision — the knowability of God is such that it beckons the human person to press up against her limitations. This first article, then, establishes the possibility of knowledge of God. It introduces the important Thomistic distinction between *attingere* and *comprehendere Deum,* a distinction that will grow in importance throughout Thomas' corpus. It also establishes a foundational insight, namely that that which exceeds the intellect actually strengthens the intellect. How this strengthening takes place, however, will be explored in later works.

Once the fact that God *can* in fact be known by the created intellect has been established, one may ask what this knowledge is or how it takes place. Having established that this knowledge is [*an est*], we seek to know what it is.[21] If the human person can in fact know God, what would be the characteristics of such knowledge? Would it be of the surest kind, namely self-evident knowledge or knowledge *per se?* Both the testimony of Scripture and the discoveries of the ancient philosophers claim that this knowledge is not self-evident. The familiar passage from the Book of Psalms [13:1], "The fool said in his heart, 'There is no God,' " establishes the fact that some deny the existence of God.[22] Anything that can be denied plausibly could not result from self-evident knowledge. Also, the ancient philosophers' demonstrations of the existence of God counter this claim to self-evidence. The conclusions of a demonstration are not known self-evidently, for to demonstrate the truth of something involves propositions and middle terms — its predicate is not understood in its subject. We know that the ancient philosophers demonstrated the existence of God. As a result, we cannot claim that the existence of God is self-evident.[23]

It is worth noting here that the fact that the ancient philosophers came to some knowledge of God — namely, that God exists — is assumed in this argument. It is a given. What it is *not* is a claim in demand of explanation. Whatever one says about natural knowledge of God, it must be seen that for Thomas ancient philosophers demonstrated the existence of God through the natural light of their intellects.

When one talks about knowledge, one can talk about the thing in itself or how it relates to us. Speaking of God insofar as God relates to us admits of two different possibilities. The first is to speak of God according to "a likeness [*similitudo*] and participation."[24] In this way: that God is, is self-evident. Nothing can be known except through its truth, which is copied [*exemplata*] from God. And that truth is, is self-evident. The second way of speaking about God is according to "*suppositum*," that is, to consider the reality of God Himself as God is in His nature, for example, as an incorporeal thing. In this way, that God is, is not self-evident. Many philosophers deny the existence of God. Therefore, it cannot be considered self-evident knowledge. For those things that are known self-evidently are arrived at immediately through the senses, as, for example, that the whole is greater than its part. But those who affirm the existence of God do so through demonstration [*procedendo*]. Knowledge of God through the senses is attained by proceeding from those things that are caused, to the cause of everything, to knowing that the first cause cannot be a body. Such knowledge emerges from inference or argument [*arguendo*] and as such is not self-evident. In addition, Thomas explicitly admits the possibility that philosophers had knowledge of God. Only those who did not affirm an efficient cause or agent, as Democritus and certain others, are said to deny the existence of God.[25] Thomas not only assumes that philosophers came to knowledge of God, but he also claims to know how they arrived at such knowledge — namely, by demonstration.

In denying that the existence of God is self-evident, this article, then, offers a preliminary sketch of what a natural knowledge of God looks like. More importantly, even, the possibility of this kind of inferential knowledge is assumed as a premise. Thomas does not even deem it in need of demonstration or argumentation. He presumes his listeners would agree. The nature of this knowledge begins to emerge as inferential rather than intuitive, as demonstrative rather than self-evident.

Once self-evident knowledge of God has been ruled out, the argument looks to what knowledge could serve in its place. The first contender is knowledge of God through creatures. Anything can be known either in itself or through something else. If God's being cannot be known *per se*, can God and God's attributes be known *per alia*, i.e., *per creaturas*? Here the initial groundwork is laid for what will become a robust proposal of analogical knowledge of God.[26] A distinction — later to be developed — is introduced here between knowledge of God in this life and in the beatific vision.

The way that creatures are constituted is one of the foundations for the knowledge of God. Creatures proceed from God as from a cause, and as such, they imitate God to the extent that they are able. This knowledge of God always bears within itself three attributes — cause, remotion and eminence. These moments in one's journey to knowledge of God are crucially important and will be explored in later works, but here Thomas simply mentions them. Two things are needed for this knowledge to take place. First, one has to apprehend [*capere*] God in some way. Brutes [*brutis*], therefore, are excluded from such knowledge of God. Second, this knowledge moves from creatures back to their cause, God. Since the angels and the blessed know creatures through the Creator, they are excluded from this knowledge. We are left, then, with the question of whether that God is can be known by human beings through creatures. This path to knowledge of God is reserved for persons in this state of life, both good and bad.[27] In other words, knowledge of God is available to sinners.[28]

The rest of the argument is elaborated in dialogue with the objectors. The knowledge that brutes, sinners and the angels have of God is distinguished here. In addition, an analysis of two passages from St. Paul's Letter to the Romans offers an initial attempt at what will be more fully developed in Thomas' scriptural commentary written toward the end of his life.

Since brutes lack the power of knowing anything beyond the senses and God is above all material things, they can in no way know God. The angels do not know God through creatures because they enjoy knowledge of God *per se,* seeing God in God's own essence.[29] The witness of Scripture, however, claims that sinners can know God. One needs to distinguish here between knowledge of God in the beatific vision [*in patria*], in faith [*fidei*], and in nature [*cognitio naturalis de Deo communis*]. From knowledge found in the beatific vision and in faith, nothing bad can result, but knowledge arising from reason is both good and bad, of the faithful and the unfaithful.[30] In addition, this knowledge nowhere claims to be perfect or complete. While creatures are not proportionate to their cause, God, they are somehow conducive to imperfect knowledge of God because some proportion does in fact exist. Perfect knowledge will be, of course, forever out of their reach. But this does not preclude creatures from proceeding some distance toward the knowledge of God.[31]

The seeds of later work are planted in this article,[32] both with respect to analogical knowledge of God, and with respect to the damage that sin wreaks upon such knowledge. That human creatures can know God is clearly established here — in the beatific vision, in faith, and in natural knowledge. The distinctions between each of these moments in one's journey to knowledge of God, however, will be more fully delineated in later works.

Once natural knowledge of God has been established and its triadic analogical structure introduced, one is left with the question of how far this knowledge extends in this life. This final article sets clear limits on the knowledge of God gained through creatures. In the process, however, it arrives at some astonishing conclusions. Instead of asking whether the philosophers could come to knowledge of *God* through creatures, it asks whether through creatures the philosophers came to knowledge of the *Trinity*. Why move from talking about God to talking about the Trinity unless the fact that the philosophers could come to knowledge of God is assumed? As established in the previous articles, the fact that the philosophers came to some knowledge of God was not a claim even in need of explanation. It was presented there as a premise presumably upon which all would agree. The possibilities and limits of such knowledge are now pursued. It is appropriate, therefore, to ask about the triune God, for that is precisely where the limits of natural knowledge in this life are most boldly seen. Note that a real continuity underlies the discussion of knowledge of God as One and God as Triune. The transition is so smooth that the distinction between the *de Deo Uno* and the *de Deo Trino* is made here only to highlight the limits of natural knowledge of God.

The last response in a3 asserted that natural knowledge of God is not only reserved for the faithful and holy. A4 now asks both for whom is it then reserved and how extensive is such knowledge. While it concludes that the Trinity cannot be known by natural knowledge, it reveals an optimistic stance toward philosophical knowledge about divine matters. The argument runs in the following manner. Natural reason can know God through creatures. Everything said about God through creatures, however, pertains to the essence of God and not to the Divine Persons as such. Natural reason, then, arrives at the attributes of the divine essence. But the reach of natural reason does not simply end here. Rather, it can know the attributes of the divine essence that later will be attributed to the persons: "nevertheless, the philosophers could have knowledge of the persons as it [later] attributed to them, by knowing power, wisdom and goodness [of the divine essence]."[33] Knowledge that God is, that God is One, the Cause of all, etc., is accessible to natural reason, and thus to the philosophers. But natural reason can also discover such attributes about God as power, wisdom and goodness. These attributes, however, gain their deepest significance through Christian revelation. There is, then, not only a clear continuity between natural knowledge of God and knowledge arrived at by faith, but also natural knowledge of God seems to anticipate in this very limited way the knowledge found in faith.[34]

Looking to the actual history of ancient philosophy and to Christian sources on this history, evidence points toward a possible knowledge of the Trinity of Persons. This evidence, however, must be examined carefully.

Although we find reference in ancient philosophy to attributes that are later ascribed to the Trinity, they were originally arrived at by chance rather than by design. While the ancient philosophers honored God in sacrifices and prayers of three, they did so because, as Aristotle following the Pythagoreans insists,[35] in all creatures the perfect appears in groups of three. They did not intend by this to place the Trinity of Persons in God.[36] Because of the making of the world, Plato, for example, calls the divine intellect the paternal intellect without actually intending an allusion to the Christian Trinity.[37]

Richard of St. Victor claimed that demonstrations for necessary truths are always available.[38] If this is true, one wonders whether it was possible for philosophers to gain some truth about the Trinity. Richard's claim can be understood in two ways. If understood universally, namely, that all truth can be proven through reason, then the saying is false, for self-evident first principles cannot be proven. There are, however, some self-evident principles that are hidden from us, and thus need to be proven by things more known to us. These are the effects of the principles.[39] It has already been established, however, that out of the effects of creatures, the Trinity cannot be proven. So the philosophers could not come to knowledge of the Trinity through natural reason. If we remove knowledge of the distinction of Persons, however, the attributes of God, such as goodness, happiness and charity still remain available to the reaches of human reason.

Finally, in testifying to the fact that the philosophers did not know the Holy Spirit, the *glossa* appears to imply that they knew the first two persons.[40] What knowledge the philosophers had of the Trinity, however, arose out of the effects of God as One and not of the Trinity itself. Even among these, they did not know the greatest of the effects of the goodness of God, namely the Incarnation and Redemption.[41] Natural reason, then, can know that God exists. To know the Trinity, however, the human intellect would have to know what God is. Thomas is emphatic here in denying the human intellect such knowledge.

What is treated more disparately in the *Summa theologiae*,[42] is treated in a tight and focused manner in this commentary on Lombard's *Sententiae*. This *sic et non* journey through the four articles of this question is framed by the voices of agnosticism in a1 and the startling claims of the reaches of philosophical knowledge in a4. These articles tell the following story. While the human person naturally desires to know God, she cannot fully attain this knowledge in this life, even through grace. What she can naturally know about God in this life, however, includes knowledge that God is, and attributes pertaining to the unity of the Divine Essence. She can even come to know something of the attributes of the Divine Persons, e.g., power, wisdom, and goodness — although, of course, she will know these only as attributes of the Divine Essence. The Distinction of Persons is only disclosed through the grace of faith. Natural knowledge is gained, as all human knowledge, by beginning with what is perceived by the senses, and moving from the effects of something back to its cause. It is gained by demonstration and arguments. And it can be gained even by sinners.

We now leap to Book III of Thomas' commentary on the *Sententiae*, which treats the Incarnation and Redemption. Here, knowledge of God is treated within the context of charity,[43] offering a summary of the state of the argument at this stage in Thomas' career. It is also interesting to note that the role of charity in one's journey to knowledge of God will become explicit by the writing of the *Summa theologiae*. Here, however, charity serves as the context for the discussion more than forming part of the content itself.

In order to contrast love of God to knowledge of God, the nature of knowledge of God demands review. In the process of human knowledge, the senses terminate in the imagination, producing *phantasmata*, which represent the object to be known to the intellect. In this life the intellect receives knowledge only by means of such *phantasmata*. Where knowledge comes through *phantasmata*, the human person cannot know God immediately. However, out of these *phantasmata* one does come to the knowledge of God. Knowledge as *cognitio* and knowledge by *videre* are contrasted here — the latter is reserved for the beatific vision while the former can be attained in this life.[44] How does this happen? While the intellect does not see [*videre*] God immediately, the understanding [*cognitio*] of the intellect terminates in God himself, since one apprehends that God is from His effects.[45]

The findings in Book I of this commentary stay with Thomas as he takes up knowledge of God found through love in Book III. Thomas will then organize his treatment of knowledge of God in the *Summa theologiae* according to this contrast between knowledge through *videre* of the beatific vision and knowledge through *cognitio* of this life. The *cognitio* of the present life is always an inferential knowledge, moving from the effects of God back to their cause.

Expositio Super Librum Boethii de Trinitate

Thomas' commentary on Boethius' *De Trinitate* is one of his earliest theological works. Although the dating of this work is widely contested,[46] the commentary was composed most likely between 1256–1259, during the beginning of Thomas' tenure as Regent Master at the University of Paris. The commentary possibly grew out of lectures he gave to his fellow Dominicans in the Convent of St. Jacques in Paris.[47] While the *Expositio* remained unfinished,[48] it was begun after the basic work was done on the *Scriptum super libros Sententiarum* (1252–1256), and at about the same time as the *Expositio in librum Boethii de Hebdomadibus* (1256–1259).[49] Thus we can imagine a young Thomas, approximately 31–34 years old, engaging upon this sophisticated exposition of the Trinity. What distinguishes this *Expositio* from other commentaries on Scripture, Aristotle or Pseudo-Dionysius, is its extended treatment of issues arising from the text rather than being a line-by-line explanation of the meaning and argument of the text itself. It is, therefore, modeled more on his commentary on the *Sentences* rather than on his commentary on the *Liber de causis*.[50]

Before entering into Thomas' commentary a preliminary interpretive issue needs to be addressed: are Thomas' arguments in the *Expositio* to be interpreted as his own, or are they simply an examination of Boethius' thought? Both contextual and textual observations come into play. The first observation is historical. In reading Boethius (480–524) Thomas was reaching back seven centuries, approximately the same number of years that separates the contemporary reader from Thomas.[51] The cultural, intellectual, and religious context within which Thomas found himself was in deep contrast to the age of Boethius. The second observation arises from an examination of the text itself. While the literal exposition of Boethius' text may be seen simply as an attempt to clarify the original text, Thomas adds six questions about issues that originate in the text and expands upon the literal exposition. While the first can more easily be interpreted as exegesis, the second lends itself to be understood as original analysis.[52] As Douglas Hall notes, these six questions "clearly constitute more of an exploration and expansion of Boethian themes than a mere 'commentary.'"[53] The selections chosen for our analysis fall within Thomas' six exploratory questions, and therefore will be treated as constituent of his own thought.

The *Expositio* opens with a general prologue of Thomas' distinguishing the knowledge of God gained by reason from that found in faith. This prologue outlines the subject matter, method and purpose of Boethius' *De trinitate*. It is followed by a careful explanation of Boethius' own prologue. Certain problems arising from Boethius' *Prooemium* are then selected and treated in the medieval *quaestio* format. The selections chosen for our examination fall within the first Question about the prologue. These questions treat the capacities and limitations of the human intellect with respect to knowledge of God, and therefore touch upon the central issue of this study. They continue to create a legitimate place for natural knowledge of God in Thomas' theology. Before an examination of the first two articles of Question One, a brief outline of the commentary leading to these articles will provide the immediate context, specifically noting the kind of inquiry engaged in here, its sources and goals.

In citing Wisdom 6:22: "I will seek her out from the beginning of her birth, and bring the knowledge of her to light,"[54] the *prooemium* establishes the theme of human knowledge of God. The opening lines of the *prooemium* distinguish philosophical and theological knowledge. These two paths to truth follow distinct methods. The first, knowledge by reason, begins with the knowledge obtained by the senses and moves to natural knowledge of God (i.e., metaphysics). The second, knowledge by faith, begins with knowledge of the first Truth bestowed by faith and then proceeds to knowledge of God and creatures.[55] Boethius' *De trinitate* follows the second method, namely knowledge of God by faith.[56]

While scriptural evidence abounds for natural knowledge of God (including Romans 1:20, Wisdom 13:5, and Job 36:25), those who have tried to know God using natural reason have fallen into many errors. As a result, God has provided another "safe" [*tutam*] way of knowing, namely through faith. Right from the opening sentences of the *prooemium*, St. Thomas makes clear that these two paths are legitimate ways to coming to knowledge of God. The first path might not be easy [*facile*],[57] but it is not any less genuine. It is one thing to say that the knowledge is difficult to come by and riddled with error [*facile visus decipitur*];[58] it is quite another to say that it is invalid.

The subject matter of the treatise is the Trinity of persons in the one divine essence. Relying, of course, on the authority of Scripture and the Church Fathers, Boethius employs reason in order to clarify the mysteries of the faith — as far, of course, as is possible in the present life.[59]

A brief line by line commentary on Boethius' preface follows the general introduction. Here the purpose of the preface is revealed: to establish the causes and inspiration of the work and to offer an apology. These causes are examined in a typically Aristotelian fashion, paying attention to the material, efficient, formal, and final causes of the work. The formal cause of the work is of particular interest for our purposes, as it proceeds by way of reasoning and is formulated by argumentation. For as long as a question is debated with probable arguments, its truth is not certain and it is unsettled. But when reason is brought to bear upon it, it becomes settled because reason confers on it the "certainty of truth."[60] Boethius highlights the act of understanding here because "as Augustine says, what we believe we owe to authority, but what we understand we owe to reason."[61]

The second part of the preface consists in an apology for the difficulty of the work and for its imperfections. One would be right to proceed with caution here, as one should not demand "greater certainty than human reason is capable of in mounting to the heights of the Godhead."[62] Augustine's statements about the Trinity, namely, "that the divine persons are the same with respect to what is absolute but distinct with respect to what is relative,"[63] provide the initial Trinitarian insights upon which this treatise expands.

In sum, the general prologue to and exposition upon Boethius' prologue establish the context surrounding the first two articles of Question One. Boethius' treatise begins with recognizing the First Truth, God, and then seeks to understand what has been proposed by faith, namely, that God is three in one. Reason is utilized in order to meditate upon what he already believes in faith. Whatever is said about natural knowledge in Boethius' treatise, then, is said from the perspective of the Christian faith, or in Thomist terms from theology that is part of *sacra doctrina*. Already in the *prooemium* knowledge of God by reason and by faith are introduced as two genuine paths. To be sure, the first is difficult to attain, but it is unequivocally affirmed as a possible fountain for knowledge of God.

Boethius' prologue gives rise to an extended treatment of human knowledge about God. This comprises Questions One and Two of Thomas' commentary. Question One establishes that the human mind by its very nature can know the truth about God. Question Two asks how that knowledge is made manifest, or what kind of science it involves.[64] These questions move beyond Boethius' original text, and represent Thomas' own systematic working out of various epistemological issues. Our examination of these articles will reveal Thomas' position on natural knowledge of God while he was regent master at the University of Paris.

Question One involves four issues. The first is whether the human mind by its very nature needs a new illumination by divine light in order to know the truth.[65] Once it has been established that the natural light of the intellect can in fact know truth, two further questions arise. First, the capacities of the natural light of the intellect are delineated, namely, whether this natural light is sufficient for the *mens humana* to arrive at knowledge of God (a2). One may then further ask whether God is the first object of this knowledge (a3). These capacities, once again, are put to the test when considering whether the human intellect can arrive at knowledge of the Divine Trinity (a4).

The first step in the argument establishes the epistemological groundwork for the discussion of natural knowledge of God. In sketching how the intellect understands whatever is within its reach, the abilities of the intellect begin to be revealed.

Two scriptural passages frame the objections: 2 Cor. 3–5 (*arg.* 1) and Eccl. 51:23 (*arg.* 8), which teach that the human intellect is insufficient to know the truth without some divine illumination. The remaining six objections draw from both philosophical and theological resources in order to support this claim. The human mind needs divine illumination to know a truth just like the human body needs the sun in order to see some thing (*arg.* 3 and 5). But why does the human mind need divine illumination? Actions are in our power if we have enough principles to use them. But any cursory observation of humankind would have to acknowledge that many are unable to know truth. The human person, then, in lacking enough principles to know truth, seeks outside assistance (*arg.* 4).[66] But if the human person needs outside light in order to learn truth from others — as established by both Augustine and Gregory, then all the more so does she need light to learn for herself (*arg.* 2).[67] Furthermore, if the human will requires the help of divine grace for right willing, as again established by Augustine, then the intellect requires divine light for right thinking (*arg.* 7).[68] Finally, in all causes arranged in essential (not accidental) order, the effect arises from the secondary cause through the activity of the first cause. The human mind is placed under uncreated light in essential order. The operation of the mind — that is, to know truth — is its proper effect. But this operation only works through the activity of the primary uncreated light (*arg.* 6).[69] Such a light is called divine illumination.

The *sed contra* offers a *reductio ad absurdum* argument against this position. Requiring an additional light to know truth would lead to an infinite regress. If the natural light that illumines the human mind were not able to know the truth on its own, then an additional light would not suffice, but would itself require another light, which in turn would require a third light. This pattern would repeat itself until infinity. Since this process could never be completed, it would be impossible to know any truth whatsoever.[70] Therefore, the natural light of the intellect must be able to move the intellect to understand something on its own.

This argument still needs epistemological foundations. The human soul contains two kinds of intellectual powers: an active power (the agent intellect), and a passive power (the possible intellect). Since the agent intellect is an active power, it does not need to be moved by anything else; rather, it moves the possible intellect to act. As a result, the intellect itself is sufficient for the perception of truth.[71]

Two complications, however, demand attention. First, every created active power is finite. Therefore, since the human intellect is a created active power, it is only suitable for finite acts of understanding. In other words, it is adequate to understand only limited effects.[72] There are, then, two kinds of truths. We know the first through the agency of the agent intellect, namely, "the principles a human being naturally knows and the conclusions deduced from them."[73] We do not need another intellectual light in order to understand these truths. We know the second through a new light that supplements the natural light and divinely illumines the mind, such as "the truths of faith, which transcend the faculty of reason, also future contingents and other matters of this sort."[74]

A second complication arises: although an additional light is unnecessary for knowledge attained through reason, "divine activity" [*divina operatio*] is nevertheless required. This divine activity, however, is not an additional light to the intellect infused by grace. Rather, it falls within the ambit of divine providence. *Divina operatio* is more akin to divine movement and direction[75] or a connatural light[76] rather than the *luce divina* that the objectors argue is necessary for knowledge. We do not need the latter, but we always need the former:

> Besides the act by which God establishes the natures of things, giving to all of them their forms and specific powers by which they can exercise their activities, he also accomplishes the work of providence in things by directing and moving the powers of all of them to their specific acts.[77]

In other words, the natural light of the intellect exists because God creates and governs the universe. God moves here by final cause, much like instruments come under control of the artist.[78] More specifically, "God teaches us interiorly in the case of natural objects of knowledge by creating a natural light within us and by directing it to the truth."[79] God creates, conserves and directs the natural light of the intellect, not as an external light added onto our natural powers, but rather as the primary cause of our intellect and its acts of understanding. While the intellect cannot know any truth without being moved by God, it does so without an influx of new light—except, of course, for those truths that surpass natural knowledge.[80] It is true, however, that "the perception of truth should principally be ascribed to [God], as the activity of an art is more attributable to the workman than to his saw."[81] But this does not render human acts of knowing are any less *human*.

Having established the general claim that without an additional illumination the human intellect can in fact arrive at knowledge of the truth, the specific issue arises concerning whether it can arrive at any knowledge of *God*.

The objections argue that the object of knowledge, God, escapes all human attempts to understand it. The first objection is the most crucial, for it argues from the fact that even at the peak of human knowledge, we are united to God as to one unknown.[82] The remaining four objections highlight the transcendence of God. They argue that God lies beyond all human acts of understanding, for God escapes every form of understanding (*arg.* 2), is not proportionate to the human intellect (*arg.* 3), is outside every genus (*arg.* 4), and His essence is unknowable (*arg.* 5).

The *sed contra* appeals to authority to establish that the human mind can, in fact, know God. Scripture[83] teaches that the human person can in fact know God. Augustine, commenting upon this command to love God, adds that one cannot love what one does not know.[84] The Gospel, of course, could not command the impossible. The human person, then, must in some way, namely by nature or by grace, become able to know God. It is the task of the *respondeo* to delineate how this act of knowledge takes place.

Something can be known in two ways, either through its own form (as when one sees a stone through the form of the stone) or through something else that is similar to it (as when a cause is known through the likeness of its effect). Now the first way something is known, namely, through its own form, itself can occur in two different ways. It can occur either through the form that is the reality itself, or through a form derived from the reality. God and angels know themselves according to the first way, since God knows Himself through His essence, and angels know themselves through their own essences. The second way — through a form derived from the reality — can occur whether the form is abstracted from the reality, as when the form is more immaterial than the reality. This is the case when the form of a stone is abstracted from the stone. Or it can occur when it is impressed upon the intelligence by the reality, as when the reality is simpler than the likeness through which it is known. Avicenna argues that this is the case when the Intelligences are known through the notions they implant in us.

The human intellect in its present state knows by abstracting forms by means of the senses. It cannot know God the way the blessed do, namely through the form that is His essence. Since the essence of God infinitely transcends every created form, any created likeness imprinted in the human mind will inevitably be an inadequate reflection of the essence of God.[85] All human knowledge is obtained through forms abstracted from the senses, and these will never bear a relation to the essence of God.[86] The human intellect, then, knows by *abstractio* rather than by *impressio*.

Two ways to know the essence of God have been ruled out for the human intellect: (1) through a form abstracted from the reality, and (2) through an impression upon the intelligence by the reality. The intellect can only know God, then, through God's effects. Even with respect to this kind of knowledge the human intellect is weak. There are two kinds of effects. In the first, the effect is equal to the power of its cause, so the cause can be fully known in its existence and in its essence. In the second, when the effect is unequal to the power of its cause, neither the power nor the essence of the cause fully can be grasped. One can know that the cause exists, but not what the cause is. The knowledge of the effect functions as the principle of knowing that the cause exists, as the essence of the cause itself does when it is known through its form. Since the effects of God are unequal to the power of their cause, in the present life humans can only know that God exists. Even among those people who know that God exists, the knowledge of one is more perfect than that of another, since "a cause is more perfectly known from its effect to the degree that the relation of the cause to the effect is more perfectly apprehended."[87]

Since knowledge of God can only happen through God's effects and even here the effects fall far short of their cause, the adequacy of this knowledge calls for closer inspection. When the effect falls short of the cause, it can be considered from three aspects: (a) with respect to the coming forth of the effect from the cause, (b) with respect to the effect acquiring a likeness to the cause, (c) with respect to its falling short of perfectly acquiring this likeness. In accord with these three aspects, the human mind advances in three ways in knowing God. These ways, however, do not enable the mind to reach knowledge of what God is [*quid est*], but only that God is [*an est*]. In the first, the mind advances by knowing God's agency in producing things. In the second, the mind advances by knowing God as the cause of effects that are loftier, which, because they bear some resemblance to Him, give more praise to His eminence. In the third, the mind gains an ever-growing knowledge of God as distinct from everything that appears in the effects of God. One finds here much of the content that has been suggested and will be developed by Thomas in his proposal of analogical knowledge of God: God known through causality, remotion, and eminence.[88] So much for the reaches of human reason.

To situate the possibilities of human reason, the light of faith must be introduced. The human mind is able to reach its ultimate heights when strengthened by a new light, namely, the light of faith and the gifts of wisdom and understanding. This new light does not contradict or destroy the light of human reason. In this moment:

> ...the mind is said to be raised above itself in contemplation inasmuch as it knows that God is above everything it naturally comprehends. But because it is not competent to penetrate to a vision of God's essence, it is said to be in a way to be turned back upon itself by a superior light.[89]

The climax of the human mind's journey to knowledge of God occurs when the mind is raised in contemplation to God. The journey of the knowledge of the effects of God to the power of their cause has been one of affirmation, negation, and transcendence. In the highest peak of contemplation, the mind does not transcend these three moments, but rather holds them in their proper tension.

The answers to the objections try to balance the utter transcendence of God, with the genuine human knowledge of God's existence. At the highest point of knowledge the human person knows God as an unknown, recognizing that God transcends everything She can apprehend in this life (*ad* 1). This does not lead to utter despair, however. Since God eludes every form of the intellect, the human intellect cannot know what God is [*quid est*], but it can know that God is [*quia est*] (*ad* 1 and 2).

There is no proportion between the human intellect and the divine intellect. This could easily cause despair about any knowledge of God. But two kinds of proportion must be distinguished here. In the case between the creature and God, a proportion between the effect to its cause exists as the thing made to its maker. It is a proportion of order. But since the creator infinitely transcends the creature, there is no proportion of the creature to the creator "such that the creature receives the full power of his influence or knows him perfectly, as he perfectly knows himself."[90]

Further, while God is not in a genus, God does pertain to the genus as the principle of the genus. This entails that God's effects are not outside the range of intelligible objects. Therefore, in this life God can be known through His effects and in the next in His essence. Furthermore, "[T]he term "intelligible" seems to be negative rather than affirmative, for anything is intelligible from the fact that it is free or separated from matter"; and "negative terms are true of God, while affirmative terms are inexact."[91] Note that affirmative terms about God here are not said to be meaningless or empty. Rather, they are not precise to the subject they treat. They will always fall short of full expression of God, but they are nonetheless true affirmations (*ad* 4). Finally, although we do not know the essence of God, this does not imply that we can know nothing about God. When something is not known through its form but rather through its effect, the form of the effect takes the place of the form of the thing itself. As a result, from the effect it is known that the cause exists. And so it is with God (*ad* 5).

This article echoes distinctions already made between knowing that God is and knowing what God is. But here a theory of analogical predication of God continues to take shape — although it will be more fully developed in later works. Further, among those who know that God exists, some attain this knowledge more perfectly than others. How some come to apprehend the cause, God, from God's effects more perfectly than others is a question that awaits further development. Finally, it is unequivocally stated here that affirmative expressions of God are true — not in the fullest sense in that they comprehend what God is — but they certainly do apprehend *something* about God, even though these expressions are "inexact."

Finally, that the human person cannot know the essence of God is something that is embedded in the structure of human knowing — whether by nature or by grace.

The influence of the epistemology laid out in the first two articles now begin to bear fruit. Thomas offers his epistemology in contrast to two reigning positions of his day. While the origins of the first, namely, that the human mind knows the First Truth and then everything else through Him, are not known, the origins of the second, that the human mind first knows the influx of Divine Light, can be found both in William of Auvergne and Bonaventure.[92] Thomas' own position recognizes that all knowledge is derived from the senses. Therefore, what is perceptible by the senses is known before what is knowable by the intellect. Specifically, the images that are abstracted by the agent intellect are the first things known by the intellect. Instead of first knowing God and then other things, knowledge of other things leads to knowledge of God, as is said in Romans 1:20: "Ever since the creation of the world his invisible nature, namely his eternal power and deity, has been clearly perceived in the things that have been made."

The objections use characteristics about the nature of God to suggest that they lead the human person to know God first. God is: the first truth (*arg.* 1), the primary intelligible (*arg.* 2), absolutely first and most simple (*arg.* 3), the final end (*arg.* 4), immaterial (*arg.* 5), and naturally known while He cannot be thought not to be (*arg.* 6).

Two among the answers to the objections are important for our purposes. The answer to the fourth objector unequivocally states that God is known by human reason. God is both the final end and the first in intention of our natural desire. But God need not be the first in knowledge in the person who is directed to the end. However, God "is known and desired in a general way from the very beginning, inasmuch as the mind longs to be well and to live well, which is possible for it only when it possesses God."[93] Natural knowledge here — as always in Thomas — has a general and inchoate shape. The reply to the last objector admits that taken in itself, God's existence is self-evident. But it is not self-evident to the human person who does not see His essence. However, Thomas adds, "we are said to have an innate knowledge of him insofar as we can easily perceive that he exists by means of principles implanted in us by nature."[94] Note that nowhere else that we have investigated has Thomas been so optimistic about this sort of knowledge. Here, not only is knowledge of God innate, as elsewhere, but it comes easily [*facili*] to us by inference.

The limitations of natural knowledge of God are most crisply seen when asking whether this knowledge arrives at any conclusions about the Divine Trinity. While two of the objections from the *Scriptum super libros Sententiarum* reappear in this article (*arg.* 7 and 9), the other eight objections propose more extensive evidence about the robust abilities of human reason. Each objection to this article puts forth an argument for the Divine Trinity that claims to arise from natural reason. While five of the objections draw from authorities in ancient philosophy and the Christian tradition itself, the other five put forth reasons without explicitly appealing to authority. It is evident that Thomas took these objections seriously, not only because of the unusually high number of objections, but also because of his attempt to construct arguments without appealing to authority, which was by his own admission, the weakest sort of argumentation.[95]

The *sed contra* appeals to *sacra doctrina*, philosophy, and the Christian tradition to show that the Divine Trinity is an article of faith. It follows other treatments of this same question in appealing to Hebrews 11:1, while also encapsulating the epistemology found in the previous article: all knowledge is derived from the senses. But in the natural world we find nothing similar to there being three persons in one essence. Appealing to an authority in the Christian tradition, the *sed contra* cites Ambrose's contention that the virgin birth is a matter of Christian faith. If, then, the virgin birth is a matter for faith, so is the Divine Trinity.

The *respondeo* opens by admitting that some "natural" arguments can be given in favor of the Divine Trinity, but these are neither apodictic [*necessariae*] nor very probable to anyone but the believer.[96] In the present life, we only know God from God's effects in the world. So we know, for example, the attributes that designate his causality and transcendence over his effects and that deny of him the imperfections of his effects. But the Divine Trinity cannot be known from creation since this causality belongs to what is common to the whole Trintiy. Neither is it expressed in negative terms. Therefore, it is impossible to give a demonstrative proof that God is three and one. Again, note that Thomas is contrasting a demonstrative proof of the Divine Trinity with a demonstrative proof of the Divine Existence. The former is a matter of Christian faith. The latter is a matter for analogical demonstrations of natural reason. The answers to the objections take each argument for the Divine Trinity and show how they are faulty on their own terms. The answers consistently rely upon the simplicity of God to show that human reason cannot penetrate the mystery of the Divine Trinity.

In commenting on Boethius' *De Trinitate,* we can see Thomas on the one hand guard the sheer gratuity of Christian faith and the central mystery of that faith, the Holy Trinity, while on the other hand recognize the integrity and coherence of human reason in matters divine. This commentary at times sounds even surprisingly optimistic about natural knowledge of God, an optimism, however, that never endangers the sacred mysteries of the faith.

Summa contra gentiles

Thomas most likely wrote the *Summa contra gentiles* between 1259 and 1264. While there is paleographical evidence that Thomas reread his manuscript and corrected it several times, the earliest version of the first 53 chapters of Book I was written in Paris before the summer of 1259. Back in Italy in 1260, Thomas revises these chapters and continues to write the rest of the *Summa contra gentiles*. It is very probable that Book IV was finished by the beginning of 1264, and represents, then, Thomas' movement into his most mature theological writings.[97] In this work Thomas pursues the theme of the twofold mode [*modus*] to truth on which the structure of this *Summa* is based. Our selections examine these two paths, which embody Thomas' position on the natural knowledge [*ratio naturalis*] of God at this stage in his career. These two paths are distinct yet inseparable.

Book I

The first nine chapters of *Summa contra gentiles* Book I serve as a prologue to the entire work. In this prologue Thomas delineates the wise man, who investigates the two paths to divine things. The first is attainable through reason, the second through faith. The first set of truths comprises those things "to which even natural reason can attain, for instance that God is, that God is one, and others like these, which even the philosophers proved demonstratively [*probaverunt demonstrive*] of God, being guided by the light of natural reason."[98] The second set of truths comprises things that wholly surpass the capabilities of human reason, that God is three and one, for example. These two paths to truth best express the reality of human knowledge of God: "[t]here are, consequently, some intelligible truths about God that are open to human reason; but there are others that absolutely surpass its power."[99] These two paths are introduced with such ease — each path with its own legitimacy and purpose — that they do not appear to be contentious claims. Thomas assumes here that by putting their natural reason to good use, the philosophers were able to prove demonstratively certain things about God.

An examination of the structure mapping out these paths will reveal that in this work Thomas places human knowledge of God within a philosophical and theological framework in which the human person desires to know that which by natural reason she cannot fully comprehend. There are glimpses in this life that allow her to apprehend God, thus igniting her desire for more. This desire is never fully quenched in this life — even by the gift of divine grace.

The distinction between these two paths is only understood when the requirements for something to be properly known are taken into account. Since Aristotle's *Posterior Analytics*[100] taught that the principle of a demonstration is what the thing is, it follows that our knowledge of a thing will be in proportion to our understanding of its essence.[101] But the human person cannot comprehend [*comprehendit*] the essence of God, for: (1) human knowledge originates from the senses; (2) things that are not objects of the senses can only be understood through the data given in sense perception; (3) God is not an object of the senses; (4) since things known through the senses are effects of God that are unequal to the power of their cause, they cannot lead to knowledge of the essence of God. (5) They can lead only to knowledge that God is, and other such truths ascribed inferentially to the first principle.[102] It is unequivocally and unabashedly affirmed here that "there are, consequently, some intelligible truths about God that are open to human reason."[103]

This is not, of course, to build a tower of Babel. Even with regular day-to-day sense experiences, the human person is sometimes unable to discover the properties of things perceived by the senses. How much more remote, then, is her understanding when investigating the truths of things above the senses. It is much more the case that "human reason is not equal to the task of investigating all the intelligible characteristics of that most excellent substance."[104]

Concerning even those things that fall under the first kind of truth, namely, things about God attainable through human reason, it is fitting [*convenienter*] that they also be presented as an object of belief.[105] If the human person were left solely to her own human reasoning, three disadvantages would result. First, few people would have any knowledge of God.[106] This kind of inquiry demands intellectual capability, a freedom from domestic or temporal duties, and consistent diligence. There are few people who have the native intelligence, leisure, and discipline required for such study. It is certain that "few are willing to take upon themselves this labor for the love of a knowledge, the natural desire [*appetitum*] for which has nevertheless been instilled in the mind of man by God."[107]

Second, those who would actually arrive at some knowledge of God would do so only after a long time.[108] This truth can only be grasped after much practice and study, for knowledge of many other things are required before understanding God — the entire considerations of philosophy, for example, are one such requirement. This kind of knowledge cannot be gained by youth, who are still under the sway of the passions. As a result, only those few dedicated and patient seekers who are fortunate enough to invest considerable time and energy would reach knowledge of God after many years of study. If the way of natural reason were the only available path to the knowledge of God, "the human race would remain in the blackest shadows of ignorance."[109]

Third, since the human intellect is weak, its findings are inevitably mixed with error.[110] As a result, many seekers would remain doubtful about the truth of a demonstration, especially because those who are considered wise come to different conclusions about the truth. Even after tireless years of study and dedication, the wise person does not attain untainted truth.

It is fortunate, then, that we are able to receive in faith even those truths accessible to human reason. In this way, we can all have a share in the knowledge of God — especially "without uncertainty and error."[111] The weakness of human reason, on the one hand, and its legitimate place in the human quest for God on the other are both admitted here:

> [S]ensible things from which human reason derives the source of its knowledge, retain a certain trace of likeness [*vestigium*]

to God, but so imperfect that it [*vestigium*] proves altogether inadequate to manifest the substance itself of God.[112]

An effect resembles its causes according in its own way. As a result, sensible things are completely insufficient for those seeking knowledge of the substance of God. Reason, however, does assemble probable arguments in support of the faith, which are insufficient of themselves to enable the human person to comprehend [*comprehendatur*] God.[113] While these arguments certainly are weak and insufficient, it is useful to pursue such arguments, so long as the person is not fooled into believing that she has fully comprehended the truths of the faith: "although our view of the sublimest things is limited and weak, it is most pleasant to be able to catch but a glimpse of them."[114] Thomas Hibbs observes:

> The prologue underscores both the accomplishments of, and the limitations to, speculative philosophy. Reason can reach conclusions about God; its inquiry remains incomplete. The method and structure of the first book reflect the thesis that human inquiry is located between presumption and despair. The discussion of whether God can be known by natural reason amplifies what the prologue had adumbrated: the philosophical life stands midway between the presumption of attaining and comprehending the highest good and the despair over its inaccessibility.[115]

It is in this pattern of the twofold path to truth, then, that the structure of the *Summa contra gentiles* unfolds. The first three books pertain to the first kind of truth (attainable by natural reason), as they consider those things that pertain to God in Godself (Bk. I), the procession of creatures from God (Bk. II), and the relation of creatures to God as their end (Bk. III).[116] Both demonstrative and probable arguments are enlisted here, some even drawn from the books of the philosophers, "through which truth is strengthened and its adversary overcome."[117] The second kind of truth (solely known by faith) is taken up in the last book that deals with the Trinity and the Incarnation.

Book I of this *Summa* emphatically and unequivocally legitimizes the uses of natural reason in the human person's search for knowledge of God. Natural reason is portrayed here as an inadequate tool that even the most intelligent and patient person cannot employ beyond its inherent limitations — but even so it is a tool well worth the use.

Book III

In the *Summa contra gentiles* Thomas places natural knowledge of God in a similar context to the one found in the *Summa theologiae*, namely, on a journey toward the beatific vision. Both texts deal with what a human being is by what a human being is oriented towards.[118] The *Summa contra gentiles*, however, demands a more extended treatment both of the natural desire that sets us on the journey, and the vision that awaits us. What is mentioned only in an objection in the *Summa theologiae*, that knowledge of God is naturally implanted in us (*ST* I, 2, 1, *ad* 1), is treated more extensively in this *Summa*.[119] The discussion in the *Summa contra gentiles* brings together what is treated separately in the *Summa theologiae*, namely, the doctrine of God in Q2–12 of the *Prima pars* with the first five questions on happiness in the *Prima secundae*. While in the *Summa theologiae* the vision of the intellect comes to be rooted in the specific virtue of *caritas*, here lies the more general intuition that the life of virtue will determine how the human person finds happiness in eternal life when she encounters God.

Book III places the ancient philosophical discussion of human nature and its teleology within the theological context of divine providence. Methodologically, this inquiry is a woven fabric of two main threads: *via negativa* and *via affirmativa*. These threads form a *sic et non* pattern presenting a God who is the ultimate happiness of the human person but whom the created intellect can never fully grasp. The argument is grounded upon the principle that every person acts toward an end that is good. A meditation on evil is necessary to reveal what this good end is *not* (ch. 4–15) in order to substantiate the claim that the end of each thing is good (ch. 16). Once this *via negativa* has eliminated false possibilities, a positive description of a good end comes to the fore. The end to which all things are ordered is God (ch. 17), not as an end to be produced, but rather as one to be attained (ch. 18). To determine how God is the natural end of all human things necessitates a treatment of the natural knowledge of God. Human beings are ordered to God as an end. This means they attain the divine goodness as an end, and become like God by imitating the divine goodness. While they can do this in different ways, the primary way humans imitate the divine goodness is found in the act of knowing. When human beings tend toward the truth, they tend toward God. By chapter 24 the fullest definition of what it means to be a human being is delineated, namely, a human being is a creature that is oriented toward the goodness of God by seeking to know God. This represents the first in a three-pronged argument: (1) to understand God is the end of every intellectual substance (ch. 25); (2) this desire is not ultimately fulfilled in this life (ch. 50); (3) but, it is fulfilled in the next life (ch. 63).

Let us review this argument. God is the end of all things, as what pre-exists and is to be attained (ch. 18). All things tend to become like God (ch. 19). Created things are made like God by the fact that they attain divine goodness. If all things tend toward God as the ultimate end in order to attain God's goodness, then the ultimate end of things is to become like God.[120] Since all creatures, even those lacking in understanding, are ordered to God as to an ultimate end (ch. 24), all achieve this to the extent that they participate somewhat in the likeness of God.[121] Human beings, however, participate in God in a more privileged way than other creatures by exercising their intellects to understand God.[122] The human intellect is the distinguishing and most noble characteristic of human beings. Consequently, to understand God must be the end of every intellectual creature.

There soon arises a difficulty in this argument. While the human person is naturally oriented to understand God as the end of human life, the power of the intellect seems to indicate the precise opposite. In fact, she understands the greatest intelligible object, God, just as an owl is able to see in the light of day. The weakness of the human intellect, as the weakness of the owl's eye, blinds it from the ultimate end.[123] How, then, can the ultimate end of human life be something that the intellect is too weak to attain?

Chapter 25 begins to address this question, but a more elaborate treatment is postponed until the discussion on human happiness in subsequent chapters. This first attempt argues that — while the human person is the lowest in the order of intellectual substances — what distinguishes her from all lower beings is her ability to understand. The higher the object of her understanding, the greater her fulfillment. However slight a grasp she has of divine knowledge, this slight grasp will be of much more value than perfect knowledge of lower objects of understanding.[124] As a result, the ultimate end is to understand God "in some fashion" [*quoquo modo*], for the human person "can grasp but little concerning divine things."[125]

As noted above, a person becomes most like God in the activity of her intellect. This distinguishes her from irrational created beings. This person becomes more like God not just by exercising her act of understanding in general, but most appropriately, by actually understanding its highest possible object, God. Further, she "becomes most like God by understanding God Himself, for God understands all things in the act of understanding Himself[.]"[126] To actually understand God [*intelligere Deum*] is the noblest act of the intellect because the object of this act of knowledge — God — is the noblest possible object. This implicit Trinitarian reference suggests that to become like God, a person enters into the Trinitarian life, in this case by understanding God as God understands.

The role of the will in moving the intellect to understand God, however, must not be neglected here. If the end of the intellect is God, the end of the whole person is God. For the intellect is the superior mover in the human being, and the end of the superior is the end of the inferior.[127] As a result, the more a person knows, the more a person is moved by desire to know, for in the process of knowing a person's natural desire tends toward a definite end. Since the noblest object of knowledge is God, knowledge of God is the ultimate end of the human person. It is important to note here that while the intellect is the distinguishing characteristic of the human being, it is intimately connected to human desires and actions.

This desire for the ultimate end, a desire to know God, is firmly implanted in the human person, for the human person naturally desires to know the causes of the effects she observes in the world. A sense of *admiratio* or wonder naturally arises in her, encouraging her to search for the first cause of all things, which, of course, is God. Therefore, her ultimate end is to know God.[128] The fact that the human person cannot reach this ultimate end by her own capabilities is not yet taken up here. What is merely established is that the ultimate end toward which the human person strives is knowledge of God. How she actually reaches this ultimate end is a question to be taken up in subsequent chapters.

The next step in the argument returns to the method of *via negativa* by establishing that the ultimate happiness of the human person does not consist in the goods of fortune, or of the body or of the sensitive part of the soul or of moral virtues, or action (ch. 26–36). Rather, the ultimate happiness of the human person lies in the "contemplation of truth"[129] or "wisdom, based on the considering of divine matters."[130] The *via negativa* of ch. 26–36 is strategically placed in the middle of the discussion of the ultimate end of the human person, happiness. After the possibilities in ch. 26–36 have been excluded, the lens is more focused in ch. 37 on contemplation of God as the ultimate end of the human person. As Hibbs notes:

> The end is considered for its own sake; it is the last thing sought in the chain of means-to-ends relations, and it is self-sufficient and lacking in nothing. It satisfies every appetite. No finite good or conglomeration of goods meets these criteria. It seems then that there is a natural desire, known to the *gentiles,* for an end that transcends what is given in nature.[131]

But in what does this contemplation of divine matters consist?

Several candidates have been excluded from this life for the attainment of happiness. Knowledge of God remains as the ultimate end of human life. But can humans attain this knowledge of God in this life? The various kinds of knowledge of God that are available to us in this life are examined (ch. 38–40). These include knowledge of God (1) possessed by nature, (2) gained through demonstration, (3) attained in faith. Each will be discussed in brief because each indicates the human possibilities for understanding God either by unaided reason or by grace.

The common and confused knowledge of God [*communis et confusa*] found in most people by nature does not suffice for human happiness (ch. 38). That people can "reach some sort of knowledge of God by natural reason"[132] is found when they realize that things in nature run according to a definite order, and from this infer the one who orders all. However, they do not immediately grasp who this being is, or how many beings of this kind exist.[133] People have in fact drawn different conclusions from the initial observation of an orderer of the universe.[134] As a result, this initial vague knowledge does not suffice for happiness.

A higher sort of knowledge of God, found through demonstration, also does not suffice for our ultimate happiness (ch. 39). These demonstrations more closely approach knowledge of God because they distinguish God from all other things, revealing, for example, an immutable, eternal, incorporeal, and simple God.[135] This knowledge, although proper, does not tell us *what* God is, but only *that* God is. It cannot consist in our ultimate happiness because (1) only few people reach this kind of knowledge after a long time and admixed with error, (2) this knowledge is always in potency because later thinkers add to the arguments of earlier thinkers, and questions always remain unanswered, and (3) error and uncertainty can accompany such knowledge.[136]

A yet superior knowledge, gained by faith, is also rejected as the ultimate happiness of human life (ch. 40). For ultimate happiness, a perfect operation of the intellect is required. But in knowledge by faith our intellect does not operate perfectly, for it does not grasp the object to which it assents in the act of believing. Further, ultimate happiness consists primarily in an act of the intellect; but in knowledge by faith, the will takes priority, where "the intellect assents through faith to things presented to it, because of an act of the will and not because it is necessarily moved by the very evidence of the truth."[137] Note here that the act of the will is crucial; the intellect does not assent to belief in God like it assents to a pythagorean theorem. This kind of knowledge is more like hearing than seeing. When a person believes, she believes another person. If she puts her faith in another believer, this believer puts her faith in others, etc. until she reaches a first truth that is certain in itself. When a person believes Christ, she believes immediately in the Truth, by a higher kind of knowledge than knowledge gained through faith. Even when a person receives the truth from those who see it immediately, as when she believes the Apostles and the prophets, this occurs through a higher knowledge than that gained through faith.[138]

Moreover, while the ultimate happiness of human life puts natural desire to rest, faith, rather than calming her desire, inflames it, since every person desires to see what she believes. Finally, in faith, we hope for what is absent rather than rejoice in what is present.[139] As St. Paul says, "While we are in the body we walk by faith and we are absent from the Lord" (2 Cor. 5:6–7).[140] Knowledge by faith, then, does not fulfill the natural desire to know God. Rather, it more fully ignites this desire, and offers hope to the faithful who await a final encounter with God.

We are left, then, with an ultimate end of human longing that cannot be reached in this life, for it can neither be reached by naturally implanted knowledge, nor by demonstration of the speculative sciences, nor even by faith. Rather, each of these awaits their consummation in the ultimate knowledge of the beatific vision. The knowledge of God found in this life — whether by nature or by grace — is insufficient to reach the ultimate happiness of the human person (ch. 48).

The final step in the argument delineates how the outpouring of divine goodness fulfills the ultimate human need (ch. 51–64). God unites Godself to the human intellect as its informing species in order to perfect it.[141] God becomes the medium by which it understands, and the form through which it is able to see. To see the essence of God so radically exceeds human nature that it is like water flowing upwards instead of downwards. For this movement to occur, the water must be moved by something else.[142]

Maintaining the opposite, namely, that humans cannot see the essence of God, offends both faith and reason: "This opinion both would destroy the rational creature's true happiness, which can consist in nothing but the vision of the divine substance... and is contrary to the authority of Holy Writ";[143] this position, therefore, "should be rejected as false and heretical."[144] Agnosticism is here being consummately rejected, for "the divine substance is not so outside the range of the created intellect, as to be absolutely beyond its reach, as sound is to sight, or an immaterial substance to the senses."[145]

Overstating the reaches of the human intellect, however, also misrepresents the case. In seeing the divine essence, the human person will never comprehend [*comprehendit*] God. Even when being raised by the divine light of glory, the human person does not fully comprehend God, for a finite power cannot rise to the level of an infinite object.[146] While in divine glory God becomes the intelligible form of the created intellect, this intellect does not grasp God perfectly. In other words, while the human person becomes beatified in the divine life, she does not become God Himself, except by intentionality or participation.

Now that the parameters for human knowledge of God have been set, it is important to note variances. While every person is directed to God as to an end, each person is directed differently, and participates in a particular manner in the end. Everyone is not equally prepared for the ultimate end, for "some are more virtuous, some less, and virtue is the way to happiness."[147] The ultimate happiness of the intellect, then, is deeply rooted in the will. One does not know God unless one desires God. The best preparation for the beatific vision of the intellect, then, is to lead a virtuous life. This beatific knowledge is not an intellectualization of the faith, a spiritualized act of the intellect divorced from the desires of the body. It is, rather, an act of the intellect that has been driven by a life of ordered desire, of one who walks in faith, hope, and love of God. It is also important to note here that similar patterns of incompleteness and inchoateness are found both in the use of reason and in the life of faith. The radical disjuncture occurs not between reason and faith, but rather between life as it is lived here, and the experience of the beatific vision.

Book IV: The Twofold Nature of Truth Revisited

While the fourth book deals with themes beyond the scope of this study, the first chapter places the knowledge of God found in this life in its proper context — that is, against the background of the knowledge found in the beatific vision. An overview of chapter 1, then, indicates how natural knowledge of God fits within the overall argument of the work. The fourth book returns to the initial theme of the work, the two paths to truth. It represents the transition between the first and second way, for this book will explicitly treat such topics as the Trinity, the Incarnation, and the sacraments. Before entering into such topics, however, these are properly placed within the methodology of the entire work.

Chapter 1 provides the prologue to the fourth book. It reintroduces the theme that serves as the foundation for the work: ultimate human happiness is found in knowledge of God that cannot be attained in this life. How is the human person, then, to reach her ultimate happiness?

Since the ultimate end for the human person consists in knowing God, an end unreachable by human reason, God has given the human person a way through which to rise to knowledge of God:

> [S]o that, since the perfections of things descend in a certain order from the highest summit of things — God — man may progress in the knowledge of God by beginning with lower things and gradually ascending.[148]

As a result, "the way of descending is the same as the way of ascending, distinguished by beginning and end."[149] The human person is able to rise to some sort of knowledge of God through observing the various effects of God in the world. But she cannot know perfectly even these effects that are properly grasped by the senses. How much less, then, can she know things not grasped by the senses, "though they may be perceived through certain deficient effects?"[150] The problematic is restated:

> If, then, we imperfectly know the ways themselves, how shall we be able to arrive at a perfect knowledge of the source of these ways? And because that source transcends the above-mentioned ways beyond proportion, even if we knew the ways themselves perfectly we would yet not have within our grasp a perfect knowledge of the source.[151]

The weakness of the human intellect inhibits it both with respect to things grasped by the senses and with respect to things beyond the senses. The knowledge of God gained through the senses, then, is limited at best.

As Hibbs notes throughout his commentary on the *Summa contra gentiles,* the ascent, then, becomes descent, for what we desire by nature we gain in faith. Even here, however, divine things are not understood, but are rather only "believed as heard."

The two paths to truth introduced in Book I now become three as the knowledge found in the beatific vision follows upon the knowledge gained first by reason and then by faith. Books I–III dealt with knowledge accessible through reason. Book IV will now discuss those truths known by faith alone.

Since knowledge by faith is gained by listening to the Word, the methodology of Book IV is patterned upon this reality. It takes principles from Scripture and employs reason in order to show that what is proposed by faith is not opposed to reason. Book IV, then, is properly theological: it begins with scriptural principles, and employs philosophical reasoning to defend these principles. The methodology itself reflects the fact that the descent of God to the creature leads to and empowers the ascent of the creature to God. The two modes, while distinct, are part of one reality.

We have seen, then, how the *Summa contra gentiles* furthers Thomas' understanding of natural knowledge of God by [1] continuing to insist upon a legitimate — albeit limited — place for natural knowledge of God, [2] portraying the structure of natural knowledge and the structure of faith analogously — each is anticipatory and incomplete, and [3] more clearly demarking the three stages in knowledge of God — through nature, grace and the beatific vision.

Conclusion

This analysis of the treatment of natural knowledge of God through Thomas' early and middle writings clearly establishes the following. Natural knowledge of God is one of three authentic moments in one's journey to knowledge of God, namely of nature, grace, and the beatific vision. The first moment is challenging; it is not achievable by everyone; and it always remains mixed with error. The sheer knowability of God is so strong, however, that it can draw out of the human person the best that natural reason can reach. This knowledge includes knowledge that God is, that God is One, Immutable, Simple, Eternal, etc. It also includes certain attributes that are later appropriated by the Christian tradition to the Divine Trinity, such as Wisdom, Power, and Goodness. Human limitations inhibit the person from attaining that for which she seeks — complete knowledge of God. It is always true that *comprehendere Deum* remains outside the reach of the human intellect, even in the beatific vision. But that the intellect can *attingere Deum,* or attain something of knowledge of God, is repeatedly and unabashedly affirmed. While the effect of virtue upon this knowledge develops throughout these writings, Thomas consistently maintains that even sinners are invited to enjoy this first moment of knowledge.

We can begin to see Thomas' position on natural knowledge of God take definite shape throughout these writings. It is a position that runs directly contrary to that outlined in chapter 1 by our postliberal colleagues. For we see Thomas continually insisting — sometimes assuming even — that natural knowledge of God has a distinct place in his theology.

– Five –

The Mature Fruit of Natural Knowledge: Central Texts

Introduction

The preceding two chapters traced how Thomas' position on natural knowledge of God developed throughout his career, noting consistencies and shifts in emphases. We now turn to the specific theological and scriptural loci of this issue. For the theological focal point, we must examine a set of questions from two of his most mature works, the revision of the *Scriptum super libros Sententiarum* and the *Summa theologiae*, both written while he was setting up a *studium* in Rome. The questions in the *Scriptum* ask: (1) "whether that God is is self-evident?" (2) "whether by creatures we can come to knowledge of God?" (3) "whether by natural reason one can arrive at knowledge of the Trinity of persons?" The question in the *Summa theologiae* (Q12, a12) asks, "Whether the human person can know God by natural reason?" For the scriptural focal point, we turn to the biblical commentary written during the last year of his life, *In epistolam ad Romanos*. Our selection examines an important passage from Romans: "For since the creation of the world His invisible attributes, His eternal power and divine nature, have been clearly seen, being understood through what has been made, so that they are without excuse" (1:20).

Our examination of the *Scriptum* will trace whether any changes or shifts in emphases occur between Thomas' first treatment of these articles and their revision. These articles are particularly important because they explicitly deal with both the possibilities and limits of natural knowledge of God. Our analysis of the *Summa* will begin by examining Q12, a12 and a13. Question 13 on the Divine Names will also be analyzed here, as concerns about language naturally arise out of epistemological questions. In particular, the treatment of analogical language found in Question 13 expresses in linguistic terms what Thomas had established through the epistemological work of Question 12. The selections from *In epistolam ad Romanos* comprise the commentary upon Romans 1:20, the scriptural focus of our study. These arise in *lectio* 6 and 7 of the commentary. This Romans passage is invoked consistently both throughout Thomas' treatment of natural knowledge of God in his career and throughout the postliberal account of this issue. As a result, an analysis of his commentary upon this passage is crucial to our interpretation.

It is particularly fitting to end with an analysis of these texts, as they provide a segue back into the contemporary setting for this problem. Using *In epistolam ad Romanos* to interpret the *Summa theologiae*, Eugene Rogers has produced an astonishing rereading of Thomas on natural knowledge of God. After our own textual analysis of these mature works, then, we will return in the epilogue to this contemporary discussion to ask whether the rereading outlined in chapter 1 offers a warranted and even plausible interpretation of Thomas on natural knowledge of God.

Scriptum super libros Sententiarum Revised Text[1]

Evidence now suggests that Thomas returned to his commentary on Lombard's *Sententiae* a second time while teaching at the Dominican *studium generale* at Santa Sabina in Rome (1265–1268). The Leonine Commission discovered an Italian copy of the first book of a commentary on the *Scriptum* in which there are various additional texts, many of which are *marginalia*. These appear to be a copy of or selections from a student *reportatio* of Thomas' lectures on Book I of the *Sententiae* during this time.[2] Three articles from this revision illumine Thomas' reworking of the subject at this late stage in his career. The three articles of Q1 on divine knowledge treat (1) whether knowledge that God is is self-evident, (2) whether by creatures one can come to knowledge of God, and (3) whether by natural reason one can arrive at knowledge of the Trinity of Persons. These articles mirror Question One of the earlier treatment of the *Sentences*, except that the first article asking whether the created intellect can come to any knowledge of God at all has been dropped. After denying the most secure knowledge of God known through human reason, knowledge *per se*, the Question establishes the use of knowledge *per alia*, namely, through human reason, and then takes this knowledge to its limit by investigating what it can understand about the Divine Trinity.

This revision is important because it reveals how the mature Thomas roots natural knowledge of God in the human person's innate desire for God as end, a desire that is the well-spring of *admiratio,* or wonder. While in the first version of the *Scriptum* Thomas focused on *who* could gain natural knowledge of God, and established that this knowledge is gained through demonstration, this version probes more deeply into *how* this knowledge occurs, investigating both the sources and conditions of this knowledge.

The objections mentioned in the first article on *per se* knowledge briefly review two objections already taken up in the original text of this commentary — by drawing on the authority of Damascene and Anselm — and add two more objections. Damascene is called upon here, as elsewhere, to show that knowledge of God is innate [*ad* 1]. Anselm is also again invoked to argue that something that cannot be thought not to be is known *per se* [*ad* 2]. The two new objections reflect upon what comprises self-evident knowledge. In one, the principle of a genus is self-evident. God is the principle of all human knowledge since all knowledge is directed toward Him [*ad* 3]. In the other, a proposition in which the same is predicated of itself is known self-evidently. In the proposition "God is" the same is predicated of itself because God is the greatest *esse* [*ad* 4]. The objections are structured in a typically Thomistic fashion — they move from the nature of the thing, to the thought of it, to the language in which it is expressed. The objections try to show what makes it evident that God is known in Himself, namely through: 1) our nature, 2) the definition of God, 3) the activity of knowledge itself, and 4) the activity of predication.

The argument in the *sed contra* is a familiar argument, but it appears here, as in the original text of this article, in the part of the article that appeals to authority, or to arguments that are generally agreed upon. *Per se* knowledge is not demonstrable. But the philosophers demonstrated the existence of God. Therefore, that God is is not known *per se*.[3] The part of the *sed contra* in the original text that dealt with the Anselmian argument for self-evident knowledge has been dropped here. The argument arising from the knowledge of pagan philosophers is kept, and thus becomes the focus of the *sed contra*. Thomas no longer needs to appeal to Christian sources in this *sed contra;* rather, the argument from pagan philosophy stands alone as authoritative. Pagan philosophers become witnesses here — as elsewhere — that God is to be known by demonstration rather than by self-evident knowledge, that is, that God is, is not self-evident to us. Instead that God is becomes known to us because of something else.

But how does this knowledge come about? The *respondeo* maintains the distinction from the previous version, namely that something can be known in two ways — in itself and as it involves us. But this distinction is to be explained in a different way. Here the emphasis is placed upon language. The focus is upon propositions, in particular the proposition "that God is." A proposition is known *per se* when the predicate is included in the definition of the subject, as in the proposition "man is an animal." A proposition is known *per se* in itself but not to us when the predicate is included in the definition of the subject, but we do not know the subject or its definition.[4] Sometimes, however, only the wise know both the subject and the predicate of such a proposition. The proposition "that God is" is self-evident because the predicate is included in the subject, but since we do not know who [*quid*] God is, we do not know the subject. Consequently, we do not know this proposition in a self-evident way.[5]

In addressing Damascene's position on innate knowledge, Thomas distinguishes between the desire for knowledge and the knowledge itself. The proposition "God is" is known naturally by everyone not as a principle but as an end. The difference is highlighted here between God as the fact that explains the universe and God as the object of our longings. Both our desires and our knowledge are ordered to God as an end. In naturally desiring to know the cause of everything, a sense of wonder [*admiratio*] is evoked. This *admiratio* is not satisfied until we arrive at knowledge of the First Cause.[6] This is a crucial shift in emphasis for Thomas. Whatever natural desire we have comes because we desire God as end. However natural this fundamental desire is, it cannot be fully satisfied within itself. It yearns for something distinctly beyond itself.

The response to the second objection rehearses Thomas' reply to the Anselmian argument for self-evident knowledge already developed in the original text of this article. Thomas has dealt with the Anselmian objection elsewhere, and does not seem to highlight this objection here.

The response to the third objection distinguishes between knowledge as a medium on the one hand and effectively or formally on the other. The first way is known *per se* while the second is not. One need not know that which is formally or effectively doing the knowing. In other words, one may not know that by which one is knowing.[7] The response to the fourth objection draws upon the distinction explicated in the *respondeo* between knowledge in itself and as it involves us. Since the human person only knows the subject and not the predicate, she does not know that God is *per se*.[8]

Once *per se* knowledge of God has been ruled out, the only possible alternative is knowledge *per alia*. This is investigated in the next two articles. The first explores whether human beings know at all and the second explains the range of this knowledge. The first asks whether through creatures human beings can come to any knowledge of God. This article largely differs from the one in the commentary's original text. In that text the knowledge was predicated of all creatures; here it is predicated of human beings. The theme here is the nature of the effects of God.

The first two objections offer precursors to the Barthian (*arg.* 1) and Kantian (*arg.* 2) objections to knowledge of God. The "Barthian" objector establishes that effects lead to knowledge of their cause only when they have a similitude or likeness of it by participating in some common form (*arg.* 1).[9] The "Kantian" objector adds that the human person only understands through the use of *phantasmata* or image, and no *phantasmata* can be created of a God who does not have a body or quantity (*arg.* 2). The third objector introduces Thomas' metaphysics: effects demonstrate their cause when they depend upon the cause for more than just their existence (*arg.* 3). But many effects do not depend upon God in becoming, but only in the act of existence [*esse*]. These, then, could not lead to knowledge of God.

The *sed contra* draws upon Scripture to summarize the methodology and position of this article: "For from the greatness and the beauty of created things their original author, by analogy, is seen" (Wisdom 13:5). In this passage the Israelites recognize that the created order reveals the existence of God. That there is a natural knowledge of God, then, is not just a Christian insight. It is, rather, a truth discovered by the Chosen People. This passage is one of two great sources in Scripture that neatly captures Thomas' approach to natural knowledge of God throughout his work — the other is Romans 1:20.

The *respondeo* argues that these effects can be either adequate or not to the power of their cause. In the former case, they lead to perfect knowledge of the cause. If less than the power of their cause, effects imperfectly demonstrate their cause. Because creatures are in no way adequate to their creator, through such improportionate effects one cannot come to know perfectly the First Cause. One, however, can come to know that God is the First Cause and that God is above all things.[10]

The responses to the objections respect both the radical transcendence of God and the limitedness of human understanding of God. But they do allow that while God and creatures do not share in some common form, creatures do imitate God as far as is possible.[11] This relationship of dependence of creatures upon God creates the condition for the possibility of human knowledge of God. Specifically, by negation, eminence or causality the human intellect forms a *phantasmata*, and then understands that God is not contained by what is in creatures.[12] Finally, the responses to the objections make clear that God is the cause of things both for their becoming into being and their continuance in being. So it is not just that God brings things into being, but rather that in the moment of existing, God is causing them to be. They do lead, then, to some knowledge of God, however imperfect this may be. The responses to the objections have moved from similitude to *phantasmata* and now to being. This third response about *esse* reveals the heart of Thomas' metaphysics: "But God is the cause of things insofar as their becoming and even their being, and therefore according to this they depend upon him for their being; and on account of this they lead to knowledge of him but imperfectly, as is said."[13]

While in the earlier commentary the article focused upon *for whom* this natural knowledge is reserved, this later commentary investigates *how* this knowledge is acquired. The *via* that is only suggested in the original text, namely the way of analogy, is elaborated more fully here.

The final step in the argument, as in the original text, asks whether by natural reason one can come to knowledge of the Trinity of Persons. The title of this article is a slight reworking of the title in the previous *Scriptum*. In the first version the article asked whether philosophers by natural knowledge could come to know the Trinity from creatures, whereas this article asks the same question in terms of anyone relying upon natural reasons. The same issue is treated in both articles, and the arguments put forth greatly resemble each other. With respect to natural knowledge of God, a philosopher and someone coming to knowledge through natural reason are interchangeable. We will see that while the title of this new article asks about anyone enlisting natural reason, the examples cited arise from pagan philosophers.

Five objections necessarily arise from the history of philosophy. The objections invoke Christian, Aristotelian, and Neoplatonic arguments for natural knowledge of God. They marshal evidence from ancient Greek philosophy in order to prove that one can come to knowledge of the Trinity through human reason. While they do not offer reasons for believing in God, they drive at the warrant for belief itself. In the *Confessions*[14] Augustine finds in the Platonists everything from the beginning of the Gospel of John to *and the Word was made flesh*. Augustine must have assumed, then, that the Platonists came to knowledge of the distinction of persons, since the first chapter of John contains these distinctions (*arg.* 1). This is also corroborated in *On the City of God*,[15] where the philosophers knew the first two distinctions, the Father and the Son (*arg.* 2). The objectors do not limit themselves to what other Christian authors found in ancient philosophy. They also find direct examples from representative thinkers of pagan philosophy. In *On the Heavens*[16] Aristotle groups things in terms of three because that number is employed to magnify the one God who is creator of everything in creatures (*arg.* 3). The author of many Neoplatonic writings, Trismegistus, employs what is then transformed into a typically Trinitarian image of the warmth reflected when a monad generates a monad (*arg.* 4).[17] The knowledge found in each of these four examples of pagan philosophy turns on the relationship of effect to cause. In examining this relationship, the last objection shows how pagan philosophers came to the knowledge of God. Through an effect, one comes to know the existence of the cause. Since the cause in the case of God is the Trinity of Persons, by knowing the effects of God, one comes to knowledge of the Trinity of Persons (*arg.* 5).[18]

The *sed contra* appeals to the same passage of Hebrews that was appealed to in the original text: "Now faith is the substance of things hoped for, the evidence of things not seen" [11:1]. This passage emphatically preserves the integrity of affirmations that arise out of faith. These affirmations arise out of faith rather than reason. The *respondeo* can be read as an extended reply to the last objection. The human intellect knows God through creatures to the extent that God is the cause of creatures. But everything pertaining to cause in God is found in the divine essence, not as a property of the Persons.[19] The intellect cannot arrive through this kind of "essential" knowledge, then, to the knowledge of the Trinity. The Trinitarian God is only discovered through revelation or by "hearing." It is true, however, that through natural knowledge one can come to know some attributes that are later appropriated to the Divine Persons — such as power, wisdom, and goodness. While these attributes are appropriated in Christian faith to the Divine Persons, the philosophers are not able to draw this connection on their own. Ontologically, the divine attributes pertain to the divine essence itself.

The answers to the objections apply the argument developed in the *respondeo* to the examples of pre-Christian philosophers cited above. Neither Plato nor Aristotle nor Trismegestus knew that they were referring to distinct Persons in the Trinity of Persons. They did come to know, however, some of the attributes of God that belong essentially to God. A bridge is being constructed here between natural knowledge and revelation through the attributes of power, wisdom, and goodness. This is not to imply, of course, that knowledge of the attributes will lead one to knowledge of the Divine Persons without the gift of grace. Natural knowledge of God here is not a foundation for revealed knowledge of God.

The three articles that comprise this question are structured around the two forms of knowledge: knowledge *per se* and knowledge *per alia*. While *per se* knowledge is ruled out in article one, the objections introduce the four sources of *per se* natural knowledge of God: (1) our nature, (2) the definition of God, (3) the activity of knowledge itself, and (4) the activity of predication. Article two, then, introduces the three conditions of knowledge of God. One always needs the similitude, the phantasm, and the effect of the thing in order for this knowledge to occur. Article three then asks, just as there are four sources for *per se* knowledge, what are the two sources for *per alia* knowledge? The body of this article introduces the sources of natural reason and revelation.

These three articles are important for our study since they provide a segue into the direct question of this article. They also reveal that the structure of Thomas' early thinking on natural knowledge of God is adopted and affirmed in his most mature works. We find here a strong confirmation rather than a deportation from his early writings on the subject.

ST I, 12, 12:
Can We Know God by Natural Reason in This Life?

Recall the placement of this article in Question 12. The Question opens by an examination of how the human person sees [*videre*] the essence of God in the beatific vision (a1–10). It then establishes that she cannot see [*videre*] the essence of God in this life (a11). Article 12 now shifts the question from *videre* to *cognoscere,* asking specifically whether she can know [*cognoscere*] God's essence through natural reason in this life. It therefore turns back to the *demonstrare Deum* of Q2, since the *videre Deum* of the beatific vision has already been ruled out for the human person in this life. What it means to be a human being, and in particular the capacities of this human being, become the central focus.

Article Twelve

Three significant voices from the tradition in which Thomas is firmly planted represent the objections inherent in his position: Boethius, Aristotle, and Augustine. These objections highlight the three powers that make us truly human. In examining the limitations of the human person with respect to knowledge of God, they must engage the three powers that are operative in human knowing: the intellect (*ad* 1), the phantasm (*ad* 2), and the will (*ad* 3). The limitations of these powers counter any claim that the human person is ill-equipped to attain knowledge of God.

Regarding the limitations of the human intellect, one must recall the findings of Q3, a7 that God is the supremely simple form. The simplicity of God here is essential since wherever there is composition there is cause.[20] Boethius reminds us in his *Consolations of Philosophy*[21] that the human person cannot know simple form. Consequently, she is unable to know God.

Aristotle's *de Anima* III[22] established the inescapable role of the *phantasmata* in human knowing. Since God, however, is incorporeal, no image or phantasm can be crafted of Him. Human reason, therefore, remains frustrated, never becoming able to know God. The last objection to which this position is liable moves from considering the limitations of human knowing to introducing the role of the will in such knowing. Augustine in *De Trinitate* insisted that only the good have true knowledge of God.[23] But with human persons both those who are good and those who are evil — inasmuch as they share a common nature — are capable of knowing. Therefore, they cannot know God by human reason. [This objection will prove a crucial one when analyzing *In epistolam ad Romanos*].

The *sed contra* cites Romans 1:19, the verse directly preceding the passage often cited by St. Thomas and others on natural knowledge of God. Here St. Paul writes, "That which is known of God is manifest in them." But how is "that which is known of God" attained? The *sed contra* asserts that this knowledge is gained through the use of natural reason.

A basic Aristotelian insight grounds the argument to support this Pauline assertion, namely, that all natural knowledge begins from the senses. But these can never lead the human intellect to see the essence of God. To see the essence of God, the power of the sensible effects would have to equal the power of God as their cause.[24] It is evident that created effects can never equal an uncreated cause. One is forced to conclude, then, that from knowledge arising from the senses, the whole power of God is not known, and therefore the essence of God is not seen. To know the essence of something, one must know the whole of it. While the language of *comprehendere Deum* is not used here, one can now see that this distinction is very much in the background of this article.

These sensible effects do not lead to complete knowledge of God, but sensible things are related to God as effects are related to their cause. From knowledge of an effect, one can come to know, at least, that the cause exists, even if one cannot fully describe what the cause is. It is this relationship of dependence of effect upon its cause that enables the human person to know whether God exists. One can also arrive at what necessarily belongs to God (i.e., First Cause, Unmoved Mover, etc.). Natural reason, then, can lead one to come to know the following about God:

> Hence we know His relationship with creatures so far as to be the cause of them all; also that creatures differ from Him, inasmuch as He is not in any way part of what is caused by Him; and that creatures are not removed from Him by reason of any defect on His part, but because He superexceeds them all.[25]

This passage summarizes both the three moments of analogical predication and the findings of Q2–11 where one discovers an Uncaused Cause that radically transcends everything that the human person encounters in this life.

The objections to the natural knowledge of God are to be met by drawing the distinction in this *respondeo* between knowledge *quid est* and knowledge *an est:* the former is closed to natural human reason, while the latter is available to it. The simplicity of the subject matter — God — establishes the limits upon human knowing. First, reason cannot know simple form in its essence, or what it is. It can, however, know whether it is.[26] Second, the phantasms do have a role to play in natural knowledge of God, but this role is limited to the structure of human knowing. They are capable of creating images of the effects of God, leading to knowledge that the cause exists.[27] Finally, at the end of his life, Augustine retracted what he had earlier said — that only the pure know the truth[28] — for many who are not pure know many truths. Knowledge of the essence of God, however, is attained only by grace, and, therefore, is reserved only for the good. Notice how in this mature work Thomas continues to maintain that sin does not completely obliterate the human person's capacity for knowledge of God. The replies, then, reflect Thomas' cautious approach to natural knowledge of God. While the limitations of natural reason are admittedly significant when attempting to reach such a subject as God, its capabilities do lead to authentic knowledge, while falling short, of course, of full disclosure. We are finding that this insistence upon authentic yet incomplete knowledge of God is a consistently maintained theme throughout Thomas' corpus.

Knowledge of God has three possibilities. The first is the vision that comes from the completion of grace. The second comes at the very beginning from natural reason. The third is something of a mix between the two — a knowledge that arises from grace. The three objectors come from two main sources: the knowledge arising out of mysticism [*obj.*1, 2] and the knowledge that comes from faith [*obj.* 3].

Grace plays a role in both sources. In mysticism we are united to God as to an Unknown,[29] and we remain restricted by the limitations of human imagination.[30] In faith things unseen are the objects of faith, and therefore do not seem to be of knowledge.[31] These objectors all accentuate the the mystery that still remains in knowledge found in faith.

The opening line of the *respondeo* leaves no doubt as to Thomas' position on the relationship of knowledge by nature and by grace: we have a more perfect knowledge of God by grace than by natural reason.[32] Grace clearly does not destroy reason here, but rather enhances it. The human person is able to attain a *more perfect* knowledge of God by grace than by nature. Here again, these two kinds of knowledge are placed upon a continuum for Thomas. In the knowledge gained through the help of divine grace, the intellect's natural light is strengthened by an infusion of gratuitous grace.[33] But even here, when our natural faculties are strengthened by the gift of divine grace, we are still united to God "as to one unknown."[34] The structure of the human intellect always imposes limitations upon knowledge, whether reached by the use of human reason alone, or aided by the divine gift of grace. The human person must wait until the beatific vision to see the essence of God.[35]

The reply to the first objector recognizes that even in grace we are united to God as to an unknown because we cannot know of God "what He is." But this does not mean that there can be no progress along the road to knowledge of God. Much to the contrary, we can know God more fully according to the more excellent effects of Him that are demonstrated to us, and as we attribute to Him some things known only by divine revelation, as the Trinity of Persons.[36] The reply to the second objection continues to portray knowledge of God as a journey in which the knowledge attained by nature is deepened by an encounter with divine grace. The images of revelation are infused by a divine light in the human person, producing a deeper knowledge of God.[37] The final reply argues that while faith is a kind of knowledge, strictly speaking it falls short of the knowledge belonging to *scientia*. Faith is knowledge inasmuch as the intellect is determined by faith to some knowable object.[38] But this determination, rather than proceeding from the vision of the believer, proceeds from the vision of Him who is believed. In this way, faith falls short of vision, and in turn, of *scientia,* since *scientia* determines the intellect to one object by the vision and understanding of first principles.[39]

It is crucial to note here that there is more continuity than discontinuity between knowledge gained by natural reason and that found in faith. This is not to make a grand statement about the reaches of natural reason, however. It is, rather, to recognize that even in faith, the knowledge gained is incomplete, inchoate, and inconclusive. The radical disjuncture does not occur between knowledge attained by reason and gained in faith. Rather, the real *disjuncture* occurs between knowledge found in this life and what awaits us in the beatific vision. In this way, the philosopher and the Christian have much more in common with each other than either does with the blessed.

Question Thirteen

Question 13 logically follows upon Question 12. As the opening of the prologue states, a consideration of divine names flows from a discussion of the knowledge of God since naming something indicates how we know it.[40] We can learn about how we think through reflecting about the words we employ. Examining the words chosen when talking about God will reveal the kind of knowledge used in arriving at the terms themselves. There is an intimate link, then, between knowledge and language. The governing concern of Q13 also directly follows upon Q12. Given that we do not know the essence of God, but only that God exists and the effects of God, how do we name this God? Can some things be more properly said of God than others can? Q13 picks up the *viae affirmativae* of Q2 and the *viae remotionis* of Q3–11 and asks how they logically fit together. How can our religious proclamations of God be on the one hand proper and true, and on the other respectful of the radical transcendence of God? This becomes the work of analogy in Q13. In accord with his treatment of the divine names in other works, this question is taken up in the context of knowledge of God.[41]

The structure of the articles is as follows: a1 asks whether any name at all can be applied to God. A2–7 investigate *how* this naming takes place. A8–11 turn to the particular name of "God" to see what it signifies, given the parameters of the preceding articles. The final article (a12) moves from names to propositions, and asks whether affirmative propositions can be made of God. Q13, then, moves from establishing the possibility of naming God, to an examination of the method of such naming, and concludes by exploring the meaning of such names.

First, the subject matter of the question is established by asserting that names can in fact be applied meaningfully to God. We can name something only as we understand it.[42] Words are the signs of ideas and ideas are the similitude of things. Words are related, then, to the meanings of things expressed through an idea. Since we cannot know the essence of God (Q12, a11, 12), it follows that we cannot name the essence of God. We can, however, know God from creatures as their principle, and by way of excellence and remotion.[43] And as we know God in this way, we name Him as such. Thus, language gives us the structure of the natural knowledge of God.

If we can name God, then one must ask what do these names signify? A2–7 set out to pursue these questions. Negative names that are applied to God or signify his relationship to creatures do not signify God's substance. Rather, they emphasize the distance of creatures from God, or they express God's relationship to something else, or the creatures' relationship to God.[44] Other absolute and affirmative names actually signify the divine substance, although they fall short of a full representation of Him. Since we know God as He is represented in the perfections of creatures, we name God in this manner (Q12, a2, *ad* 3). But the perfections in creatures do not represent God as something of the same species or genus. Rather, they represent God as the excelling principle of whose form all the effects fall short — even though they maintain some likeness to God. When creatures name God from the effects in this world, while they are really naming *God,* they are doing so in an imperfect manner, and in both of these ways the language is mirroring the natural knowledge creatures have of God.[45]

It is important to note the positions over and against which the *respondeo* is arguing here. In the first position, most explicitly stated in Moses Maimonides,[46] when people attribute a name to God affirmatively, they use it more to separate some predicate from God than to express anything that exists positively in Him.[47] So when they say that God lives, they mean that God is not like an inanimate thing. In the second position, names only signify God's causal relationship to creatures. So when they say that "God is good," they mean only that

God is the cause of goodness in things. Thomas rejects both of these positions for three reasons: (1) neither allows some names to be more appropriately applied to God than others,[48] (2) all names applied to God would be taken in their secondary sense,[49] and (3) both positions go against the intentions of those who speak of God. Surely those who say that God lives mean more than to say that God is the cause of life or that God is different than inanimate bodies.[50]

Since humans predicate names of God's divine substance, they intend to speak in the literal as opposed to metaphorical sense. But a distinction must be drawn between what is signified [*quod significant*] and the mode of signification [*modum significandi*]:

> As regards what is signified by these names,[51] they belong properly to God, and more properly than they belong to creatures, and are applied primarily to Him. But as regards their mode of signification, they do not properly and strictly apply to God; for their mode of signification applies to creatures.[52]

The name "good," for example, applies literally, fully, and primarily to God. But when humans claim "God is good" they never capture the goodness of God. They do not fully understand how what they are predicating is realized in God. The mode of signification [*modus significandi*] always carries its human limitations, while the perfection that is actually signified [*res significata*] is properly stated of God (a3).

Since names are applied substantially and literally to God, are they, then, applied synonymously to each other since God is simple? In order to attempt to understand God, human beings form conceptions [*conceptiones*] proportional to the perfections flowing from God to creatures. These perfections pre-exist in God unitedly and simply. But in creatures they are received, divided, and multiplied. Although the names of God signify one thing, they do so under many different aspects or intelligibilities. As a result, they are not synonymous.[53]

What, then, most appropriately represents this in-between place in which language about God resides? When we claim "God is good," we do not fully comprehend what we are saying, yet we know that goodness in God is causative of the goodness in us as its principle and cause. This predication, then, is not univocal, for goodness in God and goodness in the creature do not mean the same thing.[54] But neither is it equivocal, since a relationship exists between the goodness in the effect and in its principle.[55] Further, that the names of God are equivocal is against both reason and Scripture. It is both against the philosophers *"who demonstrated many things about God"*[56] — in their natural knowledge of God — and the testimony of Romans 1:20. Analogy best represents how we speak when we make statements about God — and consequently how we know God naturally, for "whatever is said of God and creatures is said according to the relation of a creature to God as its principle and cause, wherein all things pre-exist excellently."[57]

There are two kinds of analogy. In one kind, many things are proportionate to one, and in another, one thing is proportionate to another. A term used analogically "in a multiple sense signifies various proportions to some one thing."[58] This question about the names of God clearly echoes the previous question about knowledge. While one can make true claims about God, such claims are always tempered by the recognition that one has never fully captured, grasped, or comprehended the subject.[59]

While language about God is analogical in nature — as is the knowledge of God, there are some terms that are metaphorical when applied to God. These are predicated primarily of creatures than of God. When predicated of God they mean only similitudes to such creatures. For instance, "smiling" applied to a field means only that the field in the beauty of its flowering is like the beauty of the human smile by proportionate likeness. In a similar manner, the name "lion" applied to God means only that God shows strength in His works, as a lion in his. Here, the meaning of "lion" in God can be defined only from what is said of creatures.[60] Analogical terms, however, are meant essentially of God. With respect to what the name signifies, they apply to God primarily rather than to creatures because these perfections flow from God to creatures. But as regards the mode of signification, we primarily apply them to creatures since, of course, we know them first.[61]

Since both analogical and metaphorical language about God imply a certain relation between God and creatures, the nature of that relationship must be examined. While names that imply a relation to creatures are predicated of God temporally, they do not change who God is:

> Since, therefore God is outside the whole order of creation, and all creatures are ordered to Him, and not conversely, it is manifest

that creatures are really related to God Himself; whereas in God there is no real relation to creatures, but a relation only in idea, inasmuch as creatures are referred to Him.[62]

Therefore, human predications of God do not indicate a change in God. Rather, they represent a change in humans. This analogical naming of God from creatures also indicates the structure proper to the natural knowledge of God.

A8–11[63] apply the theory developed in a2–7 to one particular name, "God." They ask what the name means (a8), whether and how it is communicated (a9, 10), and what is its most proper name (a11). They establish that while we name God from God's operations or effects, the name "God" signifies the divine nature (a8), and argue that the name "God" is incommunicable in reality, but communicable in idea (a9). "God" is communicable, not in its whole signification, of course, but in some part of it by way of similitude.[64] The name "God" is applied analogically, where a word taken in one signification is placed in the definition of the same word taken in other senses (a10). Finally, the name "He Who Is" is the most proper name of God (a11). For it does not signify form, but rather existence itself, it is the most universal name, and it signifies present existence, which most properly applies to God.

The final article, a12, moves the discussion from naming and language to concepts and predication. The crucial importance here is that it is in judgments that the question of truth and falsity lie. Most fundamentally, what is of faith cannot be false. Some affirmative propositions about God are of faith. Therefore, true affirmations may be formed of God.[65] In every true affirmation the predicate and the subject somehow signify the same thing in reality, and different things in idea. Although God considered in Godself is altogether one and simple, our intellect knows God by different conceptions. All the while, though, our intellect knows that one and the same subject corresponds to its conceptions. Therefore, the plurality of the predicate and subject represents a plurality of idea, and the intellect represents the unity by composition.

The responses to the objections grant that the simplicity of God governs what can be claimed about Him, but deny that this leaves the speaker speechless. While affirmations about God are certainly "vague or incongruous," this means that no name can be applied to God according to its mode of signification (*ad* 1). We cannot, of course, comprehend simple subsisting forms as they are in themselves. But we can apprehend [*apprehendere*] them as compound things by understanding the simple form as a subject and attributing something else to it (*ad* 2). In this act of apprehension we are not understanding the simple form *to be composite*. Rather, we understand it according to our own mode, which is in a composite manner. Therefore, we can form composition in our ideas about God (*ad* 3). This, then, is not a statement about God, but is instead a statement about human beings.

In sum, Q13 is a meditation upon the possibility, method and meaning of the names of God. A1 began by establishing that names can in fact be given to God, a2–6 examine how these names can be applied to God, a7–11 analyze what the particular name "God" signifies, and a12 concludes that these names can be stated affirmatively about God. Most importantly, these articles put into linguistic terms what Thomas had established in epistemological terms in Question 12: the religious faithful must be cautious in their language about God, but they can speak about God from observing God's pulse in the world. They must recognize continuously that these claims belie a greater ignorance of the essence of God. While religious claims must be open to further refinement, revision, and even rejection, they are justified attempts at true statements about their subject matter, God. Whether in ordinary discourse, in religious worship, or in theological examination, Thomas assures the faithful that their pursuit is not fruitless, that their proclamations really do signify something true in God. They will never have the last word, but the words they use are meaningful and true.

Methodologically, Questions 12 and 13 cap the first cluster of questions in the *Summa*, questions that are braided together with *quia* and *per remotionis* demonstrations. These two strands of demonstrations hold firm to both the knowledge that one can attain about God, and the backdrop of ignorance within which that knowledge is always held. As Michael Dodds, O.P., observes:

> ...Aquinas opened a way into the mystery of God, a way of knowing God as unknown: "We say that at the limit of our knowledge God is known as unknown since our mind has come to the extreme of its knowledge of God when it knows that his

essence is above all that it is able to know in this life."⁶⁶ Since we cannot know the essence of God, we speak of him not by trying to look into his being, but by looking at his effects — at the creatures that tell the glory of the creator: "Although we cannot know in what consists the essence of God, nevertheless in this [divine] science we make use of his effects, either of nature or of grace...in regard to whatever is treated of in this science concerning God."⁶⁷ Through the things God has made, we can come to know God's relationship to creation. The better we know that relationship, the better we know God as the cause of creation.⁶⁸

Thomas thinks believers can make true claims about God, even if in doing so they radically fall short of representing their subject. Question 12, then, takes the data about the subject matter of Questions 2–11 and reflects methodologically upon how such knowledge of God is attained. It is a knowledge that is born out of a natural desire that leads to human wonder. It is a knowledge that we naturally desire but can only catch glimpses of in this life through the help of divine grace. It is a knowledge that will give way to a clear, steadfast vision by supernatural grace in the next. Question 13 reflects linguistically upon what has been established epistemologically, and offers a method of analogy that does not give way to either agnosticism or fideism. While respecting the radical transcendence of God, analogical language best expresses the real relationship between creatures and their Creator, between effects and their First Cause. It is the reality of this relationship that calls forth both knowledge and language.

In epistolam ad Romanos

In the Spring of 1272 Thomas left Paris to spend what would become his final days in Naples, setting up a *studium generale* of theology. The mendicants in this *studium* comprised the faculty of theology — while not of the stature of the one in Paris, it could more easily be compared to those existing in Bologna, Padua, and Montpellier.⁶⁹ Both historical evidence and internal clues in the text suggest that Thomas taught a course on the Epistle to the Romans during this time, and the commentary that has been passed down is a result of this course. The first eight chapters of his Romans commentary reveal a quick correction by his own hand, while the rest of the commentary survives in the form of notes from the course, a *reportatio*.[70] The sections selected for examination, chapters 6 and 7, reveal one of Thomas' last attempts at scholarship during the final stage of his life.

The passage from Romans that is cited often by Thomas, and that Rogers uses as test case for his argument, appears in *lectio* 6 and is further discussed in *lectio* 7: "[e]ver since the creation of the world, his invisible attributes of eternal power and divinity have been able to be understood and perceived in what he has made" (Rom. 1:20). Examining the commentary on this passage and the surrounding context will enable us to decipher how Thomas' understanding of this scriptural insight shapes his mature views on natural knowledge of God. It also directly takes up the commentary that Rogers uses as the key to his reading of Thomas on this issue.

Ch. 1, lectio 6

This *lectio* contains a commentary on Romans 1:16b–20a, whose theme is the universality both of the gift of faith and the pervasive presence of sin:

v. 16a [*lectio* 5:] For I see no reason to be ashamed of the gospel;

v. 16b [n.97:] it is the power of God for the salvation of everyone who believes — Jews first, then Greeks —

v. 17 [n.102:] for in it is revealed the righteousness of God from faith to faith, as it is written in Scripture: *the one who is righteous by faith will live.*

v. 18 [n.109:] The wrath of God is indeed being revealed from heaven against every impiety and injustice of those who suppress the truth by their wickedness.

v. 19 [n.113:] For what can be known about God is evident to them, because God has made it evident to them.

v. 20a [n.117:] Ever since the creation of the world, his invisible attributes of eternal power and divinity have been able to be understood and perceived in what he has made.

The first part of the commentary, §99 through §108, comprises a meditation on the power of the grace of the gospel by reflecting upon

Romans 1:16b–17. The rest of the commentary turns to the necessity of the grace of the gospel both for the Gentiles and the Jews, for neither the wisdom of the Gentiles nor the laws of the Jews were able to save them.[71] Natural knowledge of God, then, will become the way to show that no one, not even the ancient Greek philosophers, can claim ignorance as an excuse for refusing to worship God.

If the power of the grace of the gospel is necessary for salvation, the following question immediately arises, "Necessary to save them from what?" The wrath of God is at stake here. It is manifested in the penalties that God imparts to those who commit sins.[72] The sin that has been committed is double: an impiety against God and an injustice against one's fellow human beings. The perpetrators include those "who suppress the truth by their wickedness" (Rom.1:18). If the perpetrators are suppressing the truth, then they must in some way know the truth:

> [H]e [St. Paul] asserts the knowledge which they had of Him [God] when he adds "of those men who held the truth of God," that is, the "true knowledge of God," "held it in injustice," that is, captive. For the true knowledge of God in itself leads human beings to good, but it is bound, as held in a kind of captivity, by the condition of injustice through which, as Ps. 11:1 has it "truths are diminished by the children of human beings."[73]

What does "to hold the truth of God in captivity" mean? It means that the knowledge leads one into impiety rather than piety.[74] *These perpetrators detained the truth in injustice, holding captive the truth about God.* Thomas analyzes each proposition embedded in verse 18.[75] This verse presents the following coherent argument: [1] the wise men among the Gentiles knew God; [2] but in them was found impiety and injustice; [3] as a result, they incurred the wrath of God.[76]

The first proposition gives rise to three important questions that are addressed generally at first, and then further specified into specific questions. What did the wise men know about God? From whom did they get this knowledge? By what method did they attain this knowledge?

These wise men did in fact know God through reason, which was manifest in them through a "luminosity" that was intrinsic to what they were as human beings:

> For the true knowledge of God was in them in some respects. For "what can be known about God," i.e., what is knowable about God by human beings through their reason "is manifest to them," that is, from that which is in them, i.e., from the light that is intrinsic [to human beings].[77]

A caveat must be inserted here, however: this knowledge could not provide valid information about *what* God is. Humans are totally ignorant of the essence of God in this life. Knowledge of God begins from things that are connatural to humans, namely sensible things, and these could never adequately represent the divine essence.[78]

This caveat, however, certainly does not preclude humans from knowing *anything* about God. Humans can in fact use analogical predication to come to know certain truths about God. This kind of predication is explained as the way of cause, the way of excellence, and the way of negation:

> ...man can know God from such creatures in three ways, as Dionysius says in "On the Divine Names" [ch. 7, lect.4]. In fact, one way is through causality. Since indeed such creatures are defective and changeable, it is necessary to reduce them to some unmoved and perfect principle. And according to this, it is known about God whether God is. Second, through the way of excellence. Indeed, everything is reduced to the first principle, not just as to its particular and univocal cause, as man generates man, but just as to its common and surpassing cause. And from this it is known that God is above everything. Third, through the way of negation. Since if the cause exceeds [all things], nothing of those things which are in creatures can correspond to it, just as also a celestial body is not properly called heavy or light or hot or cold.[79]

The combination of these three operations leads the human person to know whether God is, that God is above everything, and that God is infinite, unmoveable, etc. This knowledge is arrived at "through the light of reason."[80]

Where did the wise men receive such knowledge? God "has made [this knowledge] evident to them" (Rom.1:19). Just as we use words to explain something to others, so does God. But in God we become the words with which God writes.[81] God "writes" in two ways, either by infusing a light internally through which the human person knows, or by providing visible creatures externally, "in which, as in a book, the knowledge of God is read."[82]

Now that it has been established where these men received such knowledge, one can now prod more deeply into how they knew God. This question is addressed from three angles: what are the things they knew about God, through which medium did they know those things, and who is actually doing the knowing?

The wise men knew three things about God. First, they knew the invisible attributes of God, although they did not see or know the essence of God in itself. Rather, they came to know God through certain similitudes found in creatures that participate in various ways in the one God. This, of course, is why St. Paul uses the word *invisibilia* in the plural. Consequently, the human intellect "considers the unity of the divine essence in the mode [*ratione*] of goodness, wisdom, power and such things, which are one in God."[83] They also knew the everlasting power of God, according to which things proceed from God as from a principle. Finally, they knew the divinity of God, or in other words, God as the ultimate end toward which everything tends. This knowledge is attained through analogical reasoning:

> These three, however, refer to three ways of knowing, as is said above. For the invisible things of God are known by way of negation, everlasting power by way of causation, divinity by way of excellence.[84]

The wise men among the pagan Gentiles attained knowledge of God through a series of analogical moments that both asserted and set limits upon what could rationally be known about God.

Through what medium did the philosophers know these things? God's "invisible attributes of eternal power and divinity have been able to be understood and perceived in what he has made" (Rom. 1:20). Just as art is made manifest through the work of an artist, so too is the wisdom of God revealed through creatures. These things are perceived by the intellect rather than by the senses or imagination, which cannot transcend corporeal things.

Finally, if these things are known, who is the knower? This question frames the reflection on "[e]ver since the creation of the world" in Romans 1:20. Thomas curiously understands "*a creatura mundi*" to mean "by the creatures of the world," which he then glosses into meaning both the human person (in particular and in general) on the one hand, and "from the creation of the world" on the other. It is striking that if interpreted as the latter, the invisible things of God are understood through those things that have been made since the creation of the world, not only through the time of grace, or, what has more generally been taken to be the meaning: "since the creation of the world men began to know God through those things that are made."[85] The Book of Job offers further proof of this interpretation, "All men contemplate him" (36:25).

The *lectio* concludes with the strongest affirmation of what the philosophers knew about God yet formulated.[86] A gloss is cited, affirming that by the "invisible things of God" is understood the person of the Father, by "eternal power" the person of the Son, and by "divinity" the person of the Holy Spirit. This does not mean, however, that the philosophers knew the Trinity confessed by the Christian faith:

> Not that the philosophers, drawing from reason, could have arrived — through those things that are made — to the knowledge of [the divine] persons, these do not signify the relationship of cause to creatures, but what is appropriated [to each person]. Nevertheless, [the philosophers] are said to have been lacking in the third sign, i.e. in the Holy Spirit, since they did not assert anything that corresponded to the Holy Spirit, as they asserted that something corresponded to the Father, namely the first principle itself, and something corresponded to the Son, namely the first created mind, which they called the father understanding. . . .[87]

Instead of being a denial of natural knowledge of God, *lectio* 6 ends with the following most startling claim. While the philosophers did not quite know the Trinity appropriately (which, Thomas has already established, can only be known through the gift of faith), they did have some knowledge of the attributes of what would later be fully revealed by the coming of Christ. Just where one would expect a disjuncture, this reveals a real continuity between the God of the ancient philosophers and the God of Christian belief.

Ch. 1, lectio 7:

The *lectio* that follows pursues the consequences that fall upon these wise men who knew God but failed to honor Him. The critical question posed here is whether the consequences of misusing this philosophical knowledge lead to its utter falsification, or whether the validity of that original knowledge persists. Herein lies the crux of our disagreement with the postliberal reading of Thomas outlined in chapter 1. The *lectio* establishes that human reason can be corrupted, but it is corrupted through misuse, not because it is inherently ineffective. The moral life, then, is inextricably tied up with the intellectual life, as the use of human reason is critical to its proper functioning. The scriptural text upon which this commentary reflects is the following:

v. 20b [n.123:] Therefore, they are inexcusable,

v. 21 [n.126:] for though they knew God, they did not honor him as God or give thanks to him, but they became futile in their thinking, and their senseless minds were darkened.

v. 22 [n.131:] Claiming to be wise, they became fools;

v. 23 [n.132:] and they exchanged the glory of the immortal God for images resembling a mortal human being or birds or four-footed animals or reptiles.

v. 24 [n.137:] Therefore God gave them up in the lusts of their hearts to impurity, to the degrading of their bodies among themselves,

v. 25 [n.141:] because they exchanged the truth about God for a lie and worshiped and served the creature rather than the Creator, who is blessed forever! Amen.

The chapter opens with a summary of the prior reflection and encapsulates the upcoming passages: "After the apostle shows that the truth of God was known by men, he shows that they were liable to guilt, impiety, and injustice."[88]

The most crucial question asks whether the philosophers[89] could claim ignorance as an excuse from the fault [*culpa*] of impiety and injustice. Ignorance excuses fault whenever it causes this fault. For example, although applying due diligence, a person believes he is killing his enemy, but he mistakenly — and tragically — kills his father. On the other hand, if this ignorance is caused by this fault, it cannot excuse the subsequent fault. If someone commits a homicide because of drunkenness, for example, she is not excused from guilt because drunkenness itself is a sin. Instead, she would deserve twice the punishment. The philosophers fall into this latter category, for while knowing the right thing to do, they chose not to do it.[90] In their specific case they had knowledge of God but did not use it for good.[91] It is critical to note here — as elsewhere — that these philosophers *had* knowledge of God.

These philosophers knew God in two ways. First, they knew God as one who is eminent over all things, and therefore, they owed Him surpassing honor and glory. Their failures were either total or partial. They did not honor Him as God either because they did not devote to Him the worship that was due or because they imposed a limit to God's virtue and knowledge. They also knew God as the cause of all goodness. But instead of devoting themselves to the thanksgiving due to God in all things, they attributed these acts to their own genius and power. Their failure, then, was rooted in pride [*superbia*], a pride that resulted in impiety before God and injustice to their neighbors.[92] The sin of pride is the philosophers' crucial downfall:

> Indeed just as he whose corporeal eyes turn away from solely material things, runs into corporeal obscurity, so that which is averted from God, presuming on himself and not on God, is spiritually darkened. Prov. 11:2, "when there is humility," through which namely man attaches himself to God, "there is wisdom; when there is pride, there is disgrace."[93]

The ignorance that grows out of this guilt has serious consequences. First, the philosophers' "senseless minds were darkened" (Rom. 1:21). But how were they darkened? The commentary suggests that the philosophers were "deprived of the light of wisdom through which man truly knows God."[94] In claiming to be wise, then, they became fools. Their guilt was that "however much was in them, they transferred divine honor to another."[95] The natural knowledge that the pagans enjoyed was darkened, then, because they did not use this knowledge for good. This darkening of the mind affects the person so entirely, that it inevitably leads to the sexual sins catalogued by St. Paul in Romans.[96]

Three main groups were the target of St. Paul's condemnations here. The priests, who engaged in civic theology, adored the idols in the temple. They "exchanged the glory of the immortal God." The poets delivered fictional [*fabularem*] theology in the theaters. Consequently, they "exchanged the truth of God for a lie." The philosophers who observed and worshipped the world engaged in natural [*naturalem*] theology. They, in turn, "worshipped and served the creature rather than the Creator."

One of the central themes that arises out of *lectio* 7, then, is that while the philosophers had natural knowledge of God, they used it for ill, sinning against God because of their impiety and against their neighbors because of their injustice. What is crucial to note here, however, is that ignorance of God would have excused them from guilt. Thomas is emphatic in denying these philosophers such ignorance.

The foregoing examination of Thomas' three mature works on this issue — the revised *Scriptum,* the *Summa theologiae,* and *In epistolam ad Romanos* — has shown that the broad contours of Thomas' position on natural knowledge of God remained constant throughout his career. We have observed, however, a clarification of the role of the virtues in this knowledge, a development of the analogical language that reflects this knowledge, and a deeper specification about the kind of knowledge that pagan philosophers had of God.

– Epilogue –

Thomas Reexamined: The Contemporary Conversation

The textual analysis in the foregoing pages has discovered an unwavering consistency about the natural knowledge of God present throughout Thomas' career and development: God can be known in this life through the light of natural reason. Under this conviction, grace does not violate or counter nature but brings it to a supereminent completion. Admittedly, Catholic theologians sometimes have made too much of this. The fact remains that Thomas does reserve a crucial place for this natural knowledge of God in his theology — even if perhaps a small place, even if such knowledge is not of itself salvific.

Since the chapters of this study traced textually the development of this thesis, there is no need to review them here. This epilogue will serve not as a conclusion or a summary, but rather as an appendix to the argument of this study.[1] In this we follow a pattern not unlike that of the *quaestio disputata* of the medieval universities. After the body of an article had made its determination of the truth of the issue before it, the article returned to the initial objections to resolve them in light of what had been demonstrated in the *determinatio*. These responses to individual objections did not so much demonstrate the conclusion of an inquiry as answer the objections in light of the conclusion reached and, in this way, expand it. This epilogue will follow suit.

Three alternatives to our central thesis have arisen in the contemporary conversation, explicitly set forth by distinguished postliberal theologians. Chapter 1 delineates Eugene Rogers' detailed and contrary interpretation of Thomas on the natural knowledge of God, an interpretation that brings the work of George Lindbeck and Bruce Marshall to its natural conclusion. All three theologians agree that in Thomas there is no natural knowledge of God strictly speaking; that whatever knowledge of God obtained by the consideration of nature must be in the context and under the influence of grace; and that consequently those thinkers and philosophies untouched by Christian revelation cannot come to any true knowledge of God. In the cumulation of these considerations — rather surprisingly — Thomas is found to be in agreement with Karl Barth.

The preceding textual study of Thomas' coordinate and parallel texts, however, find that he consistently asserted precisely the opposite — namely, that the human person can come to some knowledge of God through natural reason. This study must now return to these contemporary readings to see how the postliberal interpretations are addressed by our textual analysis. These theologians specifically contend that any knowledge of God: (1) only comes through revelation (Rogers); (2) cannot, therefore, come from nature as such (Marshall); and (3) cannot be examined outside the Christian context (Lindbeck). The first proposal provides the founding principle for the second and third proposals. It is the affirmation of (1) that makes the negation of (2) and (3) possible. I will offer only a cursory summary of these postliberal proposals, and — like Thomas — directly respond to them.

These three proposals are framed as interpretive questions of Thomas' text. First, Rogers asks what is the role of *sacra doctrina* in the *Summa theologiae,* and how does this affect Thomas' understanding of natural knowledge of God? Second, Marshall asks whether the philosopher knows anything that is true about God, and, if so, is this something that the Christian theologian can recognize as such and even incorporate into her theology? Third, Lindbeck asks whether there is any vantage point outside of a religious narrative from which truth claims can be assessed and whether this has consequences for theological knowledge?

Sacra Doctrina

Rogers' contention that knowledge of God only comes through revelation affects his understanding both of *sacra doctrina* and of the pagan philosophers' knowledge of God.

According to Rogers, *sacra doctrina* is a science like those of Aristotle, but one that takes its first principles from revelation. *Sacra doctrina* is not a human inquiry that leads to knowledge of God.

Rather, it is a science that is established by the *"subject's* inquiry after *us,"*[2] by the self-revelation of God. While we have a natural desire to know God, we receive a provisional answer in this life by a *"praecognitum finis"* and in the next, by the *"scientia Dei et beatorum."*[3] But, Rogers argues, we do not have the ability to know God on our own; "the effective structure of the soul that results from revelation is the infused habit of *formed faith.*"[4] This faith is formed into propositions by the discipline of sacred doctrine whose first principles are revealed and then believed. Believers enjoy only "textual access" to these revealed first principles today.[5] Consequently, *sacra doctrina* is a science with believers only.

It could very well be that Thomas' fluid handling of terms like *sacra doctrina, sacra scriptura* and *theologia* invite varying interpretations of these terms. But Rogers' restrictive understanding of *sacra doctrina* and *theologia* do not fully capture both Thomas' theory and his own practice in the *Summa.* While *sacra doctrina* is, of course, a science with believers only, it is the architectonic discipline within which other sciences conduct inquiry. What, for example, are we to do with *theologia quae pars philosophiae ponitur* introduced in the very first article of the *Summa?* Here Thomas affirms that there are two ways of understanding divine matters or of formulating a theology. The first theology pertains [*pertinet*] to *sacra doctrina;* the second is part of philosophy [*pars philosophiae ponitur*].[6] God is the author of *sacra doctrina;* human beings are the authors of theology. Stated differently, when the conclusions are matters of faith, one is engaging *sacra doctrina;* when they are matters of human knowledge, one is pursuing theology. In the *Summa theologiae* Thomas not only affirms this latter kind of theology — or what would elsewhere be called natural theology or metaphysics — but there are even moments in the text where he engages in this theology. The context is always that of *sacra doctrina.* But within this context the integrity of metaphysical or philosophical argument remains. It is crucial to maintain this integrity, for it affects how we understand God. As Thomas stated in the *Summa contra gentiles,* "To take away the perfection of created things is to detract from the perfection of divine power."[7] These arguments, however, have no place in Rogers' reading of Thomas.

Let us examine this issue more closely. As seen more fully in chapter 2, *sacra doctrina* is God's teaching both about God and whatever is related to God as its source or its end.[8] The theology employed in the *Summa* is an attempt to understand *sacra doctrina*. Thus, this kind of theology begins from Sacred Scripture — the texts that comprise *sacra doctrina* and document such revelation. Sacred Scripture and *sacra Doctrina* can be used interchangeably here, whereas one could never interchange Sacred Scripture with any of the distinct forms of theology. *Sacra doctrina* expounds upon Scripture by using some passages to illumine others and by drawing from other disciplines. It ensures that what God revealed has not only been heard, but that it has been understood.

This theology that pertains to *sacra doctrina* in the *Summa* presupposes Christian revelation. While the formation of theology from *sacra doctrina* draws fundamentally from Scripture by incorporating scriptural assertions as premises, it also incorporates insights from philosophy, from the sciences, in order to illumine and reflect upon the content of *sacra doctrina*. In formulating theology, sources other than Scripture, however, are used alone as extraneous and probable arguments [*quasi extraneis argumentis et probabilibus*].[9] *Sacra doctrina* does not take its principles from these other disciplines; its principles are fully provided by revelation. Rather, theology uses these other disciplines both as preambles to its own work or for the greater clarification [*ad maiorem manifestationem*] of its teaching. These disciplines, then, have a subsidiary and ancillary role [*inferioribus et ancillis*]. They are, in fact, brought into *sacra doctrina* to constitute theology not because of a defect or insufficiency within itself, but because human beings are more easily led to the things above reason through human disciplines.[10] They act as handmaidens or preliminary guides set forth to draw people into the study of *sacra doctrina*.[11] There is, then, an organic relationship between all knowledge and *sacra doctrina*. The *Summa* expounds the theology that reflects upon *sacra doctrina*, an attempt that examines the truths of *Christianam religionem*. Within this exercise, however, Thomas engages in *theologia quae pars philosophiae ponitur*. But these philosophical arguments are subsumed under the architectonic discipline that is *sacra doctrina*. This act of subsumption, however, never violates the philosophical integrity of the arguments themselves. Rather, it takes up these arguments and deepens their significance.

According to the present study, then, *sacra doctrina* makes use of all sorts of human knowledge — including natural knowledge — to formulate a theology. Recall that according to Rogers, the "intelligible structure of reality to which the science's intelligibility corresponds remains altogether unknown to us in this life even as faith unites us to it (I, 12, 13 *ad* 1) by a self-revelation of God... to which we now enjoy only textual access."[12] But this neglects the organic relationship between *sacra doctrina* and all kinds of human knowledge, and trivializes the powers that the human person was created to exercise.

Rogers interprets Thomas to be engaging in *sacra doctrina* in the *Summa*. We understand Thomas, however, to be reflecting upon this *sacra doctrina* by doing the theology both that pertains to *sacra doctrina* and that is part of philosophy. Rogers' restrictive reading of *sacra doctrina* has significant consequences for his understanding of the capabilities of human knowledge.

These consequences are most clearly exposed by Rogers' interpretation of the pagan philosophers in *In epistolam ad Romanos*. In this reading, there is no room for a positive natural knowledge of God, for natural knowledge can be only "detained" and "redeemed," depending on the disposition of the will. In the first case, natural knowledge is not neutral. But on the contrary, it is "feckless," ineffective, and culpable.[13] Natural knowledge is a category that has no real content:

> It exists only in order to show what is being denied. It does not show what people possess, but what they lack. Their cognition amounts, in Preller's words, to "a felt ignorance" and it is in that sense alone a cognition rather than a failure of cognition.[14]

This knowledge is "at once entrapping and culpable, like the loss of powers of someone drunk";[15] it *would have* been effective had it not been destroyed by human sin. This means, then, that any treatment of God from the point of view of philosophy in the present history of human beings is simply erroneous.

For Rogers, natural knowledge of God depends upon the will, which was created to "lean upon grace."[16] It functions, then, only in the presence of grace, leading human beings to do the good. Thus, Rogers maintains that one has to be a good person in order to come to any knowledge of God. In addition, faith, not *scientia*, makes this natural knowledge effective.[17] In the Romans commentary, then, Thomas ascribes natural knowledge of God to the Gentiles only to point out the knowledge that they *would have had* if their wills had turned toward God. He refers to this as "knowledge" only out of "courtesy"; it actually turns out not to be knowledge *at all,* but sounds rather more like ignorance.[18] Rogers concludes:

> So in the concrete situation of human beings the natural cognition of God is explicitly and logically dependent upon the revealed cognition of God... Thomas uses the term *theologia naturalis* only in that negative sense. Thomas never uses the phrase 'natural theology' to describe what he is up to in the Romans commentary or the *Summa*. He thinks of both as biblical, dogmatic theology....[19]

He further claims that for Thomas there are two lights (one of the intellect, and the other of faith) that come from the grace of God. What Rogers calls "grace 1" is what is traditionally meant by the category of nature. There are, then, two kinds of grace for Rogers. The first light is that by which the Gentiles have any knowledge of God whatsoever:

> That a human being can have *cognitio* of some truth without grace, which Thomas affirms at I-II.109.1, does not deny that the cognition in question is defective, and does not affirm that the cognition in question has anything to do with our elevation — except as it gets taken up into the nature that is shot through with *grace*.[20]

Here, he insists that "nature without grace — in the technical sense of God's will to save — does not concretely exist."[21] This "grace" cannot achieve anything on its own. It simply works proleptically, keeping us alive and functioning, until God's plan takes place in us; "it is not a human power so much as a divine mercy."[22]

But against Rogers Thomas does not grant the excuse of ignorance to the pagan philosophers. Theirs was not immediately a failure of knowledge but rather of reverence. Their blame emerged from failing to worship God, a failure that resulted in damage both to their neighbors, and eventually to their own intellects. The Commentary clearly establishes that the philosophers knew God through a light that was intrinsic [*lumine intrinseco*] to them.[23] They employed human reason — in their case through analogical reasoning — to know God through certain similitudes found in creatures that participate in various ways in the one God. But they erred in misusing this knowledge by not honoring God. They knew the right thing to do, but they chose not to do it.[24] Specifically, they had knowledge of God [*cognitionem habentes*], but did not use it for good [*usi ad bonum*].[25] In other words, their knowledge of God did not lead them to honor him. But Thomas is emphatic here — as elsewhere — in affirming that they *had knowledge of God*. If they had not had knowledge of God, they would be freed from blame — something that both St. Paul and Thomas are at pains to deny.

It is of course true that this knowledge was not salvific — that, in fact, is exactly where they erred; they did not use the knowledge for the purposes to which it should have led. But this does not render useless their knowledge of God. Rogers blurs the distinction here between knowledge being effective or true and knowledge being effective for salvation. Thomas nowhere claims that all human knowledge is salvific, and he always claims that all human knowledge is inadequate, even when it is elevated by grace. Here specifically, the human knowledge of God discovered by the pagan philosophers, while not salvific, was in fact true knowledge.

What he does claim is that the philosophers had inadequate knowledge of God, when he states, for example, that human reason cannot lead to knowledge of the Trinity. But Rogers fails to distinguish here between inadequate and erroneous. Recall that one can recognize that *someone* is coming without realizing that it is in fact Peter who is coming. It is this initial recognition that the philosophers had of God.

Rogers' misconstrual of natural knowledge of God also affects how he understands the relationship between the act of the intellect and movement of the will. What a human person knows inevitably affects how she acts. But Rogers finds in Thomas that only the good possess knowledge of God. The fact that the philosophers did not use their knowledge of God for good renders this knowledge completely "ineffective." But that Thomas disagrees with Rogers on this point has already been clearly shown. Knowledge of the essence of God can only be reached by grace, and therefore, only the good enjoy this sort of knowledge. But knowledge that God is can be enjoyed by both saints and sinners. Thomas even clarifies that "to know" in this context means "to know by natural knowledge."[26] While this knowledge is not salvific, even sinners can come to the knowledge of God. The quality and extent of this knowledge are affected, of course, by one's acts of charity in this life.

In sum, Thomas preserves a legitimate place for natural knowledge of God in the *Summa theologiae*, a place that is filled by the pagan philosophers in the Romans commentary.

The Philosophers

To delve further into the contrasts between our reading of Thomas and the postliberal one, we must continue to pursue this question of whether the philosophers can know anything true about God. We therefore turn to Bruce Marshall's interpretation of Thomas on this issue. Thomas, he states, would agree with the following fundamental claim: utterances of Christian belief are ontologically true *only* if they cohere with specific linguistic and practical paradigms *internal* to the religion itself, and, indeed, that this coherence is an adequate justification of their ontological truth.[27] Consequently, unbelievers cannot utter true statements about God. Unbelievers do not believe that God exists "or hold any other beliefs about God which Christians hold" because "they do not believe that God exists under those conditions which faith determines (*determinet*)."[28] In other words, they cannot believe that God exists without also believing in Scripture and the creeds. An unbeliever, then, can know nothing meaningful about God. For Marshall, knowledge is subsumed under belief — where the pre-Christian philosopher "holds beliefs about God" on the basis of demonstrative arguments.[29] The article that Marshall uses as evidence here, however, considers the act of faith, which unbelievers quite obviously do not have of God. But it neither affirms nor denies that unbelievers can come to knowledge of God. Marshall seems to conflate here knowledge and belief in Thomas.

His argument for a bold coherentism in Thomas leads Marshall to offer this startling interpretation on *scientia Dei*:

> If faith is the necessary beginning of the process which ends in complete *scientia*, then there simply is no *scientia Dei*, no correspondence of the mind to God, outside of faith...only the believer means by "God" what one must mean in order to refer to God at all.... The Christian and the philosopher both say "God is one," but because they do so under different "conditions," they in fact hold different beliefs about God.[30]

Therefore, even a philosopher's formally valid argument cannot bring about any *adaequatio mentis ad rem* in relation to God, while the same demonstration can yield such knowledge when it happens in the context of faith. For Thomas *scientia* about God, then, is confined to the context of Christian faith.

The pre-Christian philosophers knew certain attributes about God available to human reason while not knowing about the Trinity and the incarnation. However, " 'Even if [the Gentiles] err in the smallest way regarding the knowledge of God, they are said to be completely ignorant of him.' "[31] Believing that God exists and that God is one, then, are only true when one also believes that God is Triune and Incarnate.[32] Marshall concludes that the pre-Christian philosopher and the Christian believer mean two *contradictory* things when they say that God exists.

Let us briefly examine the passage in Thomas' commentary of the Gospel of John that Marshall cites as evidence for his position. We do not find here the claim that in order to know anything about God a person must first believe that God is Triune. In fact, the passage states quite the opposite.

In this selection, Thomas comments upon John 17:25, "O righteous Father, although the world has not known You, yet I have known You; and these have known that You sent Me." By neither of the two kinds of knowledge — speculative and affective — can one know God perfectly. But *"granted that some of the Gentiles knew God insofar as is knowable by reason; nevertheless, they did not know Him as the Father of an ungenerated and consubstantial son: the Lord is speaking about this kind of knowledge* [in the Gospel of John]."[33] Here, once again, we find Thomas unequivocally affirming that the Gentiles knew God by human reason.

Three observations should be made about this passage. First, Thomas strongly affirms that the pagan philosophers knew God; second, he is referring to knowledge of the *Triune* God in the selection cited by Marshall; and third, he is careful to make a cultural or descriptive rather than a normative statement about what the philosophers knew about God.

To the first point, Thomas claims that the pagan philosophers knew God. But this claim does not arise in the text as something toward which Thomas argues, or a statement he needs to defend. Rather, here as elsewhere it is introduced as a given, as something upon which his readers or listeners would all agree: [*l*]*icet enim aliqui gentilium Deum quantum ad aliqua quae per rationem cognoscibilia erant, cognoverint*. It is simply *granted* that the pagan philosophers knew some things about God as far as is knowable through human reason.

Second, what follows is a reflection upon *Trinitarian* knowledge of God, not knowledge of God in general. Thus, when Thomas writes that "even if some err in some small way with regard to the knowledge of God, they are said to be totally ignorant [of Him],"[34] he is specifically referring to knowledge of the Trinity. "The Lord is speaking of this kind of knowledge [*de qua cognitione loquitur dominus*]"; the knowledge referred to here concerns the Trinity. It is of course true that acknowledging one part of the Trinity without the others is not to acknowledge the Trinity at all. However, it would be a misconstrual of the text to claim that Thomas is considering knowledge of God in general here—when in fact, it is the particular knowledge of the Trinitarian God that is at issue. Knowledge of the Triune God is emphatically reserved for believers throughout the Thomistic corpus. But what is up for contention and what is *not* taken up in this text is the more modest claim that God exists.

Finally, it is crucially important to note that even in treating Trinitarian knowledge, Thomas is not talking about the fact of what the pagans *de facto* did know, but rather what they are said to have known. He uses *"dicuntur"* three times to emphasize that the Gentiles *are said* to be totally ignorant of God.[35] Thomas chooses not to make this normative statement here absolute. Instead, he restricts himself to making a cultural observation about what the pagans are said to know about God, not what they actually know.

Marshall does not allow the distinction between knowledge of the essence of God on the one hand and that God is on the other. This is a crucial distinction in Thomas that continually arises in his corpus. The philosophers could know about the existence of God without knowing about God's essence. They could, therefore, *attingere Deum* but not *comprehendere Deum*. They could come to recognize that God is, and some attributes of God—perhaps as one recognizes that someone approaches, although not fully realizing that it is Peter who approaches. This knowledge is, of course, incomplete and inchoate, but it is knowledge nonetheless. Human claims arising from natural reason still mean *something*, even if they never tell the whole story.

Finally, it is one thing to say that statements about God have to cohere with doctrine of the church; but it is quite a different thing to say that every statement has to be recognized within the context of faith *formaliter*. While it is certainly true that every statement about the reality of God must not materially contradict Christian faith, it certainly does not follow that one must be formally cognizant of this faith when making such a statement. Neither does it follow that one's statements must be contextualized by the faith in order for them to be true. As seen previously, *sacra doctrina* is an architectonic discipline. Statements that are not formally recognized as being of faith can be materially subsumed into Christian faith. This is in fact what Thomas actually does in the *Summa* itself.[36]

Religio

Let us turn, finally, to the ramifications for contemporary theology of this postliberal reading. Lindbeck asserts that there is no independent vantage point from which the truth claims of any religion can be assessed. This is, really, the underlying concern of the postliberal approach.

Lindbeck argues against the "meaningfulness of the notion that there is an inner experience of God common to all human beings and all religions."[37] There is no room for such a core experience in this outlook because the interpretive frameworks, i.e., the cultural *a priori*, of different religions simply give rise to totally different experiences. If experience is dependent upon language and if religions do not share a common language, then there is no way that people of different religions can have a generic core experience of God. The postliberal approach, in fact, claims that any such supposition is illusory. All religions do share, however, a formal cultural-linguistic aspect, rather than a material experiential core. Consequently, comparing religions is like comparing languages: what is common to all languages is the fact that they are spoken. But this universal formal feature tells us nothing significant about the languages themselves.

Religious truth (or any truth for that matter), then, is utterly context-dependent for Thomas, Lindbeck argues. Until one has mastered the skills needed for the Christian faith, for example, one has no way of either affirming or denying the statement that "Jesus is Lord": "One must be, so to speak, inside the relevant context; and, in the case of religion, this means that one must have some skill in *how* to use its language and practice its way of life before the propositional meaning of its affirmations becomes determinate enough to be rejected."[38]

Within this concept of religion, theological or doctrinal statements are, like grammatical statements, second-order activities. They affirm nothing true or false *about* things. Rather, they are, like grammar, statements about the use of statements. Theology and doctrine are, of course, propositional; but they are second-order propositions that "affirm nothing about extra-linguistic or extra-human reality."[39] For Lindbeck, theology does not deal primarily with ontology or truth; it is strictly a second-order discourse. This does not mean, however, that theology simply repeats the words of Scripture and disregards non-theological knowledge. Quite the contrary, theology makes use of philosophical, historical, and other resources on an *ad hoc* basis. These other disciplines are always subsumed under the theological task. There is no outside standard from which to measure the truthfulness of theological statements. As a result, there are no independently formed standards of reasonableness in postliberal theology. Lindbeck always insists that "intelligibility comes from skill, not theory, and credibility comes from good performance, not adherence to independently formulated criteria."[40]

Even for Thomas — while insisting that revelation dominates every aspect of theology — theology still uses philosophy and other knowledge in defense of the faith.[41] Thomas even argues that reason in support of the faith is only meritorious after faith. Or, in Lindbeck's terms, "[T]he logic of coming to believe... like that of learning a language, has little room for argument, but once one has learned to speak the language of faith, argument becomes possible."[42]

Like Rogers, Lindbeck interprets the more restrictive reading of *sacra doctrina* — one that is interchangeable with *sacra scriptura* — for the wider reading of *sacra doctrina*. So in some instances it is certainly true that there are no independent standards of truthfulness from which to measure a religious claim, such as, for example, that God is Triune. But this does not then mean that all arguments within *sacra doctrina* admit of no outside standards. Thomas in fact employs such arguments when arguing with pagans.

Lindbeck's more general questionable move — one that is shared by all three postliberal theologians — is that he subsumes theological knowledge under belief. This move has serious consequences for their understanding of the knowledge of God, and, more importantly, it renders their interpretation of Thomas on the subject inadequate. As has been found repeatedly in the previous chapters, it is not that arguments arising from natural reason only become possible after the assent of faith, but rather that these can reach limited conclusions and always remain incomplete. They can never tell the whole story, but the chapters that they tell are *true*. Neither is what they proclaim salvific, but this does not render their proclamations useless or ineffective. Thomas has never claimed that for knowledge to be true, it needs to be salvific.

This same limitation of incomplete and inchoate knowledge holds, of course, for arguments arising from the faith. In moving from natural knowledge to knowledge received in faith, these patterns of inchoateness and inconclusivity are certainly not overcome. They are simply the limitations of being human. Denys Turner offers a detailed argument on this point:

> ...human reason replicates, as it were "by anticipation" and in an inchoate way, the "shape" of faith itself, first because the shape of reason in its deployment in proof of God "anticipates" that interactivity of "affirmative" and "negative," of the "cataphatic" and "apophatic" moments, which are inherent to the epistemic structure and dynamic of faith itself.[43]

Faith, then, deepens rather than erases the sense of mystery found in philosophical reasoning.[44] It is not that the universe of discourse between the Christian and the philosopher are so different as to render them foreign tongues to each other. It is, rather, the language of the beatific vision that will be foreign to both.

The denial of the legitimacy of natural knowledge, at the very least, misconstrues the texts of Thomas Aquinas. But it also has radical ramifications for interreligious dialogue and ecclesiological issues generally, for the ethical and sacramental life, and for theories in education. It is a foundational issue whose importance cannot be exaggerated.

It might be that the proper use of natural reason has been so adulterated in our cultural context as to be hostile rather than preparatory for the reception of divine revelation, as Tracey Rowland has persuasively argued in *Culture and the Thomist Tradition*.[45] But what has been adulterated in actual practice must not be forgotten as a philosophical category. This forgetfulness would be yet one more concession to the contemporary nihilism that Rowland so convincingly outlines. It might also be that the conceptions of reason for Thomists have to become clearly distinguished both from "Enlightenment-derived alternatives on the one hand, and from the Genealogical tradition on the other."[46] One step in the right direction, however, is to recognize the strictly limited but still legitimate place of natural knowledge of God in Thomas' theology.

With respect to the reaches of natural knowledge of God, we would do well to end with Gilson on the subject:

> If, in spite of all, [the human person] unwearyingly applied this feeble instrument to the most exalted objects, it is because the most confused knowledge, knowledge hardly deserving the name, ceases to be despicable when it has for its object the infinite essence of God. Poverty-stricken conjectures, comparisons not totally inadequate, it is from these we draw our purest and most profound joys. The sovereign happiness of man here below is to anticipate, in however confused a fashion, the face-to-face vision of God in the quiet of eternity.[47]

This study, then, concludes that natural knowledge of God has a legitimate and proper place in Thomas' theology. While claims arising from either natural reason or Christian faith must be open to further refinement, revision, and even rejection, they are justified attempts at true statements about God. They tell us something about God, they tell us something about what it means to be a human being, a being by its very nature ordered to the knowledge of God. Whether in ordinary discourse, in religious worship, or in philosophical examination, Thomas assures us that our pursuit is not fruitless, that our proclamations really can signify something true in God. We will never have the last word, but the words we use can be meaningful and true.

Notes

Notes to Chapter One

1. *Miscellanies* (or *Stromata*) VI, v, in *The Ante-Nicene Fathers*, vol. 2, eds. Alexander Roberts and James Donaldson (Grand Rapids: Eerdmans, 1979), 489. Cf. Etienne Gilson, *History of Christian Philosophy in the Middle Ages* (New York: Random House, 1955), 31.

2. D. *Martin Luthers Werke Kritische Gesamtausgabe* (Weimar: Herman Bohlaus Nachfolger), 40/1:376.23–377, as cited in Bruce D. Marshall, "Faith and Reason Reconsidered: Aquinas and Luther on Deciding What's True," *Thomist* 63 (1999): 1–48 at 30.

3. Cf. Philip Hughes, *The Church in Crisis: A History of the General Councils 325–1870* (New York: Doubleday, 1961), 339; and Roger Aubert, *Histoire des Conciles Œcuméniques*, vol. 12, "Vatican I," ed. Gervais Dumeige, S.J. (Paris: Éditions de L'Orante, 1964), 126.

4. "*Deum, rerum omnium principium et finem, naturali humanae rationis lumine e rebus creatis certe cognosci posse,*" *De fide catholica* of Vatican I, ch. 2 *De revelatione* (Denzinger, #1785).

5. Gerald A. McCool, *The Neo-Thomists* (Milwaukee: Marquette University Press, 1994), 25.

6. George A. Lindbeck, *Nature of Doctrine: Religion and Theology in a Postliberal Age* (Philadelphia: Westminster Press, 1984), 33 [henceforth *ND*].

7. While the cluster of theological positions that could be called "postliberal," is complex, I have selected one developing argument within this wider cluster for examination. On the wider movement of postliberal theology see James J. Buckley, "Postliberal Theology: A Catholic Reading," in *Introduction to Christian Theology: Contemporary North American Perspectives* (Louisville: Westminster John Knox Press, 1998), 89–102. For a representative selection of postliberal theologies developed since the early 1980's, see *Theology After Liberalism: A Reader*, ed. John Webster and George P. Schner (Oxford: Blackwell Publishers, 2000). While it is not a consistent theological school, "[P]ostliberal theology is concerned to unsettle the stereotypical readings of the past which have at times been assumed in critical and revisionist paradigms" (John Webster, "Theology after Liberalism," in *Theology After Liberalism: A Reader*, 56). The reading traced here is one such attempt to unsettle a widely accepted reading of Thomas.

8. Although Lindbeck deals with knowledge that pertains to faith in this work, this study will examine whether Lindbeck's description of this knowledge leaves any room for knowledge of God through human reason.

9. *ND*, 67.

10. George Lindbeck, "Response to Bruce Marshall," *Thomist* 53 (1989): 403–406 at 405.

11. Lindbeck, "Response to Bruce Marshall," 135.

12. Lindbeck, "Response to Bruce Marshall," 135.

13. This characterization occurs in Lindbeck's review of Robert Jenson's *Unbaptized God: The Basic Flaw in Ecumenical Theology* (Minneapolis: Fortress Press, 1992) in *Pro Ecclesia* III (1994): 232–238 at 235.

14. It is important to note that Lindbeck applauds Marshall's elucidation of his own relationship to Thomas Aquinas. In response to Marshall's article, he writes, "If I had referred more to the Thomistic ideas [Marshall] elucidates when I was writing *Nature of Doctrine,* it would have been a better book" ["Response to Bruce Marshall," 403].

15. Bruce Marshall, "Aquinas as Postliberal Theologian," *Thomist* 53 (1989): 353–402 at 401.

16. Marshall, "Aquinas as Postliberal Theologian," 401.

17. Marshall, "Aquinas as Postliberal Theologian," 391.

18. Marshall, "Aquinas as Postliberal Theologian," 392.

19. *ND,* 118 as cited in Marshall, "Aquinas as Postliberal Theologian," 400.

20. Marshall, "Aquinas as Postliberal Theologian," 357. Marshall also argues that Thomas' Christology is another example of intratextual theology in *Christology in Conflict: The Identity of a Saviour in Rahner and Barth* (New York: Basil Blackwell, 1987), 176–189.

21. *Thomas Aquinas and Karl Barth: Sacred Doctrine and the Natural Knowledge of God* (Notre Dame: University of Notre Dame Press, 1996).

22. Otto Hermann Pesch, *Die Theologie der Rechtfertigung bei Martin Luther und Thomas von Aquin: Versuch eines systematisch-theologischen Dialogs* (Mainz: Matthias Grünewald, 1967); *Thomas von Aquin: Grenze und Größe mittelalterlicher Theologie* (Mainz: Matthias Grünewald, 1988); Michel Corbin, *Le chemin de la théologie chez Thomas d'Aquin,* Bibliothèque des archives de philosophie, nouvelle série 16 (Paris: Beauchesne, 1974); and Victor Preller, *Divine Science and the Science of God: A Reformulation of Thomas Aquinas* (Princeton: Princeton University Press, 1967).

23. Rogers claims that he cannot explicitly engage the tradition, for it asks questions that he is trying to "*un*ask. It is hard to unask questions while entertaining them" (Rogers, *Thomas Aquinas and Karl Barth,* xiii).

24. Rogers, *Thomas Aquinas and Karl Barth,* 3. The term "evangelical" here is an allusion to the Lutheran Church.

25. Rogers, *Thomas Aquinas and Karl Barth,* 3. One should note that Rogers does not distinguish between *sacra doctrina* and theology: "Question 1 of the *Summa theologiae* (I.1.1–10) sets out the last of Thomas Aquinas' several attempts to describe what sort of discipline theology is and how it proceeds" (17).

26. Rogers, *Thomas Aquinas and Karl Barth,* 5.

27. Rogers, *Thomas Aquinas and Karl Barth,* 140. Rogers' work on Thomas has been widely reviewed favorably. See, for example, Fergus Kerr, *After Aquinas: Versions of Thomism* (Oxford: Blackwell Publishers, 2002) 63–65; David Burrell's review [*Pro Ecclesia* 7 (1998): 113–114]; James J. Buckley's review [*Thomist* 61 (1997): 320–325]; Paul Molnar's review [*Scottish Journal of Theology* 55 (2002): 496–498]; and Thomas Hibb's review [*Modern Theology* 14 (1998): 462–463].

28. Rogers, *Thomas Aquinas and Karl Barth,* 5–6.

29. Thomas uses both *ratio naturalis* and *cognitio naturalis* to refer to the knowledge that humans have of God through natural reason, as evidenced by the titles of articles 12 and 13 of Question 12: (12) *utrum per rationem naturalem Deum*

in hac vita possimus cognoscere, (13) *utrum supra cognitionem naturalis rationis sit in praesenti vita aliqua cognitio Dei per gratiam.* Therefore, I will use the English phrases "knowledge of God through human reason" and "natural knowledge of God" interchangeably.

30. Richard E. Palmer, *Hermeneutics: Interpretation Theory in Schleiermacher, Dilthey, Heidegger, and Gadamer* (Evanston: Northwestern University Press, 1969), 66.

31. Hans-Georg Gadamer, *Truth and Methods,* translation revised by Joel Weinsheimer and Donald G. Marshall (New York: Seabury Press, 1975), 236.

32. Rudolf Bultmann, *History and Eschatology* (New York: Harper, 1957), 113.

33. *Truth and Method,* 251.

34. *The Ethics of Saint Thomas Aquinas: Two Courses,* ed. Edward A. Synan (Toronto: Pontifical Institute of Medieval Studies, 1997).

35. Eschmann, *The Ethics of Thomas Aquinas,* 6–10.

36. Eschmann, *The Ethics of Thomas Aquinas,* 9–10.

37. In particular, I will examine Lib. I, dist.iii, Q1, a1: *"utrum Deus possit cognosci ab intellectu creato"*; Lib. III, dist.xxvii, Q3, a1: *"utrum Deus immediate per essentiam suam possit amari."* Thomas completed this work between 1252–1256. I follow J. P. Torrell's findings of the chronology of Thomas' works. [*Saint Thomas Aquinas: The Person and His Work,* trans. Robert Royal, vol. 1 (Washington, D.C.: Catholic University of America Press, 1996)].

38. In particular, I will examine Q1, a2: *"utrum mens humana possit ad dei notitiam pervenire."* Thomas probably wrote this work in 1257–1258, or in the beginning of 1259.

39. In particular, I will examine Bk. IV, ch. 1. Thomas began writing the *Summa contra gentiles* before the summer of 1259, and finished by 1265, possibly even by the end of 1263.

40. In particular, I will examine Q3, a1–3 of the *Scriptum* revision and Q12, a12 of the *Summa theologiae.*

41. In particular, I will examine Ch. 1, lect. 6. The commentary was most likely written between 1272–1273.

42. Alasdair MacIntyre, *Whose Justice? Which Rationality?* (Notre Dame: University of Notre Dame Press, 1988), 164–208.

43. George A. Lindbeck, "Confession and Community: An Israel-like View of the Church," *The Christian Century* 107 (1990): 492–496.

44. See George A. Lindbeck, ed., *Dialogue on the Way: Protestants Report from Rome on the Vatican Council* (Minneapolis: Augsburg Publishing House, 1965), and his article "Definitive Look at Vatican II," in *Christianity and Crisis* 25 (1966): 291–295; 26 (1966): 133–134.

45. George A. Lindbeck, "The Evangelical Possibilities of Roman Catholic Theology" *Lutheran World* (1960): 142–152 at 144 and 149.

46. Specifically, Lindbeck points to Yves Congar's *Vraie et Fausse Réforme dans l'Eglise* (Paris: Les Éditions du Cerf, 1950), L. Bouyer's *Du protestantisme à l'église* (Paris: Les Éditions du Cerf, 1954), and Hans Küng's *Rechtfertigung: Die Lehre Karl Barths und eine katholische Besinnung* (Einsiedeln: Johannes, 1957) as examples of Roman Catholic theological studies that are congenial to evangelical theology.

47. Lindbeck, "The Evangelical Possibilities of Roman Catholic Theology," 150–151.

48. George A. Lindbeck, "The *A Priori* in St. Thomas' Theory of Knowledge," in *The Heritage of Christian Thought: Essays in Honor of Robert Lowry Calhoun*, eds. Robert E. Cushman and Egil Grislis (New York: Harper and Row, 1965), 41–63.
49. Lindbeck, "The *A Priori* in St. Thomas' Theory of Knowledge," 44.
50. Lindbeck, "The *A Priori* in St. Thomas' Theory of Knowledge," 45.
51. Lindbeck, "The *A Priori* in St. Thomas' Theory of Knowledge," 45–46.
52. Lindbeck, "The *A Priori* in St. Thomas' Theory of Knowledge," 46.
53. Lindbeck, "The *A Priori* in St. Thomas' Theory of Knowledge," 47.
54. Lindbeck, "The *A Priori* in St. Thomas' Theory of Knowledge," 47.
55. Lindbeck, "The *A Priori* in St. Thomas' Theory of Knowledge," 60.
56. Lindbeck, "The *A Priori* in St. Thomas' Theory of Knowledge," 60.
57. Lindbeck, "The *A Priori* in St. Thomas' Theory of Knowledge," 60.
58. Lindbeck, "The *A Priori* in St. Thomas' Theory of Knowledge," 61.
59. Lindbeck, "The *A Priori* in St. Thomas' Theory of Knowledge," 61.
60. Lindbeck, "The *A Priori* in St. Thomas' Theory of Knowledge," 62.
61. George A. Lindbeck, "Discovering Thomas (1): The Classical Statement of Christian Theism," *Una Sancta* 24 (1967): 45–52.
62. Lindbeck, "Discovering Thomas (1)," 45; Lindbeck is paraphrasing Thomas Bonhoeffer, *Die Gotteslehre des Thomas von Aquin als Sprachproblem* (Tübingen: J. C. B. Mohr, 1961), 2–3.
63. Lindbeck, "Discovering Thomas (1)," 46.
64. Lindbeck, "Discovering Thomas (1)," 52.
65. Lindbeck, "Discovering Thomas (1)," 46.
66. Lindbeck, "Discovering Thomas (1)," 46.
67. Lindbeck, "Discovering Thomas (1)," 47; *ST* Ia, 1, 8, *ad* 2.
68. Lindbeck, "Discovering Thomas (1)," 47.
69. Lindbeck, "Discovering Thomas (1)," 47.
70. Lindbeck, "Discovering Thomas (1)," 47.
71. Lindbeck, "Discovering Thomas (1)," 47.
72. Lindbeck, "Discovering Thomas (1)," 51.
73. Lindbeck, "Discovering Thomas (1)," 52; II-II, 2, 2, *ad* 3. Both Marshall and Rogers repeatedly draw upon this Thomistic text.
74. Lindbeck, "Discovering Thomas (1)," 52.
75. Lindbeck, "Discovering Thomas (1)," 52.
76. George Lindbeck, "Response to Bruce Marshall," 405.
77. Lindbeck, *ND*, 33.
78. Lindbeck, *ND*, 33
79. Lindbeck, *ND*, 34.
80. Lindbeck, *ND*, 34.
81. Lindbeck, *ND*, 35.
82. Lindbeck, *ND*, 36.
83. Lindbeck, *ND*, 33.
84. Lindbeck, *ND*, 36.
85. Lindbeck, *ND*, 39.
86. Lindbeck, *ND*, 39–40.
87. In a recent reflection upon his work, Lindbeck reaffirms that "cultural in combination with linguistic differences sometimes make communication almost though not entirely impossible" ["Performing the Faith: an Interview with George Lindbeck," *The Christian Century* 123 (November 28, 2006): 28–33 at 29].

Notes to Pages 16–23

88. Lindbeck, *ND*, 48.
89. Lindbeck, *ND*, 49.
90. Lindbeck, *ND*, 68.
91. Lindbeck, *ND*, 80.
92. Lindbeck, *ND*, 69.
93. Lindbeck, *ND*, 117.
94. Lindbeck, *ND*, 117.
95. Lindbeck, *ND*, 131.
96. Lindbeck, *ND*, 131.
97. Lindbeck, *ND*, 132.
98. George A. Lindbeck, "Scripture, Consensus and Community," in *Biblical Interpretation in Crisis: The Ratzinger Conference on Bible and Church*, ed. Richard John Neuhaus (Grand Rapids: Eerdmans, 1989), 74.
99. Lindbeck, "Scripture, Consensus and Community," 75.
100. Lindbeck, "Scripture, Consensus and Community," 88.
101. Lindbeck, "Scripture, Consensus and Community," 88.
102. Lindbeck, "Scripture, Consensus and Community," 95.
103. Lindbeck, "Scripture, Consensus and Community," 97.
104. Lindbeck, "Scripture, Consensus and Community," 94.
105. George A. Lindbeck, "Toward a Postliberal Theology," in *The Return to Scripture in Judaism and Christianity*, ed. Peter Ochs (New York: Paulist Press, 1993), 86.
106. Lindbeck, "Toward a Postliberal Theology," 89.
107. Lindbeck, "Toward a Postliberal Theology," 96.
108. George A. Lindbeck, "The Gospel's Uniqueness: Election and Untranslatability," *Modern Theology* 13 (1997): 423–450.
109. Lindbeck, "The Gospel's Uniqueness: Election and Untranslatability," 423.
110. Lindbeck, "The Gospel's Uniqueness: Election and Untranslatability," 429.
111. Lindbeck, "The Gospel's Uniqueness: Election and Untranslatability," 429.
112. Lindbeck, "The Gospel's Uniqueness: Election and Untranslatability," 429.
113. Lindbeck, "The Gospel's Uniqueness: Election and Untranslatability," 429.
114. Marshall, "Aquinas as Postliberal Theologian," 353–402.
115. See Louis Roy, O.P., "Bruce Marshall's Reading of Aquinas," and Frederick J. Crosson, "Reconsidering Aquinas as Postliberal Theologian," *Thomist* 56 (1992): 473–498.
116. Bruce D. Marshall, "Absorbing the World: Christianity and the Universe of Truths," in *Theology and Dialogue: Essays in Conversation with George Lindbeck*, ed. Bruce D. Marshall (Notre Dame: University of Notre Dame Press, 1990), 69–102.
117. Bruce D. Marshall,*Trinity and Truth* (Cambridge: Cambridge University Press, 2000).
118. Bruce Marshall, "Aquinas as Postliberal Theologian," 356–357. Ontological truth here is "that truth of correspondence to reality which, according to epistemological realists, is attributable to first-order propositions" (Lindbeck, *ND*, 64 as cited in Marshall, "Aquinas as Postliberal Theologian," 358).
119. Marshall, "Aquinas as Postliberal Theologian," 370.
120. Marshall, "Aquinas as Postliberal Theologian," 370.
121. Marshall, "Aquinas as Postliberal Theologian," 374.
122. Marshall, "Aquinas as Postliberal Theologian," 374.
123. Marshall, "Aquinas as Postliberal Theologian," 374.

124. *ST* II-II, 1, 2, as cited in Marshall, "Aquinas as Postliberal Theologian," 374.
125. Marshall, "Aquinas as Postliberal Theologian," 374.
126. Marshall, "Aquinas as Postliberal Theologian," 376.
127. Marshall, "Aquinas as Postliberal Theologian," 376.
128. Marshall, "Aquinas as Postliberal Theologian," 377.
129. *ST* II, 2, 2, *ad* 3, as quoted in Marshall, "Aquinas as Postliberal Theologian," 380–381.
130. Marshall, "Aquinas as Postliberal Theologian," 380.
131. Marshall, "Aquinas as Postliberal Theologian," 391–392. Marshall maintains that the difference between what a Christian and a philosopher believe about God is reflected in the difference between philosophy and *sacra doctrina:* "[t]here can be *theologia* in both philosophy and *sacra doctrina*, indeed in some cases both may make the same statements about God.... But they do so in different ways and on different grounds.... As a result, the two statements differ in kind (have different formal objects); even when they use the same words, philosophy and *sacra doctrina* are not saying the same thing" ("Aquinas as Postliberal Theologian," 392–393 note 93).
132. Lindbeck, *ND,* 118 as cited in Marshall, "Aquinas as Postliberal Theologian," 400. Marshall argues in another work that Thomas' Christology exemplifies intratextual theology (see *Christology in Conflict: The Identity of a Saviour in Rahner and Barth,* 176–189).
133. Marshall, "Aquinas as Postliberal Theologian," 401.
134. Marshall, "Aquinas as Postliberal Theologian," 402.
135. Marshall adopts Kathryn Tanner's definition of the "plain sense of Scripture": " 'what a participant in the community automatically or naturally takes a text to be saying on its face insofar as he or she has been socialized in a community's conventions for reading the text as Scripture' " [Kathryn E. Tanner, "Theology and the Plain Sense," in *Scriptural Authority and Narrative Interpretation,* ed. Garrett Green (Philadelphia: Fortress Press, 1987), 63]. See Marshall, "Absorbing the World: Christianity and the Universe of Truths," 72–73.
136. Beliefs and practices are "internal" to Christiantiy "when the Christian community, in a given historical context, regards that belief or practice as (maximally) necessary or (minimally) beneficial in order for it to be faithful to its own identity" ("Absorbing the World: Christianity and the Universe of Truths," 73).
137. Marshall, "Absorbing the World: Christianity and the Universe of Truths," 76.
138. Marshall, "Absorbing the World: Christianity and the Universe of Truths," 77.
139. Marshall, "Absorbing the World: Christianity and the Universe of Truths," 77.
140. Marshall, "Absorbing the World: Christianity and the Universe of Truths," 79.
141. Marshall, "Absorbing the World: Christianity and the Universe of Truths," 84.
142. Marshall, "Absorbing the World: Christianity and the Universe of Truths," 75. Marshall here draws on Donald Davidson's philosophy of language [see "A Coherence Theory of Truth and Knowledge," in *Truth and Interpretation: Perspectives on the Philosophy of Donald Davidson,* ed. Ernest LePore (Oxford: Basil Blackwell, 1986), especially 316–319; and "The Method of Truth in Metaphysics,"

in *Inquiries into Truth and Interpretation* (Oxford: Oxford University Press, 1984), 199-201].

143. Marshall, "Absorbing the World: Christianity and the Universe of Truths," 89.

144. Lindbeck, *ND,* 131, as cited in Marshall, "Absorbing the World: Christianity and the Universe of Truths," 97.

145. Marshall, "Faith and Reason Reconsidered: Aquinas and Luther on Deciding What is True," 2.

146. Marshall, "Faith and Reason Reconsidered: Aquinas and Luther on Deciding What is True," 2.

147. *In I Cor.* c.1, lect.3 (no.43) as cited in Marshall, "Faith and Reason Reconsidered: Aquinas and Luther on Deciding What is True," 6. Marshall claims that his interpretation of Thomas in broad terms agrees with the following interpretations: Michel Corbin, *Le chemin de la théologie chez Thomas d'Aquin; Thomas Hibbs, Dialectic and Narrative in Aquinas: an Interpretation of the Summa Contra Gentiles* (Notre Dame: University of Notre Dame Press, 1995); and Eugene Rogers, Jr., *Thomas Aquinas and Karl Barth: Sacred Doctrine and the Natural Knowledge of God* (4, note 7).

148. Marshall, "Faith and Reason Reconsidered: Aquinas and Luther on Deciding What is True," 6-7.

149. Marshall, "Faith and Reason Reconsidered: Aquinas and Luther on Deciding What is True," 9.

150. *In Joan.* c.17, lect. 6 (no.2265), as cited in Marshall, "Faith and Reason Reconsidered: Aquinas and Luther on Deciding What is True," 10. The passage cited in Thomas' commentary on the Gospel of John is found in the following section: [e]t *inde est quod apostolus dicit, quod notum est idest cognoscibile dei. Sed et si quid speculativa cognitione de deo cognoscebant, hoc erat cum admixtione multorum errorum, dum quidam subtraherent omnium rerum providentiam; quidam dicerent eum esse animam mundi; quidam simul cum eo multos alios deos colerent. Unde dicunter deum ignorare. Licet enim in compositis possit partim sciri et partim ignorari; in simplicibus tamen dum non attinguntur totaliter, ignorantur. Unde etsi in minimo aliqui errent circa dei cognitionem, dicuntur eum totaliter ignorare. Isti ergo non cognoscentes singularem dei excellentiam, ignorare dicunter; rom. i, 21...* [*Expositio in evangelium secundum Mathaeum et Joannem, in Job, Davidem, in Canticum Canticorum, Isaiam, et Jeremiam* (Neapoli, 1857) 2 vol.]

151. Marshall here cites *ST* II-II, 2, 2, *ad* 3, and III *Sent.,* d.23, Q2, a2, acla2, *ad* 2 [ed. P. Mandonnet, O.P., and M. F. Moos, O.P. (Paris: Lethielleux, 1929-47)].

152. Marshall here cites *Joan.* c.17, lect.6; "Faith and Reason Reconsidered: Aquinas and Luther on Deciding What is True," 13.

153. Marshall ["Faith and Reason Reconsidered: Aquinas and Luther on Deciding What is True," 19, note 42:] ["...Thomas seems to hold that *principia per se nota* are indeed of unrestricted epistemic *application,* in that nothing inconsistent with them is true, but not of unrestricted epistemic *primacy,* since we *decide* whether we have a *principium per se notum* by seeing whether the belief in question is consistent with the articles of faith."]

154. Marshall, "Faith and Reason Reconsidered: Aquinas and Luther on Deciding What is True," 20.

155. Marshall, "Faith and Reason Reconsidered: Aquinas and Luther on Deciding What is True," 48.

156. Bruce D. Marshall, "Theology after Cana," *Modern Theology* 16 (2000): 517–527 at 521.
157. Marshall, *Trinity and Truth*, xii.
158. Marshall, *Trinity and Truth*, xii.
159. It is important to note that Marshall regards the book as "Thomistic in spirit, even — indeed precisely — where it parts from Thomas according to the letter" ("Theology after Cana," 525).
160. Marshall, *Trinity and Truth*, 4.
161. Marshall distinguishes his proposal from a coherence view of truth because from what makes a belief justified is different than what makes a belief true (*Trinity and Truth*, 88).
162. Marshall, *Trinity and Truth*, 116.
163. Marshall, *Trinity and Truth*, 119.
164. Marshall, *Trinity and Truth*, 149.
165. Marshall, *Trinity and Truth*, 218.
166. Marshall, *Trinity and Truth*, 222.
167. Marshall, *Trinity and Truth*, 278.
168. See his "Do Christians Worship the God of Israel?" in *Knowing the Triune God* (Grand Rapids: Eerdmans, 2001) 231–264; and his "Christ and the Cultures: The Jewish People and Christian Theology," in *Cambridge Companion to Christian Doctrine* (New York: Cambridge University Press, 1997), 81–100.
169. *The Theology of Thomas Aquinas*, ed. Rik Van Nieuwenhove and Joseph Wawrykow (Notre Dame: University of Notre Dame Press, 2005).
170. Marshall, "*Quod Scit Una Uetula*," 18; see also *ST* II-II, 2, 2, *ad* 3.
171. Marshall, "*Quod Scit Una Uetula*," 18.
172. Marshall, "*Quod Scit Una Uetula*," 18.
173. Marshall, "*Quod Scit Una Uetula*," 18.
174. Marshall, "*Quod Scit Una Uetula*," 19.
175. Marshall, "*Quod Scit Una Uetula*," 20.
176. Rogers, *Thomas Aquinas and Karl Barth*, 3.
177. Rogers, *Thomas Aquinas and Karl Barth*, 5–6.
178. Rogers, *Thomas Aquinas and Karl Barth*, 18.
179. Rogers, *Thomas Aquinas and Karl Barth*, 19. Rogers refers here to *ST* I, 1, 2, *ad* 2 *in fin*.
180. Rogers, *Thomas Aquinas and Karl Barth*, 19. Rogers refers here to *ST* I, 1 *proem.* and III *prol.*
181. Rogers, *Thomas Aquinas and Karl Barth*, 20.
182. Rogers refers to *ST* I, 1, 2 where Thomas asks whether *sacra doctrina* is a *scientia*. The article "presuppos[es] that the scientific character of a discipline depends upon its proceeding from first principles" (*Thomas Aquinas and Karl Barth*, 21).
183. Rogers, *Thomas Aquinas and Karl Barth*, 21.
184. Rogers, *Thomas Aquinas and Karl Barth*, 22.
185. Rogers, *Thomas Aquinas and Karl Barth*, 22.
186. Rogers, *Thomas Aquinas and Karl Barth*, 23.
187. *Thomas Aquinas and Karl Barth*, 25. Rogers follows Michel Corbin's interpretation of Thomas on this point (*Le chemin de la théologie chez Thomas d'Aquin*, 717).
188. Rogers, *Thomas Aquinas and Karl Barth*, 27. For his interpretation of *sacra doctrina* as *scientia*, Rogers relies heavily on Corbin's *Le chemin*, 709–727.

189. Rogers, *Thomas Aquinas and Karl Barth*, 27.
190. Rogers, *Thomas Aquinas and Karl Barth*, 31.
191. Rogers, *Thomas Aquinas and Karl Barth*, 31.
192. Rogers, *Thomas Aquinas and Karl Barth*, 31.
193. Rogers, *Thomas Aquinas and Karl Barth*, 31.
194. Rogers, *Thomas Aquinas and Karl Barth*, 35–36.
195. Rogers, *Thomas Aquinas and Karl Barth*, 39.
196. Rogers refers here to *ST* I, 1, 1 and I, 1, 2.
197. Rogers, *Thomas Aquinas and Karl Barth*, 39.
198. Rogers, *Thomas Aquinas and Karl Barth*, 39.
199. Rogers, *Thomas Aquinas and Karl Barth*, 39.
200. Rogers, *Thomas Aquinas and Karl Barth*, 41.
201. Rogers, *Thomas Aquinas and Karl Barth*, 49.
202. "*Principale autem in doctrina fidei Christainae est salus per crucem Christi facta*" (*In* 1 Cor. 1:18, §45 *in med.*) as cited in Rogers, *Thomas Aquinas and Karl Barth*, 58.
203. Rogers, *Thomas Aquinas and Karl Barth*, 61.
204. Rogers, *Thomas Aquinas and Karl Barth*, 66.
205. Rogers, *Thomas Aquinas and Karl Barth*, 67.
206. Rogers, *Thomas Aquinas and Karl Barth*, 44.
207. Rogers, *Thomas Aquinas and Karl Barth*, 55. This interpretation of Question 1 moves beyond earlier interpretations that could not properly fit articles nine and ten into the overall pattern of Question 1. See, for example, James A. Weisheipl, "The Meaning of *Sacra Doctrina* in *Summa Theologiae* I, Q1," *Thomist* (1974): 49–80 at 76.
208. Rogers, *Thomas Aquinas and Karl Barth*, 159.
209. Rogers, *Thomas Aquinas and Karl Barth*, 159.
210. Rogers, *Thomas Aquinas and Karl Barth*, 159.
211. Rogers, *Thomas Aquinas and Karl Barth*, 121.
212. Rogers, *Thomas Aquinas and Karl Barth*, 129.
213. Rogers, *Thomas Aquinas and Karl Barth*, 121.
214. Rogers, *Thomas Aquinas and Karl Barth*, 164.
215. Rogers, *Thomas Aquinas and Karl Barth*, 125.
216. Rogers, *Thomas Aquinas and Karl Barth*, 131.
217. Rogers, *Thomas Aquinas and Karl Barth*, 139.
218. Rogers, *Thomas Aquinas and Karl Barth*, 162.
219. Rogers, *Thomas Aquinas and Karl Barth*, 139.
220. Rogers, *Thomas Aquinas and Karl Barth*, 140–141.
221. Rogers, *Thomas Aquinas and Karl Barth*, 146.
222. Rogers, *Thomas Aquinas and Karl Barth*, 187.
223. Rogers, *Thomas Aquinas and Karl Barth*, 188.

Notes to Chapter Two

1. Cf. A. Walz, "De genuino titulo *Summae Theologiae*," *Angelicum* 18 (1941): 142–143.
2. Walter H. Principe, C.S.B., *Alexander of Hales' Theology of the Hypostatic Union*, vol. 2 (Toronto: Pontifical Institute of Mediaeval Studies, 1967), 14.
3. M.-D. Chenu, O.P., *Toward Understanding Saint Thomas*, trans. A.-M. Landry, O.P., and D. Hughes, O.P. (Chicago: Henry Regnery Company, 1964), 298.

4. Chenu, *Toward Understanding Saint Thomas*, 299.
5. Chenu, *Toward Understanding Saint Thomas*, 298.
6. Chenu, *Toward Understanding Saint Thomas*, 299.
7. Chenu, *Toward Understanding Saint Thomas*, 299.
8. Mark D. Jordan, "Theology and Philosophy," in *The Cambridge Companion to Aquinas*, eds. Norman Kretzmann and Eleonore Stump (Cambridge: Cambridge University Press, 1993), 232.
9. Leonard E. Boyle, O.P., *The Setting of the* Summa theologiae *of Saint Thomas* (Ontario: Pontifical Institute of Medieval Studies, 1982), 2–3, 17.
10. Boyle, *Setting of the* Summa, 11.
11. Thomas' teaching at Orvieto, to those *fratres communes* who had not been able to study in the *studia generalia* or the *provincialia*, was meant to prepare his students for the two missions that Pope Honorius III had entrusted to the Dominicans, namely, that of preaching and confession (Torrell, *Saint Thomas Aquinas*, 118–119).
12. Leornard E. Boyle, *Pastoral Care, Clerical Education and Canon Law 1200–1400* (London: Variorum Reprints, 1981), 257.
13. Torrell, *Saint Thomas Aquinas*, 145; cf. Boyle, *Setting of the Summa*, 15.
14. Torrell, *Saint Thomas Aquinas*, 120, 145.
15. Leonard E. Boyle, O.P., "The Setting of the *Summa theologiae* of Saint Thomas," in *Facing History: A Different Thomas Aquinas* (Louvain: Louvain-Le-Neuve, 2000), 71–73.
16. Boyle, *Setting of the Summa*, 16.
17. Chenu, *Toward Understanding Saint Thomas*, 298.
18. John Jenkins, C.S.C., *Knowledge and Faith in Thomas Aquinas* (Cambridge: Cambridge University Press, 1997), 80, 92–93.
19. Jenkins, *Knowledge and Faith in Thomas Aquinas*, 89.
20. Jenkins, *Knowledge and Faith in Thomas Aquinas*, 86–87.
21. Jenkins, *Knowledge and Faith in Thomas Aquinas*, 86–87.
22. Jenkins, *Knowledge and Faith in Thomas Aquinas*, ch. 3, note 36, 240
23. The reviews of Jenkins' claim regarding his reading of the *incipientes* are mixed. Among the critics one finds Fergus Kerr, O.P., and Brian Davies, O.P. While Kerr suggests that Jenkins' interpretation of these beginners is "not entirely convincing," he does not offer arguments to the contrary [*New Blackfriars* 79 (1998): 204–206]. Davies argues that Jenkins' interpretation does not do justice to what Thomas says in the prologue to the work. He does recognize, however, that any interpretation is one of "conjecture" rather than something that can be proved true in an "absolute sense" [*Journal of Theological Studies* 49 (1998): 876–879]. Joseph Wawrykow, on the other hand, finds Jenkins' position on this issue "largely persuasive," one which "locate[s] well Thomas' theologizing" [*Journal of Religion* 80 (2000): 337–339].
24. Grabmann, *Introduction to the Theological Summa of St. Thomas* (St. Louis: Herder and Herder, 1930), 71.
25. Torrell, *Saint Thomas Aquinas*, 158. See also Boyle, *The Setting of the Summa*, 23–30.
26. While the tradition of *quaestiones* and *responsiones* dates back to the early church fathers, it is not until the twelfth century that this tradition moves from being spontaneous to methodological (the first documented use of the formalized question is found in Alberic in the early twelfth century): "c'est-à-dire que, par un généralisation qu'alimente la curiosité de la foi et qu'instrumentalise l'usage de

la dialectique, le *lector* pose techniquement, artificiellement, des questions sur chacune des propositions, ou du moins sur les points importants de son texte" [M.-D. Chenu, O.P., *La théologie au douzième siècle* (Paris: Librarie Philosophique J. Vrin, 1957), 337–338]. By the mid-thirteenth century, there developed a practice of disputations that consisted of a discussion of a question fixed in advance (M.-D. Chenu, *Toward Understanding St. Thomas,* 91). The *quaestiones quodlibetales* were even rarer, conducted at Christmas and Easter.

27. Grabmann maintains that in Lombard's *Sentences,* for example, the treatment of God and the Trinity are intermingled without an intelligible structure, and the treatment of the virtues is elaborated at several different points (Grabmann, *An Introduction to the Theological Summa of St. Thomas,* 95). Contemporary medieval scholar Marcia Colish disagrees. While recognizing that there are some areas of overlap in his work, she argues that Lombard did a "remarkable job of slicing through the redundancies, evasions, and confusions found in other systematic theologians of his time," so much so that "the schema he produces is by far the most coherent of his day" [Marcia L. Colish, *Peter Lombard,* v.1 (Leiden: E. J. Brill, 1994), 83–84].

28. Grabmann, *An Introduction to the Theological Summa of St. Thomas,* 120.

29. For the nature of the disputed question, confer Chenu, *Toward Understanding Saint Thomas,* 80–95.

30. Per Erik Persson, *Sacra Doctrina: Reason and Revelation in Aquinas* (Oxford: Basil Blackwell, 1970), 242.

31. Th.-André Audet, O.P., "Approches historiques de la *Summa Theologiae,*" in *Études d'histoire littéraire et doctrinale* (PIEM, XVII, 1962), 12.

32. *Anchor Bible,* eds. William F. Orr and James Arthur Walther (New York: Doubleday, 1976), 170.

33. S. Thomas Aquinatis, *Super epistolas S. Pauli lectura,* cura Raphaelis Cai, ed. 8 (Taurini: Marietti, 1953) caput III, lectio I, #123, 125.

34. Torrell dates the composition of this commentary between 1270 and 1272 during Thomas' second period of teaching at Paris (*Saint Thomas Aquinas,* 198).

35. *Commentary on the Gospel of St. John,* trans. James A. Weisheipl, O.P., and Fabian R. Larcher, O.P. (New York: Magis Books, 1980), 256. *Super Evangelium S. Ioannis* Lectura, c. IV, l. III, 635: [p]*erfectorum autem est solidus cibus: unde Origenes dicit, quod ille qui est altioris doctrinae, et aliis in spiritualibus praeest, potest hoc verbum dicere infirmis et debilioris intellectus existentibus. Et sic Apostolus loquitur, I Cor. III, 1:* Tamquam parvulis in Christo, lac vobis potum dedi, non escam. P. Raphaelis Cai, O.P., ed. (Rome: Marietti, 1952).

36. *ST* II-II, 81, 1: [i]*pse enim est cui principaliter alligari debemus tanquam indeficienti principio; ad quem etiam nostra electio assidue dirigi debet sicut in ultimum finem; quem etiam negligentes peccando amittimus, et credendo et fidem protestando recuperare debemus.* English translation: *The Summa theologica of St. Thomas Aquinas,* trans. Fathers of the English Dominican Province (Texas: Christian Classics, 1981). I make minor adjustments to this translation where necessary.

37. Cf. *ST* II-II, 58, 1: *justitia est habitus secundum quem aliquis constanti et perpetua voluntate jus suum unicuique tribuit.*

38. *ST* II-II, 80, 1.

39. *ST* II-II, 58, 3.

40. *ST* II-II, 81, 2.

41. *SCG,* Bk. I, ch. 5. *Quia ergo ad altius bonum quam experiri in praesenti vita possit humana fragilitas, homines per divinam providentiam ordinantur, ut in*

sequentibus investigabitur [lib. III], oportuit mentem evocari in aliquid altius quam ratio nostra in praesenti possit pertingere, ut sic disceret aliquid desiderare, et studio tendere in aliquid quod totum statum praesentis vitae excedit. [*Opera Omnia*. Editio altera Veneta..., t. 18: IV Libros de Veritate Catholicae Fidei Contra Gentiles etc. (Cudebat Simon Occhi, Venetiis, 1753)].

42. Thomas Aquinas, *SCG,* Bk. I, ch. 5.

43. For an overview of this tradition of interpretation beginning with Cardinal Cajetan, see James A. Weisheipl, "The Meaning of *Sacra Doctrina* in *Summa theologiae* I, Q1," 49–80.

44. Since articles two through eight have been understood by some commentators to refer to scholastic theology, their relationship to articles one, nine and ten have caused interpretative difficulties [For a brief overview of the discussion about the meaning of *sacra doctrina*, see M. F. Sparrow, "Natural Knowledge of God and the Principles of 'Sacra Doctrina' *Angelicum* 69 (1992): 471, note 1]. Chenu even suggested that articles nine and ten were actually a concession made by Thomas to the usage of his time, but that his theology would eventually eliminate the need for them [M.-D. Chenu, "La théologie comme science au xiiie siècle," *Archives d'histoire doctrinale et littéraire du moyen-âge* 2 (1927): 68–69]. It should be noted that Chenu does not repeat this claim in later editions [*La Théologie comme science au xiii siècle* (Paris: J. Vrin, 1942, 1957)]. See also Mark F. Johnson "The Sapiential Character of the First Article of the *Summa theologiae,"* in *Philosophy and the God of Abraham: Essays in Memory of James A. Weisheipl, O.P.,* ed. James R. Long (Toronto: Pontifical Institute of Mediaeval Studies, 1991), 86–88.

45. Weisheipl, "The Meaning of *Sacra Doctrina* in *Summa theologiae* I, q. 1," 64. For the roots of this division of inquiry in Aristotle, see his *Posterior Analytics,* trans. Jonathan Barnes (Oxford: Clarendon Press, 1994), II, 1–2, 48–49.

46. Weisheipl, "The Meaning of *Sacra Doctrina* in *Summa theologiae* I, Q1," 68–69.

47. Weisheipl, "The Meaning of *Sacra Doctrina* in *Summa theologiae* I, Q1," 67.

48. Weisheipl, "The Meaning of *Sacra Doctrina* in *Summa theologiae* I, Q1," 67.

49. G. F. Van Ackeren, *Sacra Doctrina: The Subject of the First Question of the Summa Theologica of St. Thomas Aquinas* (Rome: Catholic Book Agency, 1952).

50. James A. Weisheipl, *Friar Thomas D'Aquino: His Life, Thought, and Works* (Washington, D.C.: Catholic University of America Press, 1983), 223.

51. The prologue to Q2 will introduce the tripartite division of the *Summa.*

52. *ST,* I, 1, 2.

53. *ST* I, 12, 6.

54. Torrell, *Saint Thomas Aquinas,* 157.

55. Torrell, *Saint Thomas Aquinas,* 157.

56. Weisheipl, "The Meaning of *Sacra Doctrina* in *Summa theologiae* I, Q1," 79–80.

57. *ST* I, 1, 1, *ad* 2.

58. *ST* I, 1, 8, *ad* 2.

59. *ST* I, 1, 5, *ad* 2: *haec scientia accipere potest aliquid a philosophicis disciplinis, non quasi ex necessitate eis indigeat, sed ad maiorem manifestationem eorum quae in hac scientia traduntur. Non enim accipit sua principia ab aliis scientiis sed immediate a Deo per revelationem. Et ideo non accipit ab aliis scientiis tamquam*

a superioribus, sed utitur eis tamquam inferioribus et ancillis; sicut architectonicae utuntur subministrantibus ut civilis militari. Et hoc ipsum quod sic utitur eis non est propter defectum vel insufficientiam ejus, sed propter defectum intellectus nostri, qui ex eis quae per naturalem rationem ex qua procedunt aliae scientiae cognoscuntur, facilius manuducitur in ea quae sunt supra rationem quae in hac scientia traduntur.

60. *ST* I, 1, 5, sed contra: *aliae scientiae dicuntur ancillae hujus;* Prov. *Misit ancillas suas vocare ad arcem.* Thomas also treats the relationship between *sacra doctrina* and other sciences in *ST* I, 1, 6.

61. God sets this organic relationship on its course: "God himself begins this process of *manuductio* when He uses metaphorical language to set us on our way and sends His own Son, Wisdom in person, to take on a body in the world. But He calls others to enter into this process also as teachers, so that out of divine piety they assume the trust of pursuing the office of wise man and undertake to manifest the truth of Faith" [Oliva Blanchette, "Philosophy and Theology in Aquinas: On Being a Disciple in our Day," *Science et Esprit* 28 (1976): 23–53 at 40–41.] Blanchette refers the reader here to: *ST,* I, 1, 6, *ad* 1; and *SCG,* I, 1, 4.

62. See *ST* I, 1, 5, *ad* 2: *haec scientia accipere potest aliquid a philosophicis disciplinis, non quod ex necessitate eis indigeat, sed ad maiorem manifestationem eorum quae in hac scientia traduntur. Non enim accipit sua principia ab aliis scientiis, sed immediate a Deo per revelationem. Et ideo non accipit ab aliis scientiis, sed immediate a Deo per revelationem. Et ideo non accipit ab aliis scientiis tanquam a superioribus, sed utitur eis tanquam inferioribus et ancillis.... Et hoc ipsum quod sic utitur eis, non est propter defectum vel insufficientiam eius, sed propter defectum intellectus nostri; qui ex his quae per naturalem rationem (ex qua procedunt aliae scientiae) cognoscuntur, facilius manudicitur in ea quae sunt supra rationem, quae in hac scientia traduntur.* Cf I, 1, 8, *ad* 2.

63. In *ST* I, 1, 9 Thomas argues that Scripture uses metaphors because hiding the truth in figures is useful for the exercise of thoughtful minds: [*e*]*t ipsa etiam occultatio figurarum utilis est ad exercitium studiosorum....*

64. *ST,* I, 1, 7.

65. Torrell, *Saint Thomas Aquinas,* 157.

66. Torrell, *Saint Thomas Aquinas,* 152.

67. M.-V. Leroy, *Revue Thomiste* 84 (1984): 298–303, as cited in Torrell, *Saint Thomas Aquinas,* 153. For an alternate scheme see A.-M. Patfoort, "L'unité de la Ia Pars et le mouvement interne de la Somme théologique de S. Thomas d'Aquin," *Revue des sciences philosophiques et théologiques* 47 (1963): 513–544. Leroy's interpretation of the structure of the *Summa* more appropriately understands the *Tertia pars* as integral to the work as a whole. This marks a significant step toward quelling the criticisms of Thomas that Christ was an afterthought rather than central to his work.

68. Cf. *ST* I, 2, prol.: [*c*]*onsideratio autem de Deo tripartita erit. Primo namque considerabimus ea quae ad essentiam divinam pertinent....*

69. Cf. *ST* I, 27, prol.: [*c*]*onsideratis autem his quae ad divinae essentiae unitatem pertinent, restat considerare de his quae pertinent ad trinitatem Personarum in divinis.*

70. Cf. *ST* I, 45, prol.: [*d*]*einde quaeritur de modo emanationis rerum a primo principio, qui dicitur creatio.*

71. Thomas has also been avidly defended from this criticism. Among these, one finds Nicholas Lash, "When did the theologians lose interest in theology?" in

The Beginning and End of Religion (Cambridge: Cambridge University Press, 1996), 132–149.

72. Karl Rahner, S.J., *The Trinity*, trans. Joseph Donceel (New York: Crossroad, 1997); original German publication, 1967 by Benziger Verlag (Eisiedeln), 45. Cf. *ST* I, 27, prol.

73. Karl Rahner, *The Trinity*, 46.

74. Nicholas Lash, "Considering the Trinity," *Modern Theology* 2 (1986): 188.

75. This has been treated more fully by Michael J. Buckley, S.J., "Thomas Aquinas and the Rise of Modern Atheism" in *Denying and Disclosing God: The Ambiguous Progress of Modern Atheism*, (New Haven: Yale University Press, 2004), 48–69. See also an interesting defense of the structure of the *Prima pars* based on the distinction between the *essentia* and *operatio* of God in Rudi Te Velde, *Aquinas on God: the 'Divine Science' of the* Summa Theologiae (Aldershot: Ashgate Publishing, 2006), 68–72.

76. Cf. *ST* I, 3, prol.: [c]*ognito de aliquo an sit, inquirendum restat quomodo sit, ut sciatur de eo quid sit.*

77. Cf. *ST* I, 14, prol.: [p]*ost considerationem eorum quae ad divinam substantiam pertinent, restat considerandum de his quae pertinent ad operationem ipsius.*

78. For an overview of this discussion in the English-speaking world of the past several decades see Lubor Velecky, *Aquinas' Five Arguments in the Summa Theologiae* 1a 2, 3 (Kampen, Netherlands: Kok Pharos Publishing House, 1994).

79. See *ST* I, 2, 1, *ad* 1.

80. J. Châtillon, "De Guillaume d'Auxerre à saint Thomas d'Aquin: l'Argument de saint Anselme chez les premiers scolastiques," in *D'Isodore de Séville à saint Thomas d'Aquin* (London, 1985), 219–21.

81. John F. Wippel, *The Metaphysical Thought of Thomas Aquinas: From Finite Being to Uncreated Being* (Washington, D.C.: Catholic University of America Press, 2000), 397–399.

82. While Thomas has not yet established this metaphysical argument, he points the reader to the upcoming Q3, a4 in which he argues that in God *esse* and *essentia* are not differentiated. The arguments for God's existence in Q2, then, cannot be extracted from the surrounding questions in the *Summa* and stand on their own. They depend at least in part on the web of questions in which they are embedded for their persuasive force.

83. *ST* I, 2, 1, *ad* 1: [c]*ognoscere Deum esse in aliquo communi sub quadam confusione, est nobis naturaliter insertum, in quantum scilicet Deus est hominis beatitudo: homo enim naturaliter desiderat beatitudinem; et quod naturaliter desideratur ab homine, naturaliter cognoscitur ab eodem. Sed hoc non est simpliciter cognoscere Deum esse; sicut cognoscere venientem, non est cognoscere Petrum, quamvis veniens sit Petrus.*

84. Wippel maintains: "Thomas has pointed out that because God's essence is to exist, such argumentation would succeed, or at least God's existence would be evident to us, if we enjoyed direct knowledge of the divine essence or quiddity. According to Thomas' theory of knowledge, no such knowledge is available to us within the present life, at least within the natural order. Hence he cannot justify any immediate movement from our understanding of God...to his actual existence" (*The Metaphysical Thought of Thomas Aquinas*, 399).

85. Cf. *ST* I, 2, 2: [r]*espondeo dicendum quod duplex ex demonstratio. Una quae est per causam, et dicitur propter quid: et haec est per priora simpliciter. Alia est per effectum, et dicitur demonstratio quia: et haec est per ea quae sunt priora quoad nos: cum enim effectus aliquis nobis est manifestior quam sua causa, per effectum procedimus ad cognitionem causae. Ex quolibet autem effectu potest demonstrari propriam causam eius esse (si tamen eius effectus sint magis noti quoad nos): quia, cum effectus dependeant a causa, posito effectu necesse est causam praeexistere.*

86. Bk 1, Lec 23, n.2: [d]*emonstratio est syllogismus faciens scire, et quod demonstratio ex causis rei procedit et primis et immediatis. quod intelligendum est de demonstratione propter quid. sed tamen differt scire quia ita est, et propter quid ita est. et cum demonstratio sit syllogismus faciens scire, ut dictum est, oportet etiam quod demonstratio quae facit scire quia, differat a demonstratione quae facit scire propter quid* [*Opera omnia* ad fidem optimarum editionum accurate recognita...t. 18: In Aristotelis Stagiritae nonnullos libros commentaria. Vol. I (1a ed.: Typis Petri Fiaccadori, Parmae, 1865)]. English translation: *Commentary on Aristotle's* Posterior Analytic, trans. Richard Berquist (Notre Dame: Dumb Ox Books, 2007), 105.

87. Bk. 1 Lec. 23 n.6: *omne non scintillans est prope; planetae sunt non scintillantes; ergo sunt prope.*

88. *ST* I, 2, 2, ad 1: [a]*d primum ergo dicendum quod Deum esse, et alia huiusmodi quae per rationem naturalem nota possunt esse de Deo, ut dicitur Rom. 1,19, non sunt articuli fidei, sed praeambula ad articulos: sic enim fides praesupponit cognitionem naturalem, sicut gratia naturam, et perfectio perfectibile.* For a vigorous defense of the role of the *preambula fidei* in Thomas, see Ralph McInerny, Preambula Fidei: *Thomism and the God of the Philosophers* (Washington, D.C.: Catholic University of America Press, 2006).

89. *Dicionary of Theology*, Karl Rahner and Herbert Vorgrimler, eds., 2nd ed., s.v. "fideism" (New York: Crossroad, 1981), 176.

90. *Oxford Dictionary of the Christian Church*, F. L. Cross, ed. 3rd ed., s.v. "fideism" (Oxford: Oxford University Press, 1997), 609. The word "fideism" was apparently coined by Parisian Protestant theologians, A. Sabatier and E. Ménégoz (1838–1921), whose irrationalism was rooted in Kant and Schleiermacher (609).

91. *Sacramentum Mundi: An Encyclopedia of Theology*, vol. 2, s.v. "fideism," (New York: Herder and Herder, 1968), 335–336.

92. Terence Penelhum, *God and Skepticism: A Study in Skepticism and Fideism* (Dordrecht: D. Reidel Publishing Company, 1983), 1.

93. *ST* I, 2, 2, ad 3: [a]*d tertium dicendum quod per effectus non proportionatos causae, non potest perfecta cognitio de causa haberi: sed tamen ex quocumque effectu potest manifeste nobis demonstrari causam esse, ut dictum est. Et sic ex effectibus Dei potest demonstrari Deum esse: licet per eos non perfecte possimus eum cognoscere secundum suam essentiam.* It is important to note here that Thomas concludes we cannot know God perfectly as God is in God's essence. He does not say that we cannot know *anything* of God.

94. See Leo J. Elders, S.V.D., *The Philosophical Theology of Thomas Aquinas* (Leiden: E. J. Brill, 1990), 127–128.

95. Enchiridion II, PL 40, 236 as cited in *ST* I, 2, 3, *ad* 1: *Deus cum sit summe bonus nullo modo sineret aliquid mali esse in operibus suis nisi esset adeo omnipotens et bonus ut bene faceret etiam de malo.*

96. See Leo J. Elders, S.V.D., *The Philosophical Theology of Thomas Aquinas*, 127–128.

97. Denys Turner notes that *et hoc omnes dicunt Deum* "should be translated not as 'this is how all people speak of God' or even that 'this is what all people *mean* when they speak of God,' for manifestly they do not, and Thomas knows this: it should rather be translated as 'and this is the God all people speak of'" [*Faith, Reason and the Existence of God* (Cambridge: Cambridge University Press, 2004), 19].

98. For the composite character of any effect see *ST* I, 3, 7, *ad* 1: *ea quae sunt a Deo imitantur Deum sicut causata primam causam. Est autem hoc de ratione causati quod sit aliquo modo compositum, quia ad minus esse ejus est aliud quam quod est.* Cf. *ST* I, 50, 2, *ad* 3.

99. Cf. Wippel, *The Metaphysical Thought of Thomas Aquinas*, 498–500; Joseph Owens, C.Ss.R., *St. Thomas Aquinas on the Existence of God: Collected Papers of Joseph Owens C.Ss.R.*, ed. John R. Catan (Albany: State University of New York Press, 1980), 141.

100. Denys Turner, *Faith, Reason and the Existence of God*, 16.

101. Alvin Plantinga, *Does God Have a Nature?* (Milwaukee: Marquette University Press, 1980), 27–28. Cf. Robert M. Burns, "The Divine Simplicity in St. Thomas," *Religious Studies* 25 (1989): 271–293.

102. See Brian Davies "Classical Theism and the Doctrine of the Divine Simplicity" in *Language, Meaning, and God*, ed. Brian Davies (London: Geoffrey Chapman, 1987). The doctrine of divine simplicity has also recently received attention in analytic philosophy circles. For an overview of this discussion see for example Katherine Rogers "The Traditional Doctrine of Divine Simplicity," *Religious Studies* 32 (1996): 165–186, esp. note 1, 2.

103. David B. Burrell, C.S.C., *Aquinas: God and Action* (Notre Dame: University of Notre Dame Press, 1979), 13.

104. *ST* I, 1, 7, *ad* 1 (Thomas accepts Damascene's claim in his reply to this objection): *dicit enim Damascenus, In Deo quid est dicere est impossibile.*

105. *ST* I, 3, *prol.*

106. *Disputed Questions on Truth*, I, trans. Robert W. Mulligan, S.J. (Chicago: Henry Regnery Co., 1952), 58. *De veritate*, 2, 1, *ad* 9: *tunc intellectus dicitur scire de aliquo quid est, quando definit ipsum, id est quando concipit aliquam formam de ipsa re quae per omnia ipsi rei respondet. Iam autem ex dictis patet quod quidquid intellectus noster de Deo concipit, est deficiens a repraesentatione eius; et ideo quid est ipsius Dei semper nobis occultum remanet; et haec est summa cognitio quam de ipso in statu viae habere possumus, ut cognoscamus Deum esse supra omne id quod cogitamus de eo...* On interpreting *quid sit* in this restrictive sense see John Wippel, *Metaphysical Themes in Thomas Aquinas* "Chapter IX: Quiddative Knowledge of God" (Washington, D.C.: Catholic University of America, 1984), 239–240. Italics mine.

107. *ST* I, 85, 1: *intellectus noster intelligit materialia abstrahendo a phantasmatibus.*

108. *ST* I, 88, 2, *ad* 2: *ad secundum dicendum quod de superioribus rebus in scientiis maxime tractatur per viam remotionis: sic enim corpora caelestia notificat Aristoteles per negationem proprietatem inferiorum corporum. Unde multo magis*

immateriales substantiae a nobis cognosci non possunt ut earum quidditates apprehendamus; sed de eis nobis in scientiis documenta traduntur per viam remotionis, et alicujus habitudinis ad res materiales.

109. *ST* I, 88, 3: [c]*um intellectus humanus, secundum statum praesentis vitae, non possit intelligere substantias immateriales creatas, ut dictum est; multo minus potest intelligere essentiam substantiae increatae...*

110. Isaak Franck, "Maimonides and Aquinas on Man's Knowledge of God: A Twentieth Century Perspective," in *Maimonides: A Collection of Critical Essays*, ed. Joseph A. Buijs (Notre Dame: University of Notre Dame Press, 1988), 287.

111. Maimonides, *Guide of the Perplexed*, trans. Schlomo Pines (Chicago: University of Chicago Press, 1963), 118.

112. Maimonides, *Guide of the Perplexed*, 118.

113. Maimonides, *Guide of the Perplexed*, 139.

114. Maimonides, *Guide of the Perplexed*, 131.

115. Maimonides, *Guide of the Perplexed*, 137.

116. This criticism will be echoed in *ST* I, 13, 2.

117. *De Potentia* 7, 5: *unde nisi intellectus humanus aliquid de Deo affirmative cognosceret, nihil de Deo posset negare.* On the Power of God, trans. English Dominican Fathers (London: Burns, Oates & Washbourne, 1934), 28.

118. *De Potentia* 7, 5: *ita possemus dicere deum esse leonem, quia non habet esse ad modum avis.*

119. Thomas Aquinas, *The Division and Method of the Sciences: Questions V and VI of his Commentary on the* De Trinitate *of Boethius*, trans. Armand Maurer (Toronto: Pontifical Institute of Mediaeval Studies, 1986), VI, a3: *quod de nulla re potest sciri an est, nisi quoquo modo de ea sciatur quid est, vel cognitione perfecta, vel cognitione confusa... Oportet enim definitionum cognitionem, sicut et demonstrationum, ex aliqua praeexistenti cognitione initium sumere. Sic ergo de Deo et de aliis substantiis immaterialibus non possemus scire an est, nisi sciremus quodammodo de eis quid est sub quadam confusione.* Note that Thomas maintains this same vocabulary in his later *Summa* when asking whether knowledge of God is self-evident, insisting that to know God in a *general* and *confused* way is implanted in us by nature (see *ST* I, 2, 1, *ad* 1).

120. *Commentary on Boethius' De Trinitate* VI, a3: *et quanto plures negationes de ipsis cognoscimus, tanto minus est confusa earum cognitio in nobis; eo quod per negationes sequentes prior negatio contrahitur et determinatur, sicut genus remotum per differentias.*

121. *Commentary on Boethius' De Trinitate* VI, a3.

122. *De veritate* 1, 1, *ad* 7: *verum non est in plus quam ens; ens enim aliquo modo acceptum dicitur de non ente, secundum quod non ens est apprehensum ab intellectu; unde in* IV Metaph. *dicit philosophus, quod negatio vel privatio entis uno modo dicitur ens.* Thomas Aquinas, *The Disputed Questions on Truth*, vol. 1, trans. Robert W. Mulligan, S.J. (Chicago: Henry Regnery Co., 1952), 8.

123. Hilary Putnam, "On Negative Theology," *Faith and Philosophy: Journal of the Society of Christian Philosophers* 14 (1997): 407–422 at 418. Rudi Te Velde adds that one should not "overemphasize the role of the *via negativa* at the cost of the integrated dynamics of the *triplex via* as a whole" (*Aquinas on God*, 96).

124. *ST* I, 3, 7, *ad* 1.

125. *ST* I, 3, 3, *ad* 1: *de rebus simplicibus loqui non possumus, nisi per modum compositorum, a quibus cognitionem accipimus. Et ideo de Deo loquentes utimus*

nominibus concretis, ut significemus ejus substantiam; quia apud nos non subsistunt nisi composita; et utimur nominibus abstractis, ut significemus ejus simplicitatem.

126. *ST* I, 2, 3.

127. *ST* I, 3, 4, ad 2: *[s]cimus enim quod haec propositio quam formamus de Deo, cum dicimus,* Deus est, *vera est; et hoc scimus ex ejus effectibus, ut supra dictum est (quaest. II, art.2).* This answer to the objection will become very important to our analysis.

128. Cf. *On the Power of God*, 7, 2, ad 9.

Notes to Chapter Three

1. Ralph McInerny, *Being and Predication: Thomistic Interpretations* (Washington, D.C.: Catholic University America Press, 1986), 272.

2. Burrell states, "The resource [Aquinas] will rely upon most is his philosophical grammar. He is not directly engaged in praising or thanking God, of course, but in the reflective theological activity of making explicit what a religious life implies. None the less, this activity can also be considered a quest for God since its object discriminates between appropriate and inappropriate attitudes we might assume toward it. The mode of inquiry, however, remains reflective and explicitly linguistic" (*Aquinas: God and Action*, 6).

3. Burrell, *Aquinas: God and Action*, 22.

4. I do not mean to insinuate here that Burrell interprets Aquinas' position to end in "pure agnosticism," for Burrell is at pains to show otherwise [see *Analogy and Philosophical Language* (New Haven: Yale University Press, 1973), 126–128]. It is true, however, that at times, Burrell's Aquinas comes terribly close to sounding like an agnostic. See, for example, *Aquinas: God and Action*, 13–14: "Aquinas shows under one rubric after another how it is that our discourse fails to represent God. It fails not merely by falling short but by lacking the structural isomorphism requisite to any statement which purports to refer to its object. Besides being unable to say the right things about God, we can never even put our statement correctly." Burrell's reading of Aquinas has certainly been widely influential. See, for example, Herwi Rikhof, "Thomas at Utrecht," in Fergus Kerr, *Contemplating Aquinas: On the Varieties of Interpretation* (London: SCM, 2003), 105–136.

5. Burrell, *Aquinas: God and Action*, 67.

6. Nicholas Lash, "Ideology, Metaphor, and Analogy," in *The Philosophical Frontiers of Christian Theology: Essays Presented to D.M. Mackinnon*, eds. Brian Hebblethwaite and Stewart Sutherland (Cambridge: Cambridge University Press, 1982), 81. Quotations are adopted from Burrell, *Aquinas*, 7, 25. This leads Lash to assert that what seem to be positive analogical predications of God "cannot be said to be not literally applicable to God" (Lash, "Ideology, Metaphor, and Analogy," 83).

7. *ST* I, 12, *prol.*: *[q]uia in superioribus consideravimus qualiter Deus sit secundum seipsum, restat considerandum qualiter sit in cognitione nostra, idest quomodo cognoscatur a creaturis.*

8. *ST* I, 2, *prol.*

9. David Burrell, C.S.C., "Aquinas on Naming God," *Theological Studies* 24 (1963): 192.

10. Brian Davies, O.P., "Classical Theism and the Doctrine of Divine Simplicity," 61.

11. Thomas appeals to scriptural authority in the *sed contras* of this question: a1 (Psalms 13:14), a2 (Romans 1:20) and a3 (Exodus 3:14). This is to appeal to *sacra doctrina* to which his theology will pertain.

12. Cf. *ST* I, 1, 1 [*Ad ea etiam quae de Deo ratione humana investigari possunt, necessarium fuit hominem instrui revelatione divina. Quia veritas de Deo, per rationem investigata, a paucis, et per longum tempus, et cum admixtione multorum errorum, homini proveniret: a cuius tamen veritatis cognitione dependet tota hominis salus, quae in Deo est*]; *ST* I, 2, 2, ad 1 [*Deum esse, et alia huiusmodi quae per rationem naturalem nota possunt esse de Deo, ut dicitur Rom. 1,19, non sunt articuli fidei, sed praeambula ad articulos: sic enim fides praesupponit cognitionem naturalem, sicut gratia naturam, et perfectio perfectibile*]; and *SCG* I, 4, 1 [*Duplici igitur veritate divinorum intelligibilium existente, una ad quam rationis inquisitio pertingere potest, altera quae omne ingenium humanae rationis excedit...*].

13. See Brian Davies, *The Thought of Thomas Aquinas* (Oxford: Clarendon Press, 1992), 26.

14. In the *Summa contra gentiles*, for example, the demonstrations for the existence of God are discussed in much more detail.

15. *ST* I, 2, 1, ad 1: *cognoscere Deum esse in aliquo communi sub quadam confusione, est nobis naturaliter insertum, in quantum scilicet Deus est hominis beatitudo: homo enim naturaliter desiderat beatitudinem; et quod naturaliter desideratur ab homine, naturaliter cognoscitur ab eodem. Sed hoc non est simpliciter cognoscere Deum esse...*

16. This is the knowledge that moves from effect to cause of Q2.

17. *impossibile est aliquid scrire prius quam perveniatur ad individua* [*Commentary on the Metaphysics of Aristotle*, vol. 1, trans. Aristotle Rowan and John Patrick (Chicago: H. Regnery Co., 1961) Bk.2, Lsn.4, n.8].

18. 1 Jn. 3:2; *ST* I, 12, 1, *sc*.

19. *ST* I, 12, 1: [*c*]*um enim ultima hominis beatitudo in altissima ejus operatione consistat, quae est operatio intellectus, si nunquam essentiam Dei videre potest intellectus creatus, vel nunquam beatitudinem obtinebit, vel in alio ejus beatitude consistet quam in Deo; quod est alienum a fide.*

20. The verb *attingere* here is crucial to understanding Thomas' approach to knowledge of God, but it will be introduced more fully in our analysis of a7.

21. See *ST* I, 7, 1.

22. Recall *ST* I, 6, 2, ad 1: [*r*]*elatio autem qua aliquid de Deo dicitur relative ad creaturas, non est realiter in Deo, sed in creatura; in Deo vero secundum rationem; sicut scibile relative dicitur ad scientiam, non quia ad ipsam referatur sed quia scientia refertur ad ipsum.*

23. *ST* 1, 12, 1, ad 4: *...hoc intellectus creatus proportionatus esse potest ad cognoscendum Deum.*

24. These two components are the linchpins that hold together this question, for a2–7 reflect upon the power of sight at issue in this knowledge, and a8–11 turn to the information that is provided so that God may be seen.

25. *Cognoscere per similitudinem* is here introduced, but will not be explored fully until a12–13 address knowledge of God in this life.

26. *ST* I, 12, 5: [*c*]*um essentia divina naturam cujusque creati intellectus excedat, indiget creatus intellectus ad eam intuendam aliqut creato lumine.*

27. While this axiom was generally accepted among scholastics, the principle is first explicitly formulated by Plotinus in the sixth *Ennead*. Thomas attributes

this insight to Plato, but the only source for an actual formulation of the axiom is the *Liber de causis* [see John Tomarchio, "Computer Linguistics and Philosophical Interpretation," paper presented at the Twentieth World Congress of Philosophy (Boston, Massachusetts, August 10–15, 1998); see also Michael J. Buckley, *Denying and Disclosing God*, 113, esp. 161, note 49].

28. *ST* I, 12, 4: [n]*on igitur potest intellectus creatus Deum per essentiam videre, nisi inquantum Deus per suam gratiam se intellectui creato coniungit, ut intelligibile ab ipso.*

29. *ST* I, 12, 5: *ipsa essentia Dei fit forma intelligibilis intellectus.*

30. *ST* I, 12, 6: *qui plus habet de caritate, quia ubi est maior caritas, ibi est maius desiderium; et desiderium quodammodo facit desiderantem aptum et paratum ad susceptionem desiderati.*

31. It is interesting to note that when speaking negatively of not attaining comprehensive vision, Aquinas chooses the term *"pertingere."* As shall be seen, he reserves the term *"attingere"* for positive expressions of what the created intellect can attain of God without fully comprehending God.

32. *ST* I, 12, 7: *attingere vero mente Deum qualitercumque magna est beatitudo* (Augustine, *De Verb. Dom., Serm.* xxxviii).

33. *ST* I, 12, 7, ad 1: *quia et vident ipsum; et videndo, tenent sibi praesentem, in potestate habentes semper eum videre; et tenentes, fruuntur sicut ultimo fine desiderium implente.*

34. *ST* I, 12, 7 ad 2: *non propter hoc Deus incomprehensibilis dicitur, quasi aliquid eius sit quod non videatur: sed quia non ita perfecte videtur, sicut visibilis est.*

35. *ST* I, 12, 9: *sed contra: per unam speciem videtur speculum, et ea quae in speculo apparent. Sed omnia sic videntur in Deo sicut in quodam speculo intelligibili. Ergo, si ipse Deus non videtur per aliquam similitudinem, sed per suam essentiam; nec ea quae in ipso videntur, per aliquas similitudines sive species videntur.*

36. *ST* I, 12, 11: *quae habent formam in materia, vel quae per hujusmodi cognosci possunt.*

37. *ST* I, 12, 11: *[u]nde in somniis et alienationibus a sensibus corporis, magis divinae revelationes percipiuntur, et praevisiones futurorum.*

38. Already in this article Thomas confirms: *sicut Deus miraculose aliquid supernaturaliter in rebus corporeis operatur; ita etiam supernaturaliter et praeter communem ordinem mentes aliquorum in hac carne viventium, sed non sensibus carnis utentium, usque ad visionem suae essentiae elevavit* (*ST* I, 12, 11, *ad* 2).

39. See *ST* II-II, 174 on prophecy and II-II, 175 on rapture.

Notes to Chapter Four

1. For a detailed delineation of this insight in the *Summa contra gentiles*, see Thomas S. Hibbs, *Dialectic and Narrative in Aquinas: An Interpretation of the Summa Contra Gentiles.*

2. In particular, I will examine Lib. I, dist.iii, Q1., a1–4: *"de divina cognitione"*; Lib. III, dist.xxvii, Q3, a1: *"utrum Deus immediate per essentiam suam possit amari."*

3. In particular, I will examine Q1, a2: *"utrum mens humana possit ad Dei notitiam pervenire."*

4. In particular, I will examine Bk. I, ch. 1–9, various selections from Bk. III, and Bk. IV, ch. 1.

5. In particular, I will examine Bk. 3, Q1, a1–3.

6. It appears that Thomas returned to and improved upon the *Scriptum super libros Sententiarum* a decade later when teaching in Rome (Cf. Torrell, *Saint Thomas Aquinas*, 45–47). A list of the new titles of articles can be found in M. F. Johnson, "*Alia Lectura fratris thome*: A List of the New Texts found in Lincoln College, Oxford, MS. Lat.95," *RTAM* 57 (1990): 34–61. This revised commentary will be considered in its chronological order.

7. Torrell, *Saint Thomas Aquinas*, 39.

8. The *Sententiae*, written in the 1150's, became the chief textbook in schools of theology until the mid-sixteenth century. While other works from the twelfth century were superseded by the new Aristotelian science, by the 1240's, Lombard's book was a favored textbook for speculative theology at both Paris and Oxford. See Nancy Spatz, "Approaches and Attitudes to a New Theology Textbook: The *Sentences* of Peter Lombard," in *The Intellectual Climate of the Early University: Essays in Honor of Otto Gründler*, ed. Nancy Van Deusen (Kalamazoo: Western Michigan University, 1997), 27, 40.

9. Torrell, *Saint Thomas Aquinas*, 39.

10. Battista Mondin S.J., *St. Thomas Aquinas' Philosophy in the Commentary to the Sentences* (The Hague: Martinus Nijhoff, 1975), 3.

11. SSLS, I, 3, prooemium [217]: [i]*n parte ista ostendit Magister unitatem essentiae et Trinitatem personarum per rationes et similitudines quasdam...*

12. SSLS I, 3, 1, 1, co.: *sed utrum quocumque modo cognosci posit.*

13. SSLS I, 3, 1, 1, co.: *modus autem nullius creaturae attingit ad altitudinem divinae majestitatis.*

14. SSLS I, 3, 1, 1, s.c. 2: Psalm 78:48: *Surely, you did not create him in vain.*

15. SSLS I, 3, 1, 1, s.c. 3: *in hoc differt intelligibile a sensibili, quia sensibile excellens destruit sensum; intelligibile autem maximum non destruit, sed confortat intellectum.*

16. The objections speak consistently in terms of "*noster intellectus.*" The first line uses the term "*creatu intellectu*" but that line is generally not read as part of the first objection, but rather as a summary statement of the objections. Thomas here frames the question in terms of the created intellect, but is particularly interested in the human intellect—this distinction, however, is not one that he enters into yet. It is one that will be drawn explicitly in later works.

17. SSLS I, 3, 1, 1, ad 3: [u]*nde non dicimur cognoscere ea per abstractionem, sed per impressionem ipsorum in intelligentias nostras.*

18. SSLS I, 3, 1, 1, ad 5: *quod philosophus, loquitur de cognitione intellectus connaturali nobis secundum statum viae; et hoc modo Deus non cognoscitur a nobis nisi per phantasmata, non sui ipsius, sed causati sui per quod in ipsum devenimus.*

19. This crucial distinction between *comprehendere* and *attingere* will gain importance in Thomas' discussion of natural knowledge of God in his later works.

20. SSLS I, 3, 1, 1, s.c. 3.

21. Cf. Aristotle, *Posterior Analytics* II.1.89b30–89b35 [trans. Jonathan Barnes (Oxford: Clarendon Press, 1994)].

22. Thomas spends more time in article 2, which asks whether the knowledge of God just established is self-evident, on Anselm's objection than in later works. But his reasoning remains the same.

23. *SSLS* I, 3, 1, 2, *s.c.* 2: [*i*]*tem, quidquid est conclusio demonstrationis non est per se notum. Sed Deum esse demonstrator etiam a philosophis. Ergo Deum esse non est per se notum.* See our discussion of the *Summa contra gentiles*, Book I.

24. *SSLS* I, 3, 1, 2, *co.*: [*a*]*ut secundum suam similitudinem et participationem.*

25. *SSLS* I, 3, 1, 2, *co.*: *immo multi inveniuntur negasse Deum esse, sicut omnes philosophi qui non posuerunt causam agentem, ut Democritus et quidam alii.*

26. *SSLS* I, 3, 1, 3, *co.*: *cum creatura exemplariter procedat a Deo sicut a causa quodammodo simili secundum* analogiam, *eo scilicet quod quaelibet creatura eum imitatur secundum possibilitatem naturae suae, ex creaturis potest in Deum deveniri tribus illis modis quibus dictum est, scilicet per causalitatem, remotionem, eminentiam.*

27. *SSLS* I, 3, 1, 3, *co.*: [*s*]*ed convenit iste processus hominibus, secundum statum viae, bonis et malis.*

28. This insight will gain importance in the *In epistolam ad Romanos* because the will can lead natural knowledge to fall into error. This, in fact, happens to the philosophers in the commentary. The Romans commentary addresses the question whether the sins of the will completely obliterate the original capacity of the intellect.

29. *SSLS* I, 3, 1, 3, *arg.* 6: [*q*]*uod enim per se cognoscitur, non cognoscitur per aliquid aliud. Sed Deum cognoscunt Angeli per se, videntes ipsum in sua essentia. Ergo non cognoscunt ipsum per creaturas.*

30. *SSLS* I, 3, 1, 3, *ad* 8: *quod Ambrosius loquitur de visione Dei per essentiam, quae erit in patria, ad quam nullus malus poterit pervenire. Similiter etiam ad cognitionem fidei nullus venit nisi fidelis. Sed cognitio naturalis de Deo communis est bonis et malis, fidelibus et infidelibus.*

31. *SSLS* I, 3, 1, 3, *ad* 5: *quod creatura est effectus non proportionatus creatori; et ideo non ducit in perfectam cognitionem ipsius sed in imperfectam.*

32. As shown by Fr. George Klubertanz. S.J., Thomas' treatment of analogy is first introduced in the *De fallaciis* (1244–1245). Torrell shows that today the *De fallaciis* is considered too spurious to be attributed to Thomas (*St. Thomas Aquinas*, 11). The first text that can assuredly be attributed to Thomas in which he deals with analogy, then, is the *De ente et essentia* [before 1256]. For a list of texts that deal with analogy, see George P. Klubertanz, S.J., *St. Thomas Aquinas on Analogy: A Textual Analysis and Systematic Synthesis* (Chicago: Loyola University Press, 1960), Appendix I, 158–293.

33. *SSLS* I, 3, 1, 4, *co.*: [*t*]*amen personas, secundum appropriata eis, philosophi cognoscere potuerunt, cognoscentes potentiam, sapientiam, bonitatem.*

34. This is not to claim, of course, that this knowledge is in any way *foundational*. Knowledge received by faith is always and everywhere a sheer gift. This interpretation is not liable to the criticisms that Marshall lodges (whether rightly or wrongly) against many Thomists since the mid-nineteenth century, who "have seen a consummate natural theology as Aquinas' greatest achievement. He put belief in God's existence and nature on a firm rational foundation, whence it coud be defended against the assults of modern skepticism, and serve as a basis for the acceptance of revealed truths about God beyond reason's grasp" ("*Quod Scit Una Uetula*," 18).

35. "On the Heavens" I, 1 in *The Complete Works of Aristotle* I, ed. Jonathan Barnes (Princeton: Princeton University Press, 1984), 268a1–268b1: "For, as the Pythagoreans say, the universe and all that is in it is determined by the number three, since beginning and middle and end give the number of the universe, and the number they give is the triad. And so, having taken these three from nature as (so

to speak) laws of it, we make further use of the number three in the worship of the Gods."

36. *SSLS* I, 3, 1, 4, *ad* 1: *secundum expositionem Commentatoris, Aristoteles non intendit Trinitatem personarum in Deo ponere; sed propter hoc quod in omnibus creaturis apparet perfectio in ternario, sicut in principio, medio et fine, ideo antiqui honorabant Deum in sacrificiis et orationibus triplicatis.*

37. *SSLS* I, 3, 1, 4, *ad* 1: *Plato autem dicitur multa cognovisse de divinis, legens libros veteris legis, quos invenit in Aegypto. Vel forte intellectum paternum nominat intellectum divinum, secundum quod in se quodam modo concipit ideam mundi, quae est mundus archetypus.*

38. *SSLS* I, 3, 1, 4, *arg.* 3: *Richardus de s. Victore, dicit:* credo sine dubio quod ad quamcumque explanationem veritatis, quae necesse est esse, non modo probabilia, immo et necessaria argumenta non desunt. [*De trinitate I cap.* 4 PL196.892]. See Charles H. Lohr, *St. Thomas Aquinas Scriptum Super Sententiis: An Index of Authorities Cited* (Aldershot, U.K.: Avebury Publishing Co., 1980), 333.

39. *SSLS* I, 3, 1, 4, *ad.* 3: *quia prima principia per se nota non probantur. Si autem aliqua sunt in se nota quae nobis occulta sunt, illa probantur per notiora quo ad nos. Notiora autem quo ad nos sunt effectus principiorum.*

40. *SSLS* I, 3, 1, 4, *arg.* 4: *dicitur Rom. 1 in Glossa quod philosophi non pervenerunt ad notitiam personae tertiae, scilicet spiritus sancti, et idem habetur super Exod. 8, ubi dicitur, quod magi Pharaonis defecerunt in tertio signo. Ergo videtur ad minus quod ad notitiam duarum personarum venerunt.*

41. *SSLS* I, 3, 1, 4, *ad.* 4: *quod philosophi non pervenerunt in cognitionem duarum personarum quantum ad propria, sed solum quantum ad appropriata, non inquantum appropriata sunt, quia sic eorum cognitio dependeret ex propriis, sed inquantum sunt attributa divinae naturae. Et si objiciatur, quod similiter devenerunt in cognitionem bonitatis, quae appropriatur spiritui sancto, sicut in cognitionem potentiae et sapientiae, quae appropriantur patri et filio: dicendum, quod bonitatem non cognoverunt quantum ad potissimum effectum ipsius, incarnationem scilicet et redemptionem. Vel quia non tantum intenderunt venerationi bonitatis divinae, quam etiam non imitabantur, sicut venerati sunt potentiam et sapientiam.*

42. Cf. *ST*: I, 12, 12; I, 2, 1; and I, 32, 1.

43. The discussion of the theological virtues found in distinctions 23 through 32 is rooted in the reparation of Christ, specifically in the habits with which the grace of Christ informs the soul (*SSLS* III, 23, 1, *prol.*)

44. *SSLS* III, 27, 3, 1, *co.*: [*u*]*nde in statu viae, in qua accipit a phantasmatibus, non potest Deum immediate videre; sed oportet ut ex visibilibus, quorum phantasmata capit, in ejus cognitionem deveniat.*

45. *SSLS* III, 27, 3, 1, *co.*: [*q*]*uamvis autem ipsam essentiam non videat immediate, tamen cognitio intellectus ad ipsum Deum terminatur, quia ipsum esse ex effectibus apprehendit; unde cum ad intellectum affectus sequatur, ubi terminatur operatio intellectus, ibi incipit operatio affectus, sive voluntatis.*

46. See Douglas C. Hall, *The Trinity: An Analysis of St. Thomas Aquinas' Expositio of the De Trinitate of Boethius* (Leiden: E.J. Brill, 1992), 39–41.

47. Ralph McInerny, *Boethius and Aquinas* (Washington, D.C.: Catholic University of America Press, 1990), 106.

48. The *Expositio* ends after only the "Prologue" and Sections I and II of Boethius' work have been analyzed.

49. Hall, *The Trinity*, 41.

50. McInerny, *Boethius and Aquinas*, 106–107.
51. McInerny, *Boethius and Aquinas*, 1.
52. Cf. I.T. Eschmann, O.P., "A Catalogue of St. Thomas's Works," in Etienne Gilson, *The Christian Philosophy of St. Thomas Aquinas* (Notre Dame: University of Notre Dame Press, 1994), 405–406.
53. Hall, *The Trinity*, 46.
54. Thomas Aquinas, *Faith Reason, and Theology: Questions I–IV of his Commentary on the* De Trinitate *of Boethius*, trans. Armand Maurer (Toronto: Pontifical Institute of Mediaeval Studies, 1987), 3. For the Latin edition, *Expositio super librum Boethii de Trinitate*, ed. Bruno Decker (Leiden: E.J. Brill, 1955, repr. with corrections, 1959, 1965). *Expositio, pr.* 1: *[a]b initio nativitatis investigabo et ponam in lucem scientiam illius.*
55. *Expositio, pr.* 1: *[s]icut ergo naturalis cognitionis principium est creaturae notitia a sensu accepta, ita cognitionis desuper datae principium est primae veritatis notitia per fidem infusa. Et hinc est quod diverso ordine hinc inde proceditur. Philosophi enim, qui naturalis cognitionis ordinem sequuntur, praeordinant scientiam de creaturis scientiae divinae, scilicet naturalem metaphysicae. Sed apud theologos proceditur e converso, ut creatoris consideratio considerationem praeveniat creaturae.*
56. *Expositio, pr.* 2.
57. *Expositio, pr.* 1: *[n]aturalis mentis humanae intuitus pondere corruptibilis corporis aggravatus in primae veritatis luce, ex qua omnia sunt facile cognoscibilia, defigi non potest.*
58. *Expositio, pr.* 1: *[c]reaturae enim, per quas naturaliter cognoscitur Deus, in infinitum ab ipso distant. Sed quia in his, quae procul videntur, facile visus decipitur, idcirco ex creaturis in Deum cognoscendum tendentes in errores multiplices inciderunt.*
59. *Expositio, pr.* 6: *[f]inis vero huius operis est, ut occulta fidei manifestentur, quantum in via possibile est…*
60. *Expositio I, pr.* 3: *[q]uaestio namque quamdiu probabilibus rationibus sub dubio exagitatur, quasi informis est, nondum ad certitudinem veritatis pertingens, et ideo formata dicitur esse, quando ad eam ratio additur, per quam certitudo de veritate habetur.*
61. *Expositio I, pr.* 3: *[e]t in hoc providit intelligentiae, quia quod credimus, debemus auctoriati, quod intelligimus, rationi, ut Augustinus dicit.*
62. *Expositio I, pr.* 6: *non debet requiri ab eo in hoc opere plus certitudinis quam quantum humana ratio valet ad alta divinitatis conscendere.*
63. *Expositio I, pr.* 6: *quod in absolutis divinae personae conveniunt et in relativis distinguuntur.*
64. The pattern here of discussing the subject itself and then reflecting upon the epistemological foundations of such a subject will be followed in the first thirteen questions of the *Summa theologiae*.
65. Note how this question will be echoed in *ST* I, 1, 1.
66. *Expositio,* I, 1, 1, *arg.* 4: *illi actus in nobis esse dicuntur, ad quos exercendos principia sufficientia in nobis habemus. Sed in nobis non est cognoscere veritatem, cum quandoque multi laborent ad veritatem cognoscendam, qui eam cognoscere nequeunt. Ergo non habemus sufficientia principia in nobis ad veritatem cognoscendam. Ergo oportet ad hoc, quod eam cognoscamus, ab exteriori nos iuvari, et sic idem quod prius.*

67. *Expositio*, I, 1, 1, arg. 2: *facilius est ab alio veritatem addiscere quam per se ipsum eam inspicere. Unde qui per se ipsos sciunt praeferuntur illis, qui ab aliis addiscere possunt, in I Ethicorum. Sed homo non potest ab aliis addiscere, nisi mens eius interius doceatur a Deo, ut dicit Augustinus in libro de magistro et Gregorius in homilia Pentecostes. Ergo nec per se ipsum potest aliquis veritatem inspicere, nisi de novo mens eius illustretur a Deo.*

68. *Expositio*, I, 1, 1, arg. 7: *sicut se habet voluntas ad bene volendum, ita se habet intellectus ad recte intelligendum. Sed voluntas non potest bene velle, nisi divina gratia adiuvetur, ut Augustinus dicit. Ergo nec intellectus potest veritatem intelligere, nisi divina luce illustretur.*

69. *Expositio*, I, 1, 1, arg. 6: *in omnibus causis ordinatis per se et non secundum accidens effectus non procedit a causa secunda nisi per operationem causae primae, ut patet in libro de causis. Sed mens humana ordinatur sub luce increata ordine essentiali et non accidentali. Ergo operatio mentis quae est eius effectus proprius, scilicet cognitio veritatis, non potest provenire ex ea nisi operante prima luce increata. Eius autem operatio non videtur alia esse nisi illustratio. Et sic idem quod prius.*

70. *Expositio*, I, 1, 1, s.c. 1: *[s]i ergo hoc lumen, quia creatum est, non sufficit ad veritatem conspiciendam, sed requirit novam illustrationem, pari ratione lumen superadditum non sufficiet, sed indigebit alio lumine, et sic in infinitum, quod numquam compleri potest, et sic impossibile erit cognoscere aliquam veritatem. Ergo oportet stare in primo lumine, ut scilicet mens lumine naturali sine aliquo superaddito possit veritatem videre.*

71. *Expositio*, I, 1, 1, co. 1 and 2: *[s]ed in genere intellectus invenitur duplex potentia: activa, scilicet intellectus agens, et passiva, scilicet intellectus possibilis... ideo in anima ponitur respectu intelligibilis operationis, quae est cognitio veritatis, et potentia passiva et potentia activa. Unde sicut aliae potentiae activae naturales suis passivis coniunctae sufficiunt ad naturales operationes, ita etiam anima habens in se potentiam activam et passivam sufficit ad perceptionem veritatis.*

72. *Expositio*, I, 1, 1, co. 3: *[c]um autem quaelibet virtus activa creata finita sit, est eius sufficientia ad determinatos effectus limitata.*

73. *Expositio*, I, 1, 1, co. 3: *sicut principia quae naturaliter homo cognoscit et ea quae ab his deducuntur.* Translation altered.

74. *Expositio*, I, 1, 1, co. 3: *sicut sunt ea quae sunt fidei, facultatem rationis excedentia, et futura contingentia et alia huiusmodi...*

75. *Expositio*, I, 1, 1, co. 4: *[s]ic ergo in omni cognitione veritatis indiget mens humana divina operatione, sed in naturalibus cognoscendis non indiget nova luce, sed solo motu et directione eius, in aliis autem etiam nova illustratione.*

76. *Expositio* I, 1, 1, ad 3: *oculus corporalis ex illustratione solis materialis non consequitur lumen aliquod sibi connaturale, per quod possit facere visibilia in actu, sicut consequitur mens nostra ex illustratione solis increati.*

77. *Expositio*, I, 1, 1, co. 4: *[p]raeter operationem enim qua deus rerum instituit naturas, singulis formas et virtutes proprias tribuens, quibus possent suas operationes exercere, operatur etiam in rebus opera providentiae omnium rerum virtutes ad actus propriors dirigendo et movendo.* Cf. *ST* I, 105, 5.

78. *Expositio*, I, 1, 1, co. 4: *[i]ta enim universa creatura divinae gubernationi subicitur, sicut instrumenta subduntur gubernationi artificis et qualitates naturales virtutibus animae nutritivae, ut dicitur in* II *de anima.*

79. *Expositio*, I, 1, 1, ad 2: *deus nos interius docet in naturalibus cognitis, quod lumen naturale in nobis causat et ipsum dirigit in veritatem...*

80. *Expositio*, I, 1, 1, ad 7: *similiter intellectus non potest sine divino motu veritatem quamcumque cognoscere, potest autem sine novi luminis infusione, quamvis non ea quae naturalem cognitionem excedunt.*

81. *Expositio*, I, 1, 1, ad 8: *perceptio veritatis praecipue sibi debet ascribi, sicut operatio artis magis attribuitur artifici quam serrae.* In his later work (ST I, 105, 5) Thomas establishes that God not only acts as the primary cause and final end of every human operation, but God also gives created beings their forms and preserves them in being.

82. *Expositio* I, 1, 2, arg. 1: [s]*ed in perfectissimo gradu nostrae cognitionis Deo non coniungimur nisi quasi ignoto, ut dicit Dionysius 1 c. mysticae theologiae.*

83. Romans 1:20; Jeremiah 9:24.

84. See St. Augustine, *De Trinitate* 8, 4, 6 and 13, 20, 26. in *Corpus Christianorum, series latina. Continuatio mediaevalis* (Turnhout: Brepols, 1951).

85. *Expositio*, I, 1, 2 co. 1: [q]*uia igitur intellectus noster secundum statum viae habet determinatam habitudinem ad formas, quae a sensu abstrahuntur, cum comparetur ad phantasmata sicut visus ad colores, ut dicitur in III de anima, non potest ipsum Deum cognoscere in hoc statu per formam quae est essentia sua, sed sic cognoscetur in patria a beatis.*

86. *Expositio*, I, 1, 2 co. 2: [n]*ec etiam in statu huius viae cognoscitur Deus a nobis per formas pure intelligibiles, quae sint aliqua similitudo ipsius propter connaturalitatem intellectus nostri ad phantasmata, ut dictum est.*

87. *Expositio*, I, 1, 2, co. 2: [e]*t tamen unus cognoscentium quia est alio perfectius cognoscit, quia causa tanto ex effectu perfectius cognoscitur, quanto per effectum magis apprehenditur habitudo causae ad effectum.*

88. *Expositio*, I, 1, 2, co. 3: [u]*nde dicit Dionysius in libro* de divinis nominibus *quod cognoscitur ex omnium causa et excessu et ablatione.*

89. *Expositio*, I, 1, 2, co. 4: *... per quod mens in contemplatione supra se elevari dicitur, in quantum cognoscit deum esse supra omne id, quod naturaliter comprehendit. Sed quia ad eius essentiam videndam penetrare non sufficit, dicitur in se ipsam quodammodo ab excellenti lumine reflecti.* Translation altered.

90. *Expositio*, I, 1, 2, ad 3: *...ut recipiat influentiam ipsius secundum totam virtutem eius, neque ut ipsum perfecte cognoscat, sicut ipse se ipsum perfecte cognoscit.*

91. *Expositio*, I, 1, 2, ad 4: *...intelligibile videtur magis dici per remotionem quam per positionem. Ex hoc enim est unumquodque intelligibile quod est a materia immune vel separatum. Negationes autem in divinis verificantur, quamvis affirmationes sint incompactae...*

92. *Faith, Reason and Theology*, 26, note 10 and 11. This work cites the following sources for the objections. On the unknown origins of the first position see M. Grabmann, *Die Theologische Erkenntnis- und Einleitungslehre des hl.Thomas von Aquin auf Grund Seiner Schrift "In Boethium de Trinitate," im Zusammenhang der Scholastik des 13. und beginnenden 14. Jarhunderts dargestellt* (Freiburg in Schweiz: Paulusverlag, 1948), 76–80; L. Elders, *Faith and Science: An Introduction to St. Thomas' Expositio in Boethii De Trinitate* (Rome: Herder, 1974), 36. On the second position, see William of Auvergne, *De anima* 7.6 (Orleans-Paris. 1674. Repr. Frankfurt: Minerva, 1963), 211–212; Bonaventure, *Sententiae commentaria in IV libros sententiarum* I, d.3, pt.1, a1; Q1, 2; and 2 d.3, pt.2, a2, Q2, ad 4, ed Quaracchi 1:68 snf 2:123. See J. F. Quinn, *The Historical Constitution of St. Bonaventure's Philosophy* (Toronto: Pontifical Institute of Medieval Studies, 1973), 430–435.

93. *Expositio*, I, 1, 3, *ad* 4: [c]*ognoscitur tamen a principio et intenditur in quadam generalitate, prout mens appetit se bene esse et bene vivere, quod tunc solum est ei, cum Deum habet.*

94. *Expositio*, I, 1, 3, *ad* 6: [s]*ed tamen eius cognitio nobis innata esse dicitur, in quantum per principia nobis innata de facili percipere possumus Deum esse.*

95. *ST* I, 1, 8, *ad* 2: [n]*ec hoc derogat dignitati huius doctrinae, nam licet locus ab auctoritate quae fundatur super ratione humana, sit infirmissimus; locus tamen ab auctoritate quae fundatur super revelatione divina, est efficacissimus.*

96. *Expositio*, I, 1, 4, *co*.: *et nullo modo potest demonstrative probari, quamvis ad hoc aliquales rationes non necessariae nec multum probabiles nisi credenti haberi possint.* Note that Thomas specifically *does not* make this claim when treating arguments for the existence of God. That he makes it here rather than there is significant, for many today argue as if this were Thomas' position on natural knowledge of God.

97. Torrell, *Saint Thomas Aquinas*, 101–102.

98. *SCG* I, 3, 2: [q]*uaedam vero sunt ad quae etiam ratio naturalis pertingere potest, sicut est Deum esse, Deum esse unum, et alia huiusmodi; quae etiam philosophi demonstrative de Deo probaverunt, ducti naturalis lumine rationis.*

99. *SCG* I, 3, 3: [s]*unt igitur quaedam intelligibilium divinorum quae humanae rationi sunt pervia; quaedam vero quae omnino vim humanae rationis excedunt.*

100. See Aristotle, *Posterior Analytics*, II, 3, 9. See also Thomas Aquinas, *Expositio Posteriorum*, lib. 2, lect. 2 n. 5.

101. *SCG* I, 3, 4: *oportet quod secundum modum quo substantia rei intelligitur, sit modus eorum quae de re illa cognoscuntur.*

102. *SCG* I, 3, 3: [d]*ucitur tamen ex sensibilibus intellectus noster in divinam cognitionem ut cognoscat de Deo quia est, et alia huiusmodi quae oportet attribui primo principio.*

103. *SCG* I, 3, 4: [s]*unt igitur quaedam intelligibilium divinorum quae humanae rationi sunt pervia; quaedam vero quae omnino vim humanae rationis excedunt.*

104. *SCG* I, 3, 6: [m]*ulto igitur amplius illius excellentissimae substantiae omnia intelligibilia humana ratio investigare non sufficit.*

105. *SCG* I, 4, 1: [d]*uplici igitur veritate divinorum intelligibilium existente, una ad quam rationis inquisitio pertingere potest, altera quae omne ingenium humanae rationis excedit, utraque convenienter divinitus homini credenda proponitur.*

106. *SCG* I, 4, 3.

107. *SCG* I, 4, 3: [q]*uem quidem laborem pauci subire volunt pro amore scientiae, cuius tamen mentibus hominum naturalem Deus inseruit appetitum.*

108. *SCG* I, 4, 4: [s]*ecundum inconveniens est quod illi qui ad praedictae veritatis inventionem pervenient, vix post longum tempus pertingerent.*

109. *SCG* I, 4, 4: [r]*emaneret igitur humanum genus, si sola rationis via ad Deum cognoscendum pateret, in maximis ignorantiae tenebris...*

110. *SCG* I, 4, 5.

111. *SCG* I, 4, 6: *ut sic omnes de facili possent divinae cognitionis participes esse et absque dubitatione et errore.*

112. *SCG* I, 8, 1: *res quidem sensibiles, ex quibus humana ratio cognitionis principium sumit, aliquale vestigium in se divinae imitationis retinent, ita tamen imperfectum quod ad declarandam ipsius Dei substantiam omnino insufficiens invenitur.*

113. *SCG* I, 8: *ita se habet quod ad eam potest aliquas verisimilitudines colligere, quae tamen non sufficiunt ad hoc quod praedicta veritas quasi demonstrative vel per se intellecta comprehendatur.*

114. *SCG* I, 8, 2: *quia de rebus altissimis etiam parva et debili consideratione aliquid posse inspicere iucundissimum est...*

115. Hibbs, *Dialectic and Narrative in Aquinas*, 35.

116. I do not mean to suggest here that the first three books constitute for Thomas an autonomous philosophy, while theology is only introduced in Book IV. Here, I agree with Thomas Hibbs against Norman Kretzmann. See Hibbs, *Dialectic and Narrative*, 63–64, 124; Norman Kretzmann, *The Metaphysics of Creation: Aquinas's Natural Theology in Summa Contra Gentiles 2* (Oxford: Oxford University Press, 1999).

117. *SCG* I, 9, 3: *[s]ingularis vero modus convincendi adversarium contra huiusmodi veritatem est ex auctoritate Scripturae divinitus confirmata miraculis: quae enim supra rationem humanam sunt, non credimus nisi Deo revelante.*

118. In the early chapters here in Book III, for example, Thomas defines a human being by the very good that she is oriented towards. See *SCG* III, 3.

119. While the question of audience in the *Summa contra gentiles* is a controverted one, it is clear that even if it was not intended for missionary purposes, the question of the role of natural reason in knowledge of God is central to this work. On the issue of audience see Hibbs, *Dialectic and Narrative*, 9–14, and Hibbs, *Aquinas, Ethics and the Philosophy of Religion: Metaphysics and Practice* (Bloomington: Indiana University Press, 2007), 100–106.

120. *SCG* III, 19, 1: *[s]i igitur res omnes in Deum sicut in ultimum finem tendunt ut ipsius bonitatem consequantur, sequitur quod ultimus rerum finis sit Deo assimilari.* Thomas presents four other parallel arguments in this chapter to prove that all things tend to become like God.

121. *SCG* III, 25, 1: *[c]um autem omnes creaturae, etiam intellectu carentes, ordinentur in Deum sicut in finem ultimum: ad hunc autem finem pertingunt omnia inquantum de similitudines eius aliquid participant.*

122. *SCG* III, 25, 1: *intellectuales creaturae aliquo speciaiori modo ad ipsum pertingunt, scilicet per propriam operationem intelligendo ipsum.*

123. *SCG* III, 25, 4: *habet enim se ad cognoscendum illud quod est maximum intelligibile sicut oculus noctuae ad solem.*

124. *SCG* III, 25, 6: *intellectus igitur quantumcumque modicum possit de divina cognitione percipere, illud erit sibi pro ultimo fine, magis quam perfecta cognitio inferiorum inteligibilium.*

125. *SCG* III, 25, 7: *quamvis modicum quidem de illis percipere possit.*

126. *SCG* III, 25, 8: *[i]n genere autem huius similitudinis magis assimilatur Deo secundum quod intelligit actu, quam secundum quod intelligit in habitu vel potentia: quia Deus semper actu intelligens est... et in hoc quod intelligit actu, maxime assimilatur Deo secundum quod intelligit ipsum Deum: nam ipse Deus intelligendo se intelligit omnia alia...,* cf. *SCG* I, ch. 56 and ch. 49.

127. *SCG* III, 25, 10: *[f]inis igitur intellectus est finis omnium actionum humanarum.*

128. *SCG* III, 25, 11: *[n]aturaliter inest omnibus hominibus desiderium cognoscendi causas eorum quae videntur: unde propter admirationem eorum quae videbantur, quorum causae latebant, homines primo philosophari coeperunt, invenientes autem causam quiescebant. Nec sistit inquisitio quousque perveniatur ad*

primam causam: et tunc perfecte nos scire arbitramur quando primam causam cognoscimus. Desiderat igitur homo naturaliter cognoscere primam causam quasi ultimum finem. Prima autem omnium causa Deus est. Est igitur ultimus finis hominis cognoscere Deum.

129. *SCG* III, 37, 1: *ultima hominis felicitas sit in contemplatione veritatis.*

130. *SCG* III, 37, 8: [r]*elinquitur ititur quod in contemplatione sapientiae ultima hominis felicitas consistat.*

131. Hibbs, *Dialectic and Narrative*, 105.

132. *SCG* III, 38, 1: *quia naturali ratione statim homo in aliqualem Dei cognitionem pervenire potest.*

133. *SCG* III, 38, 1: [q]*uis autem, vel qualis, vel si unus tantum est ordinator naturae, nondum statim ex hac communi consideratione habetur...*

134. Some have found, for example, that heavenly bodies are the orderers, others that natural operations are the cause of order, and yet others that human beings cause order in the universe. See *SCG* III, 38, 1: [q]*uidam enim rerum mundanarum non alium ordinatorem esse crediderunt quam corpora caelestia: unde corpora caelestia deos esse dixerunt. Quidam vero ulterius ipsa elementa et quae ex eis generantur: quasi aestimantes motus et operationes naturales quas habent, non ab alio ordinatore eis inesse, sed ab eis alia ordinari. Quidam vero, humanos actus non alicuius ordinationi subesse credentes nisi humanae, homines qui alios ordinant, deos esse dixerunt.*

135. *SCG* III, 39, 1: [o]*stendit enim demonstratio Deum esse immobilem, aeternum, incorporeum, omnino simplicem, unum, et alia huiusmodi...*

136. *SCG* III, 39, 2–4. Cf. *ST* I, 1, 1.

137. *SCG* III, 40, 3: *intellectus enim assentit per fidem his quae sibi proponuntur, quia vult, non autem ex ipsa veritatis evidentia necessario tractus.*

138. *SCG* III, 40, 4: [e]*st igitur aliqua hominis cognitio de Deo altior cognitione fidei: sive ipse homo proponens fidem immediate videat veritatem, sicut Christo credimus; sive a vidente immediate accipiat, sicut credimus apostolis et prophetis.*

139. *SCG* III, 40, 6: *quia fides de absentibus est, non de praesentibus.*

140. As quoted in *SCG* III, 40, 6.

141. *SCG*, III, 52, 3: [v]*idere autem substantiam Dei impossibile est nisi ipsa divina essentia sit forma intellectus qua intelligit, ut probatum est.*

142. *SCG*, III, 52, 6: [q]*uiquid excedit limites alicuius naturae, non potest sibi advenire nisi per actionem alterius: sicut aqua non tendit sursum nisi ab aliquo alio mota.*

143. *SCG* III, 54, 8: [q]*uae quidem positio et veram creaturae rationalis beatitudinem tollit, quae non potest esse nisi in visione divinae substantiae... et auctoritati Sacrae Scripturae contradicit...*

144. *SCG* III, 54, 8: [u]*nde tanquam falsa et haeretica abiicienda est.*

145. *SCG* III, 54, 9: [d]*ivina enim substantia non sic est extra facultatem creati intellectus quasi aliquid omnino extraneum ab ipso, sicut est sonus a visu, vel substantia immaterialis a sensu...*

146. *SCG* III, 55, 3: [v]*irtus finita non potest adaequare in sua operatione obiectum infinitum.*

147. *SCG* III, 58, 4: *quaedam enim sunt maioris virtutis, et quaedam minoris; virtus autem est via ad felicitatem.*

148. *SCG* IV, 1, 3: *quia omnes rerum perfectiones quodam ordine a summon rerum vertice Deo descendunt, ipse, ab inferioribus incipiens et gradatim ascendens, in Dei cognitionem proficiat.*

149. *SCG* IV, 1, 3: *nam et in corporalibus motibus eadem est via qua descenditur et ascenditur, ratione principii et finis distincta.*

150. *SCG* IV, 1, 6: *etsi per quosdam deficientes effectus percipiantur.*

151. *SCG* IV, 1, 6: *[s]i igitur ipsae viae imperfecte cognoscuntur a nobis, quomodo per eas ad perfecte cognoscendum ipsarum viarum principium poterimus pervenire? Quod quia sine proportione excedit cognosceremus perfecte, nondum tamen perfecta principii cognitio nobis adesset.*

Notes to Chapter Five

1. I am deeply indebted to John F. Boyle for sharing these articles with me before they were published. They have now been published: Thomas Aquinas, *Lectura Romana in primum Sententiarum Petri Lombardi*, ed. Leonard E. Boyle, O.P., and John F. Boyle (Toronto: Pontifical Institute of Mediaeval Studies, 2006).

2. Mark F. Johnson "*Alia lectura fratris thome*: A List of the New Texts of St. Thomas Aquinas found in Lincoln College, Oxford, MS. Lat.95," *Recherches de Théologie Ancienne et Médiévale* 57 (1990): 34–61. Johnson draws largely from the work of Leonard E. Boyle, O.P. to make this argument, and shows that nothing has appeared in Thomistic literature to argue against Boyle's conclusion.

3. *SSLS* Revised Text, 3, 1, 1, s.c.: *[i]llud quod est per se notum non est demonstrabile. Sed philosophi demonstraverunt Deum esse.*

4. *SSLS* Revised Text, 3, 1, 1: *[c]ontingit autem aliquando quod aliquid est per se notum quantum in se, quod non est notum quoad nos, quia nescimus subiectum seu definitionem eius.*

5. *SSLS* Revised Text, 3, 1, 1: *[d]ico ergo quod haec propositio "Deus est" est per se nota quantum in se cum praedicatum sit idem cum subiecto; sed quia nos nescimus quid est Deus, ideo nobis non est per se nota.*

6. *SSLS* Revised Text, 3, 1, 1, ad 1: *quod [canc quod. et quia add. sup. lin.]Deum esse est naturaliter notum omnibus non ut principium sed ut finis, quia desiderium et cognitio nostra ordinatur in Deum ut in finem. Homo enim naturaliter vult scire causam, et inde venit admiratio; non ergo stat desiderium hominis quousque veniat ad causam primam.*

7. *SSLS* Revised Text, 3, 1, 1, ad 3: *[n]on enim cognoscunt <omnes> intellectum possibilem quo cognoscimus omnia effective; et ideo non oportet quod omnes cognoscant principium effectivum cognitionis omnium quod est Deus.*

8. *SSLS* Revised Text, 3, 1, 1, ad 4: *quantum de se est, ista propositio "Deus est" est per se nota; sed nescimus subiectum, propter hoc non est per se nota nobis.*

9. This objection can be found in the modern voice of Karl Barth. We will see how Thomas anticipates and treats this Barthian objection.

10. *SSLS* Revised Text 3, 1, 2: *[s]ed quia non potuit esse talis effectus, cum creatura nullo modo possit aequari creatori, ideo per effectus huiusmodi improportionatos non possumus pervenire in cognitionem perfectam primae et altissimae causae. Scimus tamen per huiusmodi effectos nihilominus quod Deus qui est prima causa, est aliquid supra ipsos.*

11. *SSLS* Revised Text 3, 1, 2, ad 1: *non solum ducimur in cognitionem Dei per similitudinem creaturarum ad Deum, sed etiam per quandam dependentiam.*

Nihilominus tamen est aliqualis imitatio, secundum quod possibile est, creaturae ad Deum.

12. SSLS Revised Text 3, 1, 2, ad 2: [*i*]*ntelligimus enim Deum sive cognoscimus vel per negationem vel per eminentiam vel per causalitatem, et semper intellectus noster format sibi phantasma.*

13. SSLS Revised Text 3, 1, 2, ad 3: [*s*]*ed Deus est causa rerum quantum ad fieri et etiam quantum ad esse, et ideo secundum esse dependent ab eo et secundum fieri; et propter hoc ducunt in cognitionem ipsius licet imperfectam.*

14. Augustine, *Confessiones*, VII.ix [13–14] (PL 32.740–41; CCSL 27.101).

15. Augustine, *De civitate Dei*, X.23 (PL 41.300; CCSL 47.296-97).

16. Aristotle, *De caelo et mundo*, I.1 (268a14).

17. Hermes Trismegistus, *Liber viginti quatuor philosophorum*, prop. 1 [ed. C. Baeumker in Abhandlungen aus dem Gebiete der Philosophie und ihrer Geschichte (Freiburg in Breisgau: Herder, 1913), 31].

18. SSLS Revised Text 3, 1, 3, arg. 5: [*p*]*er effectus ducimur in cognitionem causae. Sed tres personae in divinis sunt una causa. Ergo per effectus sive per res creatas possumus devenire in cognitionem Trinitatis.*

19. SSLS Revised Text 3, 1, 3: [*e*]*t ratio huius est quia nos non ducimur in cognitionem Dei ex creaturis, nisi quatenus ipse est causa creaturarum. Omnia autem illa quae pertinent ad causalitatem in divinis sunt essentialia, et ideo per eas nullus potuit pervenire in cognitionem Trinitatis personarum nisi per revelationem vel auditum.*

20. ST I, 3, 7: *quia omne compositum causam habet, quae enim secundum se diversa sunt, non conveniunt in aliquod unum nisi per aliquam causam adunantem ipsa. Deus autem non habet causam, ut supra ostensum est, cum sit prima causa efficiens.*

21. Book V, 154–155.

22. 431a15–431a19 [Aristotle, *On the Soul*, trans. R. D. Hicks (New York: Prometheus Books, 1991)].

23. *De Trinitate* I, 4:*et a se propterea cerni comprehendique non posse quia mentis humanae acies inualida in tam excellenti luce non figitur nisi "per iustitiam fidei" nutrita uegetetur.*

24. ST I, 12, 12: *naturalis nostra cognitio a sensu principium sumit, unde tantum se nostra naturalis cognitio extendere potest, inquantum manuduci potest per sensibilia. Ex sensibilibus autem non potest usque ad hoc intellectus noster pertingere, quod divinam essentiam videat, quia creaturae sensibiles sunt effectus Dei virtutem causae non adaequantes. Unde ex sensibilium cognitione non potest tota Dei virtus cognosci, et per consequens nec eius essentia videri.*

25. ST I, 12, 12: [*u*]*nde cognoscimus de ipso habitudinem ipsius ad creaturas, quod scilicet omnium est causa, et differentiam creaturarum ab ipso, quod scilicet ipse non est aliquid eorum quae ab eo causantur; et quod haec non removentur ab eo propter eius defectum, sed quia superexcedit.*

26. ST I, 12, 12, ad 1: *ratio ad formam simplicem pertingere non potest, ut sciat de ea quid est, potest tamen de ea cognoscere, ut sciat an est.*

27. ST I, 12, 12, ad 2: [*d*]*eus naturali cognitione cognoscitur per phantasmata effectus sui.*

28. *Retractationum* I, 4.

29. Dionysius, *De Mystica Theologiae*, i.

30. Dionysius, *De Coelesti Hierarchia*, i.

31. Gregory, Homily xxvi in Ev. [*Reading the Gospels with Gregory the Great: Homilies on the Gospels, 21–26*, trans. Santha Bhattacharji (Petersham, Mass.: St. Bede's Publications, 2001)].

32. ST I, 12, 13: *per gratiam perfectior cognitio de Deo habetur a nobis, quam per rationem naturalem.*

33. ST I, 12, 13: *nam et lumen naturale intellectus confortatur per infusionem luminis gratuiti...*

34. ST I, 2, 13, ad 1: *et sic ei quasi ignoto coniungamur.*

35. ST I, 12, 13, ad 1: *licet per revelationem gratiae in hac vita non cognoscamus de Deo* quid est, *et sic ei quasi ignoto conjugamur...*

36. ST I, 12, 13, ad 1: *tamen plenius ipsum cognoscimus, inquantum plures et excellentiores effectus eius nobis demonstrantur; et inquantum ei aliqua attribuimus ex revelatione divina, ad quae ratio naturalis non pertingit, ut Deum esse trinum et unum.*

37. ST I, 12, 13, ad 2: *[e]t sic per revelationem ex phantasmatibus plenior cognitio accipitur, ex infusione divini luminis.*

38. ST I, 12, 13, ad 3: *fides cognitio quaedam est, inquantum intellectus determinatur per fidem ad aliquod cognoscibile.*

39. ST I, 12, 13, ad 3: *[s]ed haec determinatio ad unum non procedit ex visione credentis, sed a visione eius cui creditur. Et sic, inquantum deest visio, deficit a ratione cognitionis quae est in scientia, nam scientia determinat intellectum ad unum per visionem et intellectum primorum principiorum.*

40. ST 1, 13, prol.: *[u]numquodque enim nominatur a nobis, secundum quod ipsum cogniscimus.*

41. Cf. Mark D. Jordan, *Ordering Wisdom: The Hierarchy of Philosophical Discourses in Aquinas* (Notre Dame: Notre Dame Press, 1986), section 5.3, note 2.

42. ST I, 13, 1: *secundum philosophum, voces sunt signa intellectuum, et intellectus sunt rerum similitudines. Et sic patet quod voces referuntur ad res significandas, mediante conceptione intellectus. Secundum igitur quod aliquid a nobis intellectu cognosci potest, sic a nobis potest nominari.*

43. ST I, 13, 1: *sed cognoscitur a nobis ex creaturis, secundum habitudinem principii, et per modum excellentiae et remotionis.*

44. ST I, 13, 2: *de nominibus quae de Deo dicuntur negative, vel quae relationem ipsius ad creaturam significant, manifestum est quod substantiam eius nullo modo significant; sed remotionem alicuius ab ipso, vel relationem eius ad alium, vel potius alicuius ad ipsum.*

45. ST I, 13, 2: *quod huiusmodi quidem nomina significant substantiam divinam, et praedicantur de Deo substantialiter, sed deficiunt a repraesentatione ipsius. Quod sic patet. Significant enim sic nomina Deum, secundum quod intellectus noster cognoscit ipsum. Intellectus autem noster, cum cognoscat Deum ex creaturis, sic cognoscit ipsum, secundum quod creaturae ipsum repraesentant. Ostensum est autem supra quod Deus in se praehabet omnes perfectiones creaturarum, quasi simpliciter et universaliter perfectus. Unde quaelibet creatura intantum eum repraesentat, et est ei similis, inquantum perfectionem aliquam habet, non tamen ita quod repraesentet eum sicut aliquid eiusdem speciei vel generis, sed sicut excellens principium, a cuius forma effectus deficiunt, cuius tamen aliqualem similitudinem effectus consequuntur; sicut formae corporum inferiorum repraesentant virtutem solarem..... Sic igitur praedicta nomina divinam substantiam significant, imperfecte tamen, sicut et creaturae imperfecte eam repraesentant.*

46. *Doctor Perplexorum*, part.I, c.58 (Basileae: Sumptibus & impensis Ludovici König, excudebat J. J. Genath, 1629).

47. *ST* I, 13, 2: [q]uidam enim dixerunt quod haec omnia nomina, licet affirmative de Deo dicantur, tamen magis inventa sunt ad aliquid removendum a Deo, quam ad aliquid ponendum in ipso.

48. Thomas provides an example here: God is assuredly the cause of bodies in the same way as God is the cause of good things. If the words "God is good," meant no more than, "God is the cause of good things," it might be said similarly that God is a body, insofar as God is the cause of bodies. To say that God is a body implies that God is not a mere potentiality, as is primary matter [*ST* I, 13, 2].

49. Here, too, Thomas provides an example: healthy is secondarily said of medicine, since it means only the cause of the health in the animal, which primarily is called healthy [*ST* I, 13, 2].

50. *ST* I, 13, 2: [p]rimo quidem, quia secundum neutram harum positionum posset assignari ratio quare quaedam nomina magis de Deo dicerentur quam alia. Sic enim est causa corporum, sicut est causa bonorum, unde, si nihil aliud significatur, cum dicitur Deus est bonus, nisi Deus est causa bonorum, poterit similiter dici quod Deus est corpus, quia est causa corporum. Item, per hoc quod dicitur quod est corpus, removetur quod non sit ens in potentia tantum, sicut materia prima. Secundo, quia sequeretur quod omnia nomina dicta de Deo, per posterius dicerentur de ipso, sicut sanum per posterius dicitur de medicina, eo quod significat hoc tantum quod sit causa sanitatis in animali, quod per prius dicitur sanum. Tertio, quia hoc est contra intentionem loquentium de Deo. Aliud enim intendunt dicere, cum dicunt Deum viventem, quam quod sit causa vitae nostrae, vel quod differat a corporibus inanimatis.

51. These are names applied to God.

52. *ST* I, 13, 3: [q]uantum igitur ad id quod significant huiusmodi nomina, proprie competunt Deo, et magis proprie quam ipsis creaturis, et per prius dicuntur de eo. Quantum vero ad modum significandi, non proprie dicuntur de Deo: habent enim modum significandi qui creaturis competit.

53. *ST* I, 13, 4: [i]ntellectus autem noster, cum cognoscat Deum ex creaturis, format ad intelligendum Deum conceptiones proportionatas perfectionibus procedentibus a Deo in creaturas. Quae quidem perfectiones in Deo praeexistunt unite et simpliciter, in creaturis vero recipiuntur divise et multipliciter. Sicut igitur diversis perfectionibus creaturarum respondet unum simplex principium, repraesentatum per diversas perfectiones creaturarum varie et multipliciter; ita variis et multiplicibus conceptibus intellectus nostri respondet unum omnino simplex, secundum huiusmodi conceptiones imperfecte intellectum. Et ideo nomina Deo attributa, licet significent unam rem, tamen, quia significant eam sub rationibus multis et diversis, non sunt synonyma.

54. *ST* I, 13, 5: [u]nde patet quod non secundum eandem rationem hoc nomen sapiens de Deo et de homine dicitur.

55. *ST* I, 13, 5: [e]t iste modus communitatis medius est inter puram aequivocationem et simplicem univocationem. Neque enim in his quae analogice dicuntur, est una ratio, sicut est in univocis; nec totaliter diversa, sicut in aequivocis; sed nomen quod sic multipliciter dicitur, significat diversas proportiones ad aliquid unum[.]

56. *ST* I, 13, 5: qui multa demonstrative de Deo probant[.]

57. *ST* I, 13, 5: [e]*t sic, quidquid dicitur de Deo et creaturis, dicitur secundum quod est aliquis ordo creaturae ad Deum, ut ad principium et causam, in qua praeexistunt excellenter omnes rerum perfectiones.*

58. *ST* I, 13, 5: *sed nomen quod sic multipliciter dicitur, significat diversas proportiones ad aliquid unum.*

59. With respect to analogical language, Mark Jordan notes: "[e]very act of approach is marked by a more sharply felt absence. The more intelligible the signified, the more inadequate the mode of signification. The greater the intelligibility of the mind's abstractive intention, the greater its distance from the existing things it seeks to understand. In these and many other instances hierarchies are constructed upon the opposition of the present image and the absent original. But the opposition persists only *because* the image is tied to the original. There would be no hierarchy if there were not both likeness and unlikeness" ["The Names of God and the Being of Names," in *The Existence and Nature of God*, ed. Alfred J. Freddoso (Notre Dame: University of Notre Dame Press, 1983), 180].

60. *ST* I, 13, 6: [s]*icut enim ridere, dictum de prato, nihil aliud significat quam quod pratum similiter se habet in decore cum floret, sicut homo cum ridet, secundum similitudinem proportionis; sic nomen leonis, dictum de Deo, nihil aliud significat quam quod Deus similiter se habet ut fortiter operetur in suis operibus, sicut leo in suis. Et sic patet quod, secundum quod dicuntur de Deo, eorum significatio definiri non potest, nisi per illud quod de creaturis dicitur.*

61. *ST* I, 13, 6: *secundum hoc, dicendum est quod, quantum ad rem significatam per nomen, per prius dicuntur de Deo quam de creaturis, quia a Deo huiusmodi perfectiones in creaturas manant. Sed quantum ad impositionem nominis, per prius a nobis imponuntur creaturis, quas prius cognoscimus. Unde et modum significandi habent qui competit creaturis* [.]

62. *ST* I, 13, 7: [c]*um igitur Deus sit extra totum ordinem creaturae, et omnes creaturae ordinentur ad ipsum, et non e converso, manifestum est quod creaturae realiter referuntur ad ipsum Deum; sed in Deo non est aliqua realis relatio eius ad creaturas, sed secundum rationem tantum, inquantum creaturae referuntur ad ipsum.*

63. While these articles are very rich in content, they will be briefly reviewed as they do not bear upon the central thesis of this study.

64. *ST* I, 13, 9: [e]*st nihilominus communicabile hoc nomen Deus, non secundum suam totam significationem, sed secundum aliquid eius, per quandam similitudinem, ut dii dicantur, qui participant aliquid divinum per similitudinem* [.]

65. *ST* I, 13, 12, *s.c.*: *quod fidei non subest falsum. Sed propositiones quaedam affirmativae subduntur fidei, utpote quod Deus est trinus et unus, et quod est omnipotens. Ergo propositiones affirmativae possunt vere formari de Deo.*

66. *In Librum Boethii de Trinitate* [*In de trin.*] Q1, a2, ad 1. ... *in fine nostrae cognitionis deum tamquam ignotum cognoscere, quia tunc maxime mens in cognitione profecisse invenitur, quando cognoscit eius essentiam esse supra omne quod apprehendere potest in statu viae, et sic quamvis ignotum quid est, scitur tamen quia est* [*In Isaiam prophetam, in tres psalmos David, in Boetium de Hebdomadibus et de Trinitate expositiones*, Ed.: P. A. Uccelli (Romae, 1880)].

67. *ST* I, 1, 7, *ad* 1; cf: *ST* I, 3, 4, *ad* 2.

68. "Therefore in this life we are able to know of God only that he is, and yet one person may know what God is better than another, because a cause is known more perfectly from its effect the more the relationship of the cause of the effect is known through the effect." *In de trin.* Q1, a2, co. as cited in Michael J. Dodds, O.P.,

"Ultimacy and Intimacy: Aquinas on the Relation between God and the World," in *Ordo Sapientiae et Amoris: Image et Message de Saint Thomas d'Aquin àtravers les récentes études historiques, herméneutiques et doctrinales (Hommage au Professeur Jean-Pierre Torrell, O.P.)*, ed. Carlos-Josaphat Pinto de Oliveira, O.P. (Fribourg: Éditions Universitaires, 1993), 213.

69. Torrell, *Saint Thomas Aquinas*, 249.

70. Torrell, *Saint Thomas Aquinas*, 250-254. While the dating of this commentary has not received uniform acceptance among historical scholars, we follow Torrell's chronological work.

71. *Super epistolas S. Pauli lectura Thomas Aquinas*, P. Raphaelis CAI, O.P., ed. Vol. I (Taurini: Marietti, 1953) Ch.1, *lectio* 6, n.109: [p]*rimo ostendit virtutem evangelicae gratiae esse necessariam ad salutem gentibus, quia scilicet sapientia, de qua confidebant, salvare eos non potuit; secundo ostendit quod fuit necessaria Iudaeis, quia scilicet circumcisio et lex et alia in quibus confidebant, eis salutem non attulerunt. II cap. ibi propter quod inexcusabilis es.* It is important to note here that what is at issue with the Gentiles is whether this knowledge (*sapientia*) is *salvific*, not whether it is genuine in itself. All translations from the *Super epistolas* are mine.

72. *Super epistolas S. Pauli*, Ch.I, *lectio* 6, n.110: [p]*rimo quidem poenam dicens: recte dico quod in eo iustitia Dei revelatur, revelatur enim in eo ira Dei, id est vindicta ipsius, quae dicitur ira Dei secundum similitudinem hominum irascentium, qui vindictam quaerunt extra.*

73. *Super epistolas S. Pauli*, Ch.I, *lectio* 6, n.112: [t]*ertio ponit cognitionem quam de eo habuerunt, cum subdit hominum eorum qui veritatem Dei, id est veram de Deo cognitionem, detinent in iniustitia, quasi captivatam. Nam vera Dei cognitio quantum est de se inducit homines ad bonum, sed ligatur, quasi captivitate detenta, per iniustitiae affectum, per quam, ut Ps. XI, 1, diminutae sunt veritates a filiis hominum.*

74. This will be explicated in *lectio vii*.

75. Romans 1:18: [t]he wrath of God is indeed being revealed from heaven against every ungodliness and injustice of those who suppress the truth by their wickedness.

76. *Super epistolas S. Pauli*, Ch.I, *lectio* 6, n.113.

77. *Super epistolas S. Pauli*, Ch.I, *lectio* 6, n.114: [r]*ecte dico quod veritatem Dei detinuerunt, fuit enim in eis, quantum ad aliquid, vera Dei cognitio, quia quod notum est Dei, id est quod cognoscibile est de Deo ab homine per rationem, manifestum est in illis, id est manifestum est eis ex eo quod in illis est, id est ex lumine intrinseco.*

78. *Super epistolas S. Pauli*, Ch.I, *lectio* 6, n.114: [s]*ciendum est ergo quod aliquid circa Deum est omnino ignotum homini in hac vita, scilicet quid est Deus.*

79. *Super epistolas S. Pauli*, Ch.I, *lectio* 6, n.115. [p]*otest tamen homo, ex huiusmodi creaturis, Deum tripliciter cognoscere, ut Dionysius dicit in libro de divinis nominibus. Uno quidem modo per causalitatem. Quia enim huiusmodi creaturae sunt defectibiles et mutabiles, necesse est eas reducere ad aliquod principium immobile et perfectum. Et secundum hoc cognoscitur de Deo an est. Secundo per viam excellentiae. Non enim reducuntur omnia in primum principium, sicut in propriam causam et univocam, prout homo hominem generat, sed sicut in causam communem et excedentem. Et ex hoc cognoscitur quod est super omnia. Tertio per viam negationis. Quia si est causa excedens, nihil eorum quae sunt in creaturis potest ei competere, sicut etiam neque corpus caeleste proprie dicitur grave vel leve aut calidum aut frigidum.*

80. *Super epistolas S. Pauli*, Ch.I, *lectio* 6, n.115: *[h]uiusmodi autem cognitionem habuerunt per lumen rationis inditum.*

81. *Super epistolas S. Pauli*, Ch.I, *lectio* 6, n.116: *[u]bi considerandum est quod unus homo alteri manifestat explicando conceptum suum per aliqua signa exteriora, puta per vocem vel Scripturam, Deus autem dupliciter aliquid homini manifestat.*

82. *Super epistolas S. Pauli*, Ch.I, *lectio* 6, n.116: *in quibus, sicut in quodam libro, Dei cognitio legeretur.*

83. *Super epistolas S. Pauli*, Ch.I, *lectio* 6, n.117: *et secundum hoc intellectus noster considerat unitatem divinae essentiae sub ratione bonitatis, sapientiae, virtutis et huiusmodi, quae in Deo unum sunt.*

84. *Super epistolas S. Pauli*, Ch.I, *lectio* 6, n.117: *[h]aec autem tria referuntur ad tres modos cognoscendi supradictos. Nam invisibilia Dei cognoscuntur per viam negationis; sempiterna virtus, per viam causalitatis; divinitas, per viam excellentiae.*

85. *Super epistolas S. Pauli*, Ch.I, *lectio* 6, n.121: *quod a creatione mundi homines incoeperunt Deum cognoscere per ea quae facta sunt.*

86. It is important to remember that when Thomas talks about philosophers he almost always is talking about pagan philosophers.

87. *Super epistolas S. Pauli*, Ch.I, *lectio* 6, n.122: *[n]on quod philosophi, ductu rationis, potuerint pervenire, per ea quae facta sunt, in cognitionem personarum quantum ad propria, quae non significant habitudinem causae ad creaturas, sed secundum appropriata. Dicuntur tamen defecisse in tertio signo, id est in spiritu sancto quia non posuerunt aliquid respondere spiritui sancto, sicut posuerunt aliquid respondere patri, scilicet ipsum primum principium, et aliquid respondere filio, scilicet primam mentem creatam, quam vocabant paternum intellectum...*

88. *Super epistolas S. Pauli*, Ch.I, *lectio* 7, n.123: *[p]ostquam apostolus ostendit veritatem Dei fuisse a gentibus cognitam, hic ostendit eos obnoxios culpae impietatis et iniustitiae.*

89. While Thomas is not referring only to the philosophers here, they are the focus of the present study. He mentions the ancient poets and priests as two other groups of "wise men" who knew God but failed to honor him as God.

90. *Super epistolas S. Pauli*, Ch.I, *lectio* 7, n.124: *[c]irca primum considerandum est quod tunc ignorantia culpam excusat quando sic procedit et causat culpam, quod non causatur a culpa. Sicut cum aliquis, adhibita diligentia debita, dum credit percutere hostem, percutit patrem. Si vero ignorantia causetur ex culpa, non potest subsequentem culpam ignorantia excusare. Unde si quis per ebrietatem homicidium committit, non excusatur a culpa, quia peccavit se inebriando, unde secundum philosophum meretur duplices mulctationes.*

91. *Super epistolas S. Pauli*, Ch.I, *lectio* 7, n.127: *[q]uod autem prima eorum culpa non fuerit ex ignorantia, ostenditur per hoc quod Dei cognitionem habentes ea non sunt usi ad bonum.*

92. *Super epistolas S. Pauli*, Ch.I, *lectio* 7, n.127: *[d]upliciter autem Deum cognoverunt. Uno modo sicut omnibus super eminentem, et sic ei debebant gloriam et honorem quae superexcellentibus debetur. Isti ideo dicuntur inexcusabiles quia cum cognovissent Deum, non sicut Deum glorificaverunt, vel quia ei debitum cultum non impenderunt, vel quia virtuti eius et scientiae terminum imposuerunt, aliqua eius potentiae et scientiae subtrahentes, contra id quod dicitur Eccli. XLIII, v. 37: glorificantes dominum quantumcumque potueritis. Secundo, cognoverunt eum sicut omnium bonorum causam. Unde ei in omnibus gratiarum actio debebatur,*

quam tamen ipsi non impendebant, sed potius suo ingenio et virtuti suae bona sua adscribebant[.]
93. *Super epistolas S. Pauli*, Ch.I, *lectio* 7, n.130: *[s]icut enim qui oculos corporales a sole materiali avertit, obscuritatem corporalem incurrit, ita ille qui a Deo avertitur, de seipso praesumens et non de Deo, spiritualiter obscuratur.* Prov. XI, 2: ubi humilitas, *per quam scilicet homo se Deo subiicit,* ibi sapientia; ubi superbia, ibi contumelia.
94. *Super epistolas S. Pauli*, Ch.I, *lectio* 7, n.130: *id est lumine sapientiae privatum, per quam homo vere Deum cognoscit.*
95. *Super epistolas S. Pauli*, Ch.I, *lectio* 7, n.133: *[c]ulpa quidem eorum fuit quod, quantum in ipsis erat, honorem divinum in alium transtulerunt[.]*
96. *Super epistolas S. Pauli*, Ch.I, *lectio* 7, n.137: *[c]irca quod considerandum est quod homo medium locum obtinet inter Deum et animalia bruta, et cum utroque extremorum communicat: cum Deo quidem, secundum intellectualitatem; cum animalibus vero brutis, secundum sensualitatem. Sicut igitur homo, id quod est Dei, mutavit usque ad bestias, ita Deus, id quod est divinum in homine secundum rationem, subdidit ei quod est brutale in ipso, scilicet desiderio sensualitatis, secundum illud Ps. XLVIII, 21: homo cum in honore esset non intellexit, similitudinem scilicet divinae imaginis propter rationem, comparatus est iumentis insipientibus. Hoc est ergo quod dicit propter quod tradidit illos Deus in desideria cordis, ut eorum ratio subderetur desideriis cordis, scilicet sensualis affectus, de quibus dicitur infra XIII, 14: carnis curam ne feceritis in desideriis.*

Epilogue

1. For the emergence of an epilogue as appendix rather than as conclusion or summary, see *The Compact Oxford English Dictionary*, "Epilogue" (Oxford: Oxford University Press, 1987), 524.
2. Rogers, *Thomas Aquinas and Karl Barth*, 39.
3. Rogers refers here to *ST* I, 1, 1 and I, 1, 2.
4. Rogers, *Thomas Aquinas and Karl Barth*, 39.
5. Rogers, *Thomas Aquinas and Karl Barth*, 39.
6. *ST* I, 1, 1, *ad* 2: *theologia quae ad sacram doctrinam pertinet, differt secundum genus ab illa theologia quae pars philosophiae ponitur.*
7. *SCG*, III, 69, n.15: *[d]etrahere ergo perfectioni creaturarum est detrahere perfectioni divinae virtutis.*
8. See *ST* I, 1, 7.
9. *ST* I, 1, 8, *ad* 2.
10. *ST* I, 1, 5, *ad* 2: *haec scientia accipere potest aliquid a philosophicis disciplinis, non quasi ex necessitate eis indigeat, sed ad maiorem manifestationem eorum quae in hac scientia traduntur. Non enim accipit sua principia ab aliis scientiis sed immediate a Deo per revelationem. Et ideo non accipit ab aliis scientiis tamquam a superioribus, sed utitur eis tamquam inferioribus et ancillis; sicut architectonicae utuntur subministrantibus ut civilis militari. Et hoc ipsum quod sic utitur eis non est propter defectum vel insufficientiam ejus, sed propter defectum intellectus nostri, qui ex eis quae per naturalem rationem ex qua procedunt aliae scientiae cognoscuntur, facilius manuducitur in ea quae sunt supra rationem quae in hac scientia traduntur.*
11. *ST* I, 1, 5, *sed contra: aliae scientiae dicuntur ancillae hujus;* Prov. *Misit ancillas suas vocare ad arcem.* Thomas also treats the relationship between *sacra doctrina* and other sciences in: *ST* I, 1, 6.

12. Rogers, *Thomas Aquinas and Karl Barth*, 39.
13. Rogers, *Thomas Aquinas and Karl Barth*, 121.
14. Rogers, *Thomas Aquinas and Karl Barth*, 129.
15. Rogers, *Thomas Aquinas and Karl Barth*, 121.
16. Rogers, *Thomas Aquinas and Karl Barth*, 121.
17. Rogers, *Thomas Aquinas and Karl Barth*, 164.
18. Rogers, *Thomas Aquinas and Karl Barth*, 125.
19. Rogers, *Thomas Aquinas and Karl Barth*, 131.
20. Rogers, *Thomas Aquinas and Karl Barth*, 187.
21. Rogers, *Thomas Aquinas and Karl Barth*, 187.
22. Rogers, *Thomas Aquinas and Karl Barth*, 188.
23. *Super epistolas S. Pauli*, Ch.I, *lectio* 6, n.114.
24. *Super epistolas S. Pauli*, Ch.I, *lectio* 7, n.124: [c]*irca primum considerandum est quod tunc ignorantia culpam excusat quando sic procedit et causat culpam, quod non causatur a culpa. Sicut cum aliquis, adhibita diligentia debita, dum credit percutere hostem, percutit patrem. Si vero ignorantia causetur ex culpa, non potest subsequentem culpam ignorantia excusare. Unde si quis per ebrietatem homicidium committit, non excusatur a culpa, quia peccavit se inebriando, unde secundum philosophum meretur duplices mulctationes.*
25. *Super epistolas S. Pauli*, Ch.I, *lectio* 7, n.127: [q]*uod autem prima eorum culpa non fuerit ex ignorantia, ostenditur per hoc quod Dei cognitionem habentes ea non sunt usi ad bonum.*
26. *ST* I, 12, 12, *ad* 3: *cognitio Dei per essentiam, cum sit per gratiam, non competit nisi bonis, sed cognitio eius quae est per rationem naturalem, potest competere bonis et malis. Unde dicit Augustinus, in libro Retractationum, non approbo quod in oratione dixi, Deus, qui non nisi mundos verum scire voluisti, responderi enim potest, multos etiam non mundos multa scire vera, scilicet per rationem naturalem.*
27. Bruce Marshall, "Aquinas as Postliberal Theologian," 356–357 [italics mine]. Ontological truth here is "that truth of correspondence to reality which, according to epistemological realists, is attributable to first-order propositions" (Lindbeck, *ND*, 64 as cited in Marshall, "Aquinas as Postliberal Theologian," 358).
28. *ST* II, 2, 2, *ad* 3, as quoted in Marshall, "Aquinas as Postliberal Theologian," 380–381.
29. Marshall, "Aquinas as Postliberal Theologian," 380.
30. Marshall, "Aquinas as Postliberal Theologian," 391–392. Marshall maintains that the difference between what a Christian and a philosopher believe about God is reflected in the difference between philosophy and *sacra doctrina*: "[t]here can be *theologia* in both philosophy and *sacra doctrina*, indeed in some cases both may make the same statements about God.... But they do so in different ways and on different grounds.... As a result, the two statements differ in kind (have different formal objects); even when they use the same words, philosophy and *sacra doctrina* are not saying the same thing" (ibid., 392–393 note 93). On Thomas' very different position on this very question see *ST* I, 1, 1, *ad* 2: [a]*d secundum dicendum quod diversa ratio cognoscibilis diversitatem scientiarum inducit. Eandem enim conclusionem demonstrat astrologus et naturalis, puta quod terra est rotunda, sed astrologus per medium mathematicum, idest a materia abstractum; naturalis autem per medium circa materiam consideratum. Unde nihil prohibet de eisdem rebus, de quibus philosophicae disciplinae tractant secundum quod sunt cognoscibilia lumine naturalis rationis, et aliam scientiam tractare secundum quod cognoscuntur lumine divinae revelationis.*

Unde theologia quae ad sacram doctrinam pertinet, differt secundum genus ab illa theologia quae pars philosophiae ponitur.

31. *In Joan.* c.17, lect 6, as cited in Marshall, "Faith and Reason Reconsidered: Aquinas and Luther on Deciding What is True" 10. The passage cited in Thomas' commentary on the Gospel of John is found in the following section: *[d]icendum, quod duplex est cognitio: una speculativa, et alia affectiva: et neutra mundus Deum cognovit perfecte. Licet enim aliqui gentilium Deum quantum ad aliqua quae per rationem cognoscibilia erant, cognoverint; ipsum tamen secundum quod est pater filii unigeniti et consubstantialis, non cognoverunt: de qua cognitione loquitur dominus. Et inde est quod apostolus dicit, quod notumest id est cognoscibile dei. Sed et si quid speculativa cognitione de deo cognoscebant, hoc erat cum admixtione multorum errorum, dum quidam subtraherent omnium rerum providentiam; quidam dicerent eum esse animam mundi; quidam simul cum eo multos alios deos colerent. Unde dicunter deum ignorare. Licet enim in compositis possit partim sciri et partim ignorari; in simplicibus tamen dum non attinguntur totaliter, ignorantur. Unde etsi in minimo aliqui errent circa dei cognitionem, dicuntur eum totaliter ignorare. Isti ergo non cognoscentes singularem dei excellentiam, ignorare dicunter; rom. i, 21...*

32. Marshall here cites *Summa theologiae* II-II, 2, 2, *ad* 3, and III *Sent.*, d.23, Q2, a2, ac1a2, *ad* 2 [ed. P. Mandonnet, O.P., and M. F. Moos, O.P. (Paris: Lethielleux, 1929–47)].

33. *In Joan.* c.17, lect. 6: *[l]icet enim aliqui gentilium Deum quantum ad aliqua quae per rationem cognoscibilia erant, cognoverint; ipsum tamen secundum quod est pater filii unigeniti et consubstantialis, non cognoverunt: de qua cognitione loquitur dominus* (emphasis in text).

34. *In Joan.* c.17, lect. 6: *[u]nde etsi in minimo aliqui errent circa dei cognitionem, dicuntur eum totaliter ignorare.*

35. *In Joan.* c.17, lect. 6: *[u]nde dicunter deum ignorare. Licet enim in compositis possit partim sciri et partim ignorari; in simplicibus tamen dum non attinguntur totaliter, ignorantur. [u]nde etsi in minimo aliqui errent circa dei cognitionem, dicuntur eum totaliter ignorare. Isti ergo non cognoscentes singularem dei excellentiam, ignorare dicunter[.]*

36. Cf. Louis Roy, O.P., "Bruce Marshall's Reading of Aquinas," *Thomist* 56 (1992): 473–480. Fr. Roy focuses upon Marshall's confusing the material and formal objects of faith; this leads Marshall to quite wrongly lump the unbeliever with the heretic. The fact is that for Thomas the pre-Christian philosopher can know that God exists without believing this under the formal aspect of faith.

37. Lindbeck, *ND*, 39–40.
38. Lindbeck, *ND*, 68.
39. Lindbeck, *ND*, 80.
40. Lindbeck, *ND*, 131.
41. Lindbeck, *ND*, 131.
42. Lindbeck, *ND*, 132.
43. Turner, *Faith, Reason and the Existence of God*, 23–24.
44. Hibbs, *Aquinas, Ethics and Philosophy of Religion*, 109.
45. See Tracey Rowland, *Culture and the Thomist Tradition: After Vatican II* (London: Routledge, 2003), esp. 116, 128, and 159.
46. Rowland, 116.
47. *The Christian Philosophy of St. Thomas Aquinas* (Notre Dame: University of Notre Dame Press, 1956), 24–25.

Select Bibliography

Thomas Aquinas. *Expositio super librum Boethii De Trinitate.* Leiden: Brill, 1955.

———. *In Isaiam prophetam, in tres psalmos David, in Boetium de Hebdomadibus et de Trinitate expositiones,* Ed. P. A. Uccelli. Romae, 1880.

———. *Scriptum super libros Sententiarum,* ed. Mandonnet and Moos. Paris: Lethielleux, 1929–1933.

———. *Summa Contra Gentiles.* Ed. C. Pera, P. Marc, and P. Caramello. Turin: Marietti, 1961.

———. *Summa Contra Gentiles.* Book I, trans. A. Pegis; Book II, trans. J. F. Anderson; Book II, 2 vols., trans. V. J. Bourke; Book IV, trans. C. J. O'Neill. Notre Dame: University of Notre Dame Press, 1975.

———. *Summa theologiae.* Turin: Marietti, 1948.

———. *Summa theologiae,* trans. Fathers of the English Dominican Province, 5 vols. Repr., Westminster, Maryland: Christian Classics, 1981.

Aristotle. *The Complete Works of Aristotle* I, ed. Jonathan Barnes. Princeton: Princeton University Press, 1984.

Audet, Th.-André, O.P. *Études d'histoire littéraire et doctrinale,* "Approches historiques de la *Summa Theologiae.*" PIEM, XVII, 1962.

Barth, Karl. *Church Dogmatics,* trans. G. T. Thomson. Edinburgh: T. & T. Clark, 1936–1977.

Blanchette, Oliva. "Philosophy and Theology in Aquinas: On Being a Disciple in Our Day." *Science et Esprit* 28 (1976).

Boyle, L. E. *The Setting of the Summa theologiae of Saint Thomas.* Etienne Gilson Series, vol. 5. Toronto: Pontifical Institute of Mediaeval Studies, 1982.

Buckley, Michael J., S.J. *Denying and Disclosing God: The Ambiguous Progress of Modern Atheism.* New Haven: Yale University Press, 2004.

Burell, David., C.C.C. *Analogy and Philosophical Language.* New Haven: Yale University Press, 1973.

———. *Aquinas: God and Action.* Notre Dame: University of Notre Dame Press, 1979.

———. "Aquinas on Naming God." *Theological Studies* 24 (1963).

——. *Knowing the Unknowable God: Ibn-Sina, Maimonides, and Aquinas.* Notre Dame: University of Notre Dame Press, 1986.

Burns, Robert M. "The Divine Simplicity in St. Thomas." *Religious Studies* 18 (1982): 451–471

Callus, D. A. "Les sources de saint Thomas. Etat de la question." In *Aristotle et saint Thomas d'Aquin,* pp. 93–174.

Cessario, Romanus. "Is Aquinas' Summa Only About Grace?" in *Ordo sapientiae et amoris.* Pp. 197–209.

Châtillon, J. "De Guillaume d'Auxerre à saint Thomas d'Aquin: l'Argument de saint Anselme chez les premiers scolastiques," in *D'Isodore de Séville à saint Thomas d'Aquin.* London, 1985.

Chenu, M. D. "La théologie comme science au xiiie siècle," *Archives d'histoire doctrinale et littéraire du moyen-âge* 2 (1927).

——. *Introduction à l'étude de Saint Thomas d'Aquin.* Paris: J. Vrin, 1954.

——. *La théologie au douzième siècle.* Études Philosophie Médiévale, 3d ed. Paris: J. Vrin, 1976.

——. *La théologie comme science au XIII siècle.* 3d ed. Paris: J. Vrin, 1957.

——. *Toward Understanding St. Thomas,* trans. A. M. Landry and D. Hughes. Chicago: Regnery, 1964.

Colish, Marcia L. *Peter Lombard,* vol. 1. Leiden: E. J. Brill, 1994.

Corbin, Michel. *Le chemin de la théologie chez Thomas d'Aquin.* Paris: Beauchesne, 1972.

Crosson, Frederick J. "Reconsidering Aquinas as Postliberal Theologian." *Thomist* 56 (1992): 481–498.

Davies, Brian. "Classical Theism and the Doctrine of the Divine Simplicity," *Language, Meaning, and God,* ed. Brian Davies. London: Geoffrey Chapman, 1987.

——. *The Thought of Thomas Aquinas.* Oxford: Clarendon Press, 1992.

Deferrari, Roy J., et al., eds. *A Lexicon of St. Thomas Aquinas Based on the Summa theologiae and Selected Passages of His Other Works.* Washington, D.C.: Catholic University of America Press, 1948.

Dodds, Michael J., O.P. "Ultimacy and Intimacy: Aquinas on the Relation between God and the World," *Ordo Sapientiae et Amoris: Image et Message de Saint Thomas d'Aquin à travers les récentes études historiques, herméneutiques et doctrinales (Hommage au Professeur Jean-Pierre Torrell O.P.),* ed. Carlos-Josaphat Pinto de Oliveira, O.P. Fribourg: Éditions Universitaires, 1993.

Elders, Leo J., S.V.D. *Faith and Science. An Introduction to St. Thomas' Expositio in Poethii De Trinitate.* Rome: Herder, 1974.

———. *The Philosophical Theology of Thomas Aquinas*. Leiden: E. J. Brill, 1990.

———. "Saint Thomas d'Aquin et Aristote." *Revue Thomiste* 88 (1988): 357–76.

Eschmann, I.T. "A Catalogue of St. Thomas's Works." In E. Gilson, *The Christian Philosophy of St. Thomas Aquinas*, trans. L. K. Shook, pp. 381–437. New York: Random House, 1956.

Franck, Isaak. "Maimonides and Aquinas on Man's Knowledge of God: A Twentieth Century Perspective." In *Maimonides: A Collection of Critical Essays*, ed. Joseph A. Buijs. Notre Dame: University of Notre Dame Press, 1988.

Gilson, Etienne. *The Spirit of Medieval Philosophy*, trans. A. H. C. Downes. London: Sheed and Ward, 1936.

———. *Le Thomisme: Introduction á la philosophie de saint Thomas d'Aquin*. Paris: J. Vrin, 1944.

Glorieux, P. "Répertoire des Maîtres en Théologie de Paris au XIIIe siècle." 2 vols. *Études de philosophie Médiévale*, vols. 17 and 18. Paris, 1933.

Gomez Nogales, S. "Saint Thomas, Averroés et l'Averroïsme." In *Aquinas and Problems of His Time*, ed. Gérard Verbeke and D. Verhelst, 161–77. Louvain: Leuven, 1976.

Grabmann, Martin. *Die Theologische Erkenntnis- und Einleitungslehre des hl. Thomas von Aquin auf Grund Seiner Schrift "In Boethium de Trinitate," im Zusammenhang der Scholastik des 13. und beginnenden 14. Jarhunderts dargestellt*. Freiburg in Schweiz: Paulusverlag, 1948.

Gregory, St. *Reading the Gospels with Gregory the Great: Homilies on the Gospels, 21–26*, trans. Santha Bhattacharji. Petersham, Mass.: St. Bede's Publications, 2001.

Hall, D. C. *The Trinity: An Analysis of St. Thomas Aquinas' Expositio of the De Trinitate of Boethius*. Studien und Texte zur Geistesgeschichte des Mittelalters. Leiden, 1992.

Hibbs, Thomas S. *Aquinas, Ethics and Philosophy of Religion: Metaphysics and Practice*. Bloomington: Indiana University Press, 2007.

———. *Dialectic and Narrative in Aquinas: An Interpretation of the Summa Contra Gentiles*. Notre Dame: University of Notre Dame Press, 1995.

Johnson, Mark F. "*Alia lectura fratris thome*": A List of the New Texts of St. Thomas Aquinas found in Lincoln College, Oxford, MS. Lat.95," *Recherches de Théologie Ancienne et Médiévale* 57 (1990).

———. "The Sapiential Character of the First Article of the *Summa theologiae*." In *Philosophy and the God of Abraham: Essays in Memory of James A. Weisheipl, O.P.* James R. Long, ed. Toronto: Pontifical Institute of Mediaeval Studies, 1991.

Jordan, Mark D. "The Names of God and the Being of Names," *The Existence and Nature of God,* ed. Alfred J. Freddoso. Notre Dame: University of Notre Dame Press, 1983.

———. *Ordering Wisdom: The Hierarchy of Philosophical Discourses in Aquinas.* Notre Dame: University of Notre Dame Press, 1986.

———. "The Protreptic Structure of the 'Summa Contra Gentiles.'" *Thomist* 50 (1986): 173–209.

Klubertanz, George P., S.J. *St. Thomas Aquinas on Analogy: A Textual Analysis and Systematic Synthesis.* Chicago: Loyola University Press, 1960.

Kretzmann, Norman. *The Metaphysics of Creation: Aquinas's Natural Theology in Summa contra Gentiles 2.* Oxford: Oxford University Press, 1999.

La Doctrine de la Révélation Divine de Saint Thomas d'Aquin. Ed. L. Elders. Studi Tomistici, vol. 37. Vatican City, 1990.

Lafont, G. *Structures et Méthode dans la Somme théologique de Saint Thomas d'Aquin.* Bruges: Desclee du Brouwer, 1961.

Laporta, Jorge. *La Destinée de la nature humaine selon Thomas d'Aquin.* Paris: J. Vrin, 1965.

Lash, Nicholas. *The Beginning and End of Religion.* Cambridge: Cambridge University Press, 1996.

———. "Ideology, Metaphor, and Analogy," *The Philosophical Frontiers of Christian Theology: Essays Presented to D. M. Mackinnon.* Ed. Brian Hebblethwaite and Stewart Sutherland. Cambridge: Cambridge University Press, 1982.

———. "Considering the Trinity" *Modern Theology* 2 (1986).

Lindbeck, George. *The Nature of Doctrine: Religion and Theology in a Postliberal Age.* Philadelphia: Westminster Press, 1984.

———. "A Priori in St. Thomas' Theory of Knowledge." *Heritage of Christian Thought: Essays in Honor of Robert Lowry Calhoun.* New York: Harper and Row, 1965.

———. "Confession and Community: How my Mind has Changed." *Christian Century* 107 (1990): 492–496.

———. "A Discovering Thomas: Four Points." *Una Sancta.* 24, #1 (1967): 45–52; 24, #3 (1967): 44–48; 24, #4 (1967): 67–75; 25, #1 (1968): 66–73.

———. "The Evangelical Possibilities of Roman Catholic Theology." *Lutheran World* 7 (1960): 142–152.

———. "The Gospel's Uniqueness: Election and Untranslatability." *Modern Theology* 13 (1997): 423–450.

———. "Participation and Existence in the Interpretation of St. Thomas Aquinas." *Franciscan Studies* 17 (1957): 1–22, 107–25.

———. "Toward a Postliberal Theology: Faithfulness as Intratextuality." *Return of Scripture in Judaism and Christianity*. New York: Paulist Press, 1993.

Lubac, Henri de. *Surnaturel*. Paris: Aubier, 1946.

MacIntyre, Alisdair. *Whose Justice? Which Rationality?* Notre Dame: University of Notre Dame Press, 1988.

Maimonides, Moses. *Doctor Perplexorum*, part.I, c.58. Basileæ: Sumptibus & impensis Ludovici König, excudebat J. J. Genath, 1629.

Marshall, Bruce D. "Aquinas as Postliberal Theologian." *Thomist* 53 (1989): 353–402.

———. *Christology in Conflict: The Identity of a Saviour in Rahner and Barth*. New York: Basil Blackwell, 1987.

———. "Faith and Reason Reconsidered: Aquinas and Luther on Deciding What's True." *Thomist* 63 (1999): 1–48.

———. "Lindbeck on What Theology Is." *Dialog* 31(1992): 44–47.

———. "Thomas, Thomisms, and Truth." *Thomist* 56 (1992): 499–524.

———. "What is Truth?" *Pro Ecclesia* 4(1995): 404–430.

———, ed. *Theology and Dialogue: Essays in Conversation with George Lindbeck*. Notre Dame: University of Notre Dame Press, 1990.

Matthys, M. "Quid ratio naturalis doceat de possibilitate visionis beatae secundum S. Thomam in summa contra gentiles." *Divus Thomas* (Piacenza) 39 (1936): 201–28.

McInerny, Ralph. *Boethius and Aquinas*. Washington, D.C.: Catholic University of America Press, 1990.

Mondin, Battista, S.J. *St. Thomas Aquinas' Philosophy in the Commentary to the Sentences*. The Hague: Martinus Nijhoff, 1975.

Mulard, R. "Désir naturel de connaître et vision béatifique." *Revue des sciences philosophiques et théologiques* 14 (1925): 5–19.

Owens, J. C.Ss.R. "Aquinas as Aristotelian Commentator." In *St. Thomas Aquinas 1274–1974: Commemorative Studies*. Vol. 1, 213–38.

———. *St. Thomas Aquinas on the Existence of God: Collected Papers of Joseph Owens, C.Ss.R*. John R. Catan, ed. Albany: State University of New York Press, 1980.

Patfoort, A. *Saint Thomas d'Aquin: Les clés d'une Théologie*. Paris: FAC, 1983.

———. "L'unité de la *Ia Pars* et le mouvement interne de la Somme théologique de S. Thomas d'Aquin." *Revue des sciences philosophiques et théologiques* 47 (1963).

Pegis, Anton. *At the Origins of the Thomistic Notion of Man.* St. Augustine Lecture, 1963. New York: Macmillan, 1963.

———. "Nature and Spirit: Some Reflections on the Problem of the End of Man." *Proceedings of the American Catholic Philosophical Association* 23 (1949): 62–79.

Persson, P. E. "Le plan de la Somme théologique et le Rapport *Ratio-Revelatio.*" *Revue Philosophique de Louvain* 56 (1958): 545–575.

———. *Sacra Doctrina: Reason and Revelation in Aquinas.* Oxford: Basil Blackwell, 1970.

Pieper, Josef. *Happiness and Contemplation,* trans. Richard and Clara Winston. New York: Pantheon Books, 1958.

Plantinga, Alvin. *Does God Have a Nature?* Milwaukee: Marquette University Press, 1980.

Putnam, Hilary. "On Negative Theology." *Faith and Philosophy: Journal of the Society of Christian Philosophers* 14 (1997).

Rahner, Karl, S.J. *The Trinity,* trans. Joseph Donceel. New York: Crossroad, 1997; original German publication, 1967 by Benziger Verlag Eisiedeln.

Rogers, Eugene F., Jr. *Thomas Aquinas and Karl Barth: Sacred Doctrine and the Natural Knowledge of God.* South Bend: University of Notre Dame Press, 1996.

———. "How the Virtues of an Interpreter Presuppose and Perfect Hermeneutics: The Case of Thomas Aquinas." *Journal of Religion* 76 (1996): 64–81.

Rogers, Katherine. "The Traditional Doctrine of Divine Simplicity." *Religious Studies* 32 (1996).

Roy, Louis. "Bruce Marshall's Reading of Aquinas." *Thomist* 56 (1992): 473–480.

Smith, Gerard. "Philosophy and the Unity of Man's Ultimate End." *Proceedings of the American Catholic Philosophical Association* 27 (1953): 60–83.

Sparrow, M. F. "Natural Knowledge of God and the Principles of "Sacra Doctrina." *Angelicum* 69 (1992).

Spatz, Nancy. "Approaches and Attitudes to a New Theology Textbook: The *Sentences* of Peter Lombard." in *The Intellectual Climate of the Early University: Essays in Honor of Otto Gründler,* ed. Nancy Van Deusen. Kalamazoo, Mich.: Western Michigan University, 1997.

Staley, Kevin. "Happiness: The Natural End of Man?" *The Thomist* 53 (1989): 215–234.

Torrell, Jean-Pierre, O.P. *Saint Thomas Aquinas: The Person and His Work,* trans. Robert Royal, vol. 1. Washington, D.C.: Catholic University of America Press, 1996.

Trismegistus, Hermes. *Liber viginti quatuor philosophorum,* prop. 1., ed. C. Baeumker, in Abhandlungen aus dem Gebiete der Philosophie und ihrer Geschichte. Freiburg in Breisgau: Herder, 1913.

Turner, Denys. *Faith, Reason and the Existence of God.* Cambridge: Cambridge University Press, 2004.

Van Ackeren, G. F. *Sacra Doctrina.* Rome: Catholic Book Agency, 1952.

Wawrykow, Joseph. " 'Merit' in the Theology of Thomas Aquinas." *Medieval Philosophy and Theology* 2 (1992): 97–116.

Weisheipl, James A. *Friar Thomas D'Aquino: His Life, Thought and Works.* Washington, D.C.: Catholic University of America Press, 1983.

———. "The Meaning of *Sacra Doctrina* in *Summa theologiae* I, Q1," *Thomist* 38 (1974).

Wippel, John. *Metaphysical Themes in Thomas Aquinas.* Washington, D.C.: Catholic University of America Press, 1984.

———. *The Metaphysical Thought of Thomas Aquinas: From Finite Being to Uncreated Being.* Washington, D.C.: Catholic University of America Press, 2000.

Index

Abelard, Peter, 81
Aeterni Patris, 1
agent intellect, 11, 96, 101
agnosticism, 52, 54–58, 61–68, 71, 90, 112, 174n4
Alexander of Hales, 39, 44, 52
analogy, 120, 121, 178n32
  contrasted with metaphor, 131–134
Anselm of Canterbury, 52–54, 118–119
Aristotle
  de Anima III, 125
  On the Heavens, 122
  Posterior Analytics, 104
  Thomas' use of, 13, 25–26, 33, 55, 60, 62, 124–125
Augustine, 95, 124
  Confessions, 122
  De Trinitate, 125–126
  Enchridion, 57
  On the City of God, 122

Barth, Karl, 144
  In *Nature of Doctrine* (Lindbeck), 2, 13
  Rogers' treatment of, 3–4, 36–37,
beatific vision, 48, 69–74, 76–78, 79–80, 82–86, 112, 113–115, 127–128
  natural desire for, 11
Boethius, 124
  Thomas' *Commentary on the De Trinitate*, 62, 91–103
Bonaventure, Saint, 52, 101

Boyle, Leonard, 40–41
Buckley, Michael J., S.J., 170n75, 176n27
Burrell, David, C.S.C. 58, 67–68, 174n4

Chenu, Marie-Dominique, O.P., 39, 41, 50–51
christianam religionem, 45–46
Corbin, Michel, 3

Damascene, John, 52–53, 59, 118–119
Davies, Brian, O.P., 68
Dei Filius, 1
Deism, 36

epistemology, 10, 60, 101–102
Eschmann, I.T.,O.P., 6

fideism
  Bruce Marshall and, 26
  Thomas Aquinas and, 54, 56–58
Fishacre, Richard, 52

Gilson, Etienne, 11, 30, 156
God
  as formal and material object of faith, 22–23, 195n36
  as *Ipsum Esse*, 13
  simplicity of, 63–65, 124, 132
Gregory the Great, 95

Hibbs, Thomas, 106, 110, 114
Honorius of Autun, 39

interreligious dialogue, 155

Jenkins, John, C.S.C., 42–43

Kant, Immanuel, 10
knowledge
   a posteriori vs. *a priori*, 10–12
   a priori, 15–16
   through *phantasmata*, 10, 60, 83–84, 91, 120–121, 124–126
knowledge of God
   by *abstractio* vs. impression, 83–84, 98
   through analogy, 120–121, 128, 131, 134,
   by ancient philosophers, 23–24, 27–28, 81–82, 85–86, 88–90, 103–104, 118–119, 122–123, 131, 138–142, 144, 147–150, 150–153
   apprehendere, 133
   attingere vs. *comprehendere*, 75, 80, 85, 152, 176n31
   through cause vs. through effect, 42, 47, 52, 54–56, 57–58, 70–72, 76, 97–100, 121–123, 125–126, 130–131
   cognitio vs. *videre*, 82, 91, 124
   per creaturas, 82, 86
   through divine illumination, 95
   by faith, 3, 9, 12–13, 17–18, 23–24, 27–28, 30–37, 55–56, 87–89, 92–96, 99, 103–104, 106, 110–113, 114–115, 123, 126–128, 139, 145, 148, 150–151, 153–156
   and happiness, 53, 70, 72, 89, 107–113, 156
   natural desire for, 11
   per se vs. *per alia*, 86, 118–120, 123
   pertingere Deum, 82, 176n31
   quid est vs. *an est*, 99–100, 126

knowledge of God (*continued*)
   quid est vs. *quia est*, 100
   role of charity, 80
   role of the will, 109, 125
   via negativa and *via affirmativa*, 73, 107, 109–110

Lash, Nicholas, 51, 67, 174n6
Leroy, M.-V., 51
Lindbeck, George
   and experiential-expressivism, 14–16
   and *Nature of Doctrine*, 14–18
   and religion as cultural and/or linguistic framework, 2, 14–21
Lombard, Peter, 39, 41–44, 80–81
lumen gloriae, 73–78
Luther, Martin, 27–28

MacIntyre, Alasdair, 7
Maimonides, Rabbi Moses, 60–62, 129
Maréchal, Joseph, S.J., 11
Maritain, Jacques, 11
Marshall, Bruce
   and coherentist view of justification, 29–31
   and foundationalism, 29
   and Donald Davidson, 28
   and Alfred Tarski, 28

names of God,
   modus significandi vs. *res significata*, 130
   names of God, univocal vs. equivocal, 130, 137
natural knowledge of God
   demonstrative arguments, 86, 102–106
   quia vs. *propter quid* arguments, 54–55
   as *ratio naturalis* and *cognitio naturalis*, 158n29

Index

Origen, 45

Pesch, Otto Hermann, 3
Plantinga, Alvin, 58
Platonism, 10, 89, 122–123

Rahner, Karl, S.J., 11, 51
Raymond of Peñafort, 44
Richard of St. Victor, 89
Rogers, Eugene
  and *quinquae viae*, 36
  and *sacra doctrina*, 31–37
  and *scientia*, 31–34
Rowland, Tracey, 155–156
Roy, Louis, O.P., 195n36

sacra doctrina
  and philosophy, 12
  and *scientia*. *See* Rogers, Eugene
  and scripture, 146
  as speculative, 49
  and theology, 145
similitudo, 72, 86,
sin, 9, 28, 31, 35, 45, 88, 126, 136, 141–142, 147, 149
summa, 39

theology
  as grammar, 67–68, 154, 174n2
  as intratextual, 8–20
  postliberal, 8–37
Torrell, Jean Pierre, O.P., 51, 159n37
Trinity
  knowledge of. *See under* knowledge
  and Truth. *See* Marshall, Bruce
Trismegistus, 122
truth
  and biblical narrative, 20, 29
  epistemic and justification, 27–29, 155
  incommensurability, 36, 55
  as ontological, 3, 17, 22, 24, 150
Turner, Denys, 155, 172n97

Van Ackeren, Gerald, S.J., 48

Weisheipl, James, 47–48
William of Auvergne, 101
Wippel, John F., 52, 170n84

Herder & Herder is proud to present books that celebrate what is distinctive about Catholic theology. Each of these books offers a greater appreciation for the enduring value and urgency of Catholic intellectual life in our new millennium.

David Tracy
THE ANALOGICAL IMAGINATION
Christian Theology and the Culture of Pluralism

In this great classic of Catholic thought, David Tracy introduces his idea of the religious classic and illustrates the fundamental difference between the Catholic (analogical) vision of theology and other (dialectical) visions.

"One of the most ambitious theological projects in the world. It is written with such modesty, breath of knowledge, and sense of complexity that it is the best among the rare works that try to tackle its subject matter." — *The Thomist*

978-0-8245-0694-0

Of Related Interest

Francis Cardinal George, OMI
THE DIFFERENCE GOD MAKES
A Catholic Vision of Faith, Communion, and Culture

"A scholarly and spiritual collection of essays on the role of the Catholic faith in the modern world, from one of the most thoughtful men in the American hierarchy."

— *Publishers Weekly*

In contemporary American society, it can seem as though there is little room left for religious faith. Is there any need for belief today? Does God make any difference in our lives?

In this wide-ranging vision of Catholic faith, Cardinal George, Archbishop of Chicago, calls us to reflect on how God, revealed in Jesus Christ, makes a difference in everything we do and all that we are. In the light of the risen Christ, Catholics are united to each other, to other Christians, and to people of other religions and no religion at all. By recognizing our identity in communion, we learn that we are not individuals — we can discover our identities only in and through others. Our relations, whether personal or public, make us who are.

To invite use to enter more deeply into this vision, Cardinal George draws from the great voices of Catholic faith, from Cyril of Alexandria, Maximus the Confessor, and St. Francis of Assisi to Popes John Paul II and Benedict XVI. He also weaves in his own experiences of faith — from a moving encounter with a non-Christian in Zambia to the remarkable pilgrimage of young people who observed Pope John Paul II's visit to Mexico City.

978-0-8245-2582-8 (cloth)

Of Related Interest

Grant Kaplan
ANSWERING THE ENLIGHTENMENT
The Catholic Recovery of Historical Revelation

Revelation is one of the most important concepts in Western religious thought. Since the Enlightenment, however, traditional notions of revelation have come under critique, even to the point of being wholly abandoned. In this book Grant Kaplan examines some of the well-known and lesser-known figures in the Enlightenment and post-Enlightenment, showing that a Catholic retrieval of revelation is possible and even preferable to alternative paths.

Major figures and topics include: Lessing • Kant • Fichte • Schelling • Johannes Kuhn • The philosophy of history • German idealism • The Catholic Tübingen School • The genealogy of modernity • Faith and reason

978-0-8245-2364-0 (pbk.)

Of Related Interest

Robert Barron
THOMAS AQUINAS
Spiritual Master

Catholic Press Award Winner!

Thomas Aquinas is widely considered the greatest and most influential of Catholic theologians. Yet too often his insights into the nature of God and the meaning of life are seen as somehow cold, impersonal, and divorced from spirituality. In this award-winning book, Robert Barron shows how Aquinas's profound understanding of the Christian mystical life animates and helps explain his writings on Jesus Christ, creation, God's "strange" nature, and the human call to ecstasy.

978-0-8245-2496-8 (pbk.)

Check your local bookstore for availability.
To order directly from the publisher,
please call 1-800-888-4741 for Customer Service
or visit our website at *www.CrossroadPublishing.com*.